D1569772

MSU Campus
Buildings, Places, Spaces

MSU Campus

Buildings, Places, Spaces

Architecture and the Campus Park of Michigan State University

Linda O. Stanford and C. Kurt Dewhurst

Michigan State University Press
East Lansing

Copyright © 2002 by Michigan State University Press

∞ The paper used in this publication meets the minimum requirements
of ANSI/NISO Z39.48-1992 (R 1997) (Permanence of Paper).

Michigan State University Press
East Lansing, Michigan 48823-5245
Printed and bound in the United States of America.

08 07 06 05 04 03 02   1 2 3 4 5 6 7 8 9 10

LIBRARY OF CONGRESS CATALOGING-IN-PUBLICATION DATA
Stanford, Linda Oliphant.
    MSU campus—buildings, places, spaces: architecture and the
campus park of Michigan State University / Linda O. Stanford and
C. Kurt Dewhurst.
            p. cm.
Includes bibliographical references and index.
    ISBN 0-87013-631-3 (alk. paper)
    1. Michigan State University—Buildings—Guidebooks. 2. Michigan
State University—Buildings—History. I. Title: MSU campus. II. Title:
Architecture and the campus park of Michigan State University.
III. Dewhurst, C. Kurt. IV. Title.
LD3248.M5 S83 2003
378.774'27—dc21
                                        2002008950

Cover and book design by Thomas Kachadurian
Front cover photograph by Thomas Kachadurian;
Back cover photograph courtesy Michigan State University Archives and Historical Collections

This publication was made possible by generous support from
the Office of the Provost, Michigan State University.

Printed by McNaughton and Gunn, Inc.
Saline, Michigan

Visit Michigan State University Press on the World Wide Web at: www.msupress.msu.edu

Contents

Acknowledgments

We appreciate the assistance we received from members of the Michigan State University and Greater Lansing area communities.

We would especially like to thank Dr. Frederick L. Honhart, director, Michigan State University Archives and Historical Collections; Ronald T. Flinn, assistant vice president, Physical Plant; Jeffrey R. Kacos, director, Campus Park and Planning; and their respective staffs. Dr. Honhart's critical reading of the manuscript enabled us to clarify historical facts and refine interpretations. The research assistance of Lorena Griffin, Carl Lee, Jeanine Mazak, Whitney Miller, and Robert W. Nestle, university engineer, was invaluable.

Special acknowledgment is extended to Lou Anna Kimsey Simon, provost; Robert Huggett, vice president for research and graduate studies; Barbara C. Steidle, assistant provost for undergraduate education, assessment, and academic services; Wendy K. Wilkins, dean, College of Arts and Letters; and John W. Eadie, dean emeritus, College of Arts and Letters.

The following individuals provided important information, insights, and support: Laura Ashlee, Juanita Atkinson, Susan J. Bandes, Peter Berg, Val Berryman, Raymond L. Brock, John Cantlon, Ila Church, Rebecca Clark, Brian Conway, Maurice Crane, Judy DeJaegher, Jerry Dodgson, Patricia Enos, Francie Freese, Roger L. Funk, Thomas Kehler, Roberta Kelley, Barbara Kranz, William Latta, Stuart Lingo, Carolyn Loeb, Marsha MacDowell, Pamela Marcis, Dugald McMillan, Mike Olrich, Stephanie Perentesis, Lisa Rahall, Norman W. Schleif, John M. Schnorrenberg, Terry Shaffer, Janice D. Simpson, Joy Speas, Richard M. Stanford, Tristan E. Stanford, Irving Z. Taran, Frank Telewski, Patricia Thompson, Joy Tubaugh, Bonnie Westbrook, and Michael Zieleniewski.

We thank Cheryl Snay for her professional research assistance during the early stages of this project; Gary Boynton, Thomas Kachadurian, and Derrick Turner for their excellent photographs; Thomas Kachadurian for his pleasing book design; and Kristine M. Blakeslee for her editorial guidance.

And finally, we are grateful for the encouragement of Fredric C. Bohm, director, Michigan State University Press, who shared our belief that this book was worth writing.

Preface

During our years as faculty members at Michigan State University, we have often walked or driven from one building on campus to another and spontaneously felt these buildings speak to us—aesthetically, psychologically, and socially. Occasionally, we wondered about their histories.

These fleeting experiences, on the way to teach a class, use the library, participate in a meeting, or attend a cultural event, accumulated in our minds. We began to ask ourselves questions: What are the relationships between buildings and their sites? Why do we see so many examples of certain styles? For whom are the buildings named? How different did the campus seem fifty years ago? What will the campus be like in years to come? How is it similar to or different from other campuses? We began to ask these questions a decade ago and find that they are still compelling to us today. Students, faculty, and community members continue to want to learn about our campus architecture and have shared their knowledge and reactions with us.

We decided it would be helpful to prepare this text to provide aesthetic, stylistic, and historical descriptions and interpretations of these buildings. We envision *MSU Campus—Buildings, Places, Spaces* as a useful, hands-on resource. It includes most, but not all, of the buildings on the Michigan State University campus and brief discussions of some historical sites or markers, public art, and natural areas that contribute to the spirit of the campus park as visual culture.

In the introduction and some entries, we refer to certain historically important buildings that burned or have been razed. Otherwise, we focus our attention on extant architectural examples that include academic, administrative, residential, and service buildings. We selected approximately 125 buildings, all but one of which are found north of Mount Hope Road. The area south of Mount Hope includes a large pavilion, experimental farms, laboratories, an executive development center, golf courses, and an astronomical observatory. Although this area is vitally important for aspects of instruction, research, and outreach and contains many agricultural buildings, most students attend daily classes north of this area.

We divided the campus into eight areas. Areas 1 through 7 are north of Mount Hope Road and Area 8 is south of Mount Hope Road. Each of these areas holds together as a section because its buildings share some common elements such as dating, style, size, purpose, and/or similar relationships to their surroundings. They are accessible by foot, bike, bus, or car, although some distances between buildings are greater than others. The areas have no formal boundaries. Numbers are used simply to distinguish one area from another and to provide varied ways to view, experience, and learn more about the buildings, places, and spaces of the Michigan State University campus park. For each building entry, this book uses the name offered in the "Building Data Book," Michigan State University, Physical Plant Division.

We encourage you to look at the buildings and allow them to speak to you. They have many tales to tell.

A work of art [architecture] is a challenge; we do not explain it, we adjust ourselves to it. In interpreting it, we draw upon our own aims and endeavors, inform it with a meaning that has its origin in our own ways of life and thought.[1]

We also hope you will read MSU Campus—Buildings, Places, Spaces as a historical account. It is a story that will change over time as new architecture is erected, as older examples are renovated and retrofitted, and as the concept of a campus continues to evolve.

Works of art [architecture] . . . are like unattainable heights. We do not go straight toward them, but circle round them. Each generation sees them from a different point of view and with a fresh eye; nor is it to be assumed that a later point of view is more apt than an earlier one. Each aspect comes into sight in its own time, which cannot be anticipated or prolonged.[2]

Finally, we invite you to reflect on or think about this built environment, this campus park, "in as many ways as possible," to learn with us, "how it is that works of art [architecture] come to look as they do."[3]

The Campus Park of Michigan State University

The Campus in Context

> Colleges and universities . . . bear an . . . obligation—to fulfill their roles as stewards in such a way as to ensure that the environment of learning continues to thrive.
>
> —"Turning Point,"
> *Policy Perspectives*, May 1997

For almost a century and a half, people have praised the beauty of the Michigan State University campus and its ongoing life as an educational resource. If these people were asked to define why they find this campus appealing, they might mention its gardens or natural areas, its historical or contemporary buildings, or its academic or social activities. While the campus may appeal to different people on the basis of its natural beauty, its architectural styles, or the activities that bring it to life, it is clear that these three elements are intricately interrelated; a look at one element invariably leads to a deeper understanding of the other two. This is especially true of architecture, because it is "an amalgam of context and relationships."[1]

Exploring the architecture at Michigan State University can lead us to aesthetic, stylistic, historical, and cultural meanings inherent in the built environment. Although this is possible on many other campuses also, Michigan State is distinguished for its excellent planning through the years. As we investigate approximately 125 extant buildings, it is apparent that campus leaders and planners

Aerial view of "sacred space," 1990s.

have asked an important and all-too-rare question with regard to each proposed construction, namely, "How does it fit within the overall plan suitable for a land-grant institution?" as opposed to, "How can we design a lone architectural star?"[2] This planning is evident in the way that the unfolding beauty of the campus rests in its cohesiveness as a carefully orchestrated design. The Michigan State University campus is a park, a *campus park*, where the landscape has been the "consummate companion" of its architecture.[3] This interactive relationship between landscape and built environment is what makes this attractive campus memorable.

Today, in the early twenty-first century, as we hear cries of dismay regarding urban and suburban sprawl and vanishing farmlands, we are reminded that the concept of a campus as greenspace is also being challenged. Many campuses now devote "huge acreages" to parking lots.[4] Critics already

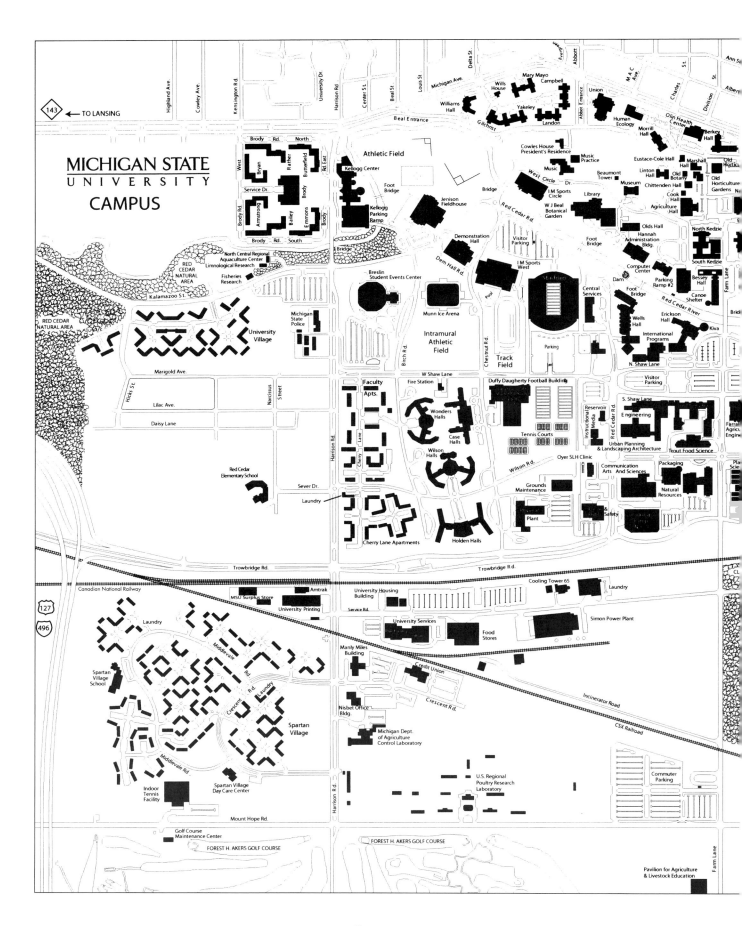

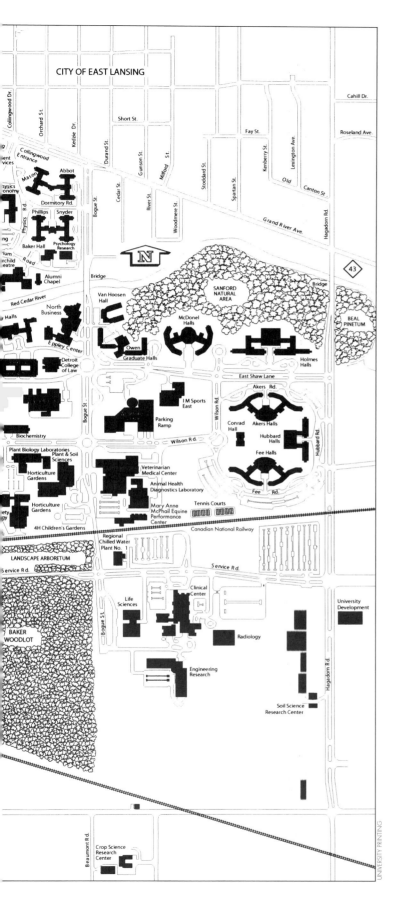

realize that, "having matured, most American campuses will not remain vital if they neglect to maintain their hard-won architectural heritage, both the built environment and binding greenery."[5] Loss of this heritage would be tragic because "The campus expresses (architecturally) something about the quality of its academic life, as well as its role as a citizen of the community in which it is located. The campus also represents many different things to various groups of people who live, learn, teach, or visit there. It plays the role of home, museum, place of employment, social center, park, arena for dissent, and forum for the search of truth. All of these functions must be designed not only for today but also for the future."[6]

Even as we create virtual universities in cyberspace, the green campus will remain relevant if we believe that public spaces matter. A college campus, particularly a state college or university campus, is a community space. This kind of "public realm" is "the connective tissue of our everyday world."[7] It is a "physical manifestation of the common good."[8] As James Kunstler writes:

> We . . . honor and embellish the public realm with architecture and design, in order to make civic life possible. This implies that the decoration of buildings and their arrangement in the landscape in order to define public space is not a frivolous matter. Relinquishing such attention to detail actually damages civic life on several counts. When buildings fail to define public space at a scale congenial to humans—as along any commercial highway strip— people cannot *be* there in safety and comfort. They will not walk there. They will not pause and mingle there with other people. They will not *communicate* there. . . . They will not contribute to a social organism that is larger than themselves.[9]

Fortunately, every day on the Michigan State University campus, people share common experiences—an impromptu conversation, a volleyball game, a jog or a reflective stroll—amidst campus buildings and landscape. Given campus size, many also ride bicycles or ride in cars or busses. Although some of these travelers are motivated by necessity and others by sheer pleasure, it is the campus planner's hope that all respond positively to the campus environment.

At Michigan State University, when people feel they

are part of their surroundings rather than feeling alienated by them, the professional challenge of "discovering, balancing, and expressing" institutional vitality is satisfied. This satisfaction, however, is always temporary, because institutions of higher education thrive on change. This explains why "college and university campuses are never completed."[10] To thrive as an institution, academic and physical changes must occur. The visual presentation of institutional vitality is reinvented each time the built environment of the campus is altered.

When the geographical location of a college or university remains the same, the amount of change needed to invigorate its image is less than were the institution to move to a new site or establish a satellite campus. The Michigan State University campus has always been on the same site, although it has grown considerably through numerous land annexations. Many other colleges and universities have grown in similar fashion, although some have abandoned their original geographical home for more space in another town or city. Since 1945, with the extensive growth of higher education, many public institutions have become part of larger state systems; many schools have a home campus as well as branch or satellite campuses. For Michigan State University, the original setting was undeveloped land. Today, its surroundings are suburban. The university has no branch campuses, although it does have statewide regional offices and facilities. The East Lansing site is not the *flagship* campus with subsidiary campuses; it is *the* campus, accessible to many by foot, bicycle, car, public transportation, and cyberspace.

Colleges and universities such as Michigan State have achieved international and national stature while they have remained firmly engaged academically in a particular geographical locale. As part of their mission, land-grant institutions such as Michigan State University are dedicated to serving the people in their home state. This is in contrast to the corporate world, where large firms move their corporate headquarters regularly and abandon downtowns for suburban corporate-park environments (ironically reminiscent of college and university campuses). Corporations justify movement from site to site as a means to provide a better environment to serve clients globally.

Colleges and universities such as Michigan State also have global clients—students and scholars from around the world who use the institution's resources, such as its libraries, laboratories, collections, and museums. These institutions also enroll students from around the corner or from the next town. Many college and university campuses that began as bucolic enclaves are now in the midst of major metropolises, from Boston to Los Angeles, and from Chicago to Houston. These institutions are not planning to move, that is, to close the "downtown store" in favor of the outskirts of town. The best among them have rethought their purpose and advanced and adapted their mission in concert with changing societal needs.

Colleges and universities thrive today in myriad environments. What, then, will happen to the college or university greenspace campus? The social ecologist Peter Drucker speculates that in thirty years large campuses such as Michigan State's will be "relics."[11] This is not a surprising prediction from the man who wrote insightfully a half-century ago about decentralization as a principle of management. Yes, we will learn increasingly via electronic resources found in our own homes, but will the campus become defunct? The question is neither surprising nor worrisome. In fact, it is invigorating. No one wants to maintain the campus as a mausoleum, and it certainly will not become one. When we look at past periods in the history of campuses across the United States, we see patterns of evolving use of both architecture and landscape. At Michigan State University, many examples of adaptive reuse exist. Linton Hall, the oldest academic building, has led several lives since it was erected in 1881. It once was the library and the museum, and then the administration building. Now it houses the College of Arts and Letters and the Graduate School. The land along Grand River Avenue near Bogue Street was once an orchard. Now it displays mature conifers and deciduous trees surrounding Mason-Abbot. Schoolchildren and other members of the public will continue to visit the campus grounds and exhibitions and attend special events, just as they have for more than a century, because in addition to being a seat of learning, the campus is also a *place*, a park, and a cultural resource.[12]

One of the most interesting and revealing ways to understand the history of this campus is to study individual buildings. Peel back the decades, layer by layer, uncover varied uses for interiors and exteriors, and witness the sheer impact of time. Then, consider these buildings as part of a larger context, in this instance, the whole campus park. By their very existence, buildings reveal that someone considers them important. Positioned with others

Above: **Entrance to State Agricultural College, showing terminus of streetcar from Lansing, ca. 1895. The former President's House is in the distance, on the site of present-day Gilchrist Hall.** *Below: Michigan State College*, **Abbot entrance marker relief by Samuel Cashwan, ca. 1939. Gift of the Class of 1938.**

amidst the landscape, they mark and create space.[13] Architecture and landscape serve as purveyors of institutional assets. They are economic indicators, a physical analog of an annual report or a financial balance sheet.

Academic years come and go. Campus trees and shrubs mature. Buildings often outlive their original purpose and their symbolic meanings and are transformed as aesthetic and cultural preferences change. This is true at Michigan State University and on other campuses. Despite the alteration of meanings, original aspects of campus plans can remain resoundingly observable. At Michigan State, examples abound. People use the winding paths and roads of the West Circle Drive area in the oldest part of campus. Across the entire campus, there are still many entrances, including the oldest one, off Michigan Avenue, known as the Beal entrance. Michigan State does not have one major portal or elaborate entry gate. If the criterion for assessing this campus plan were an interest in the hierarchy that one main entrance imposes, then Michigan State University would fail the test. The intention here is different because this is a public university, created in the land-grant tradition, where access prevails. Providing multiple entrances, and therefore different ways of approaching the campus, sends this message emphatically. All are welcome and each part of the campus is important.

College Hall, built 1856, collapsed 1918.

The Morrill Land-Grant College Act of 1862

The Michigan State University campus park we recognize today developed with the support of legislation known as the Morrill Land-Grant College Act of 1862. Since its earliest days, Michigan State leaders have viewed the campus as a testimonial to institutional success and have devoted considerable energies to its development and enhancement. On 21 January 1857, the State Board of Education charged that "the grounds around the College premises [be] properly laid out, and tastefully arranged."[14] A school dedi-cated to the study of agriculture and the mechanic arts with a "liberal and practical" curriculum should be set in an environment reflective of nature as a spiritual and utili-tarian resource.[15] Its architecture should reflect the nature of its curriculum. Therefore, early buildings were inexpen-sive, almost unadorned, and suitable for a "plain people's great practical [school]."[16] In support of the new college's mission and the legislative mandate of the Morrill Act, the earliest buildings included College Hall in 1856, the first building in the United States dedicated to the study of sci-entific agriculture; a chemical laboratory in 1869; and an armory in 1885.

Justin Smith Morrill, a congressional representative from Vermont, sponsored the original federal legislation, which was signed into law by President Abraham Lincoln on 2 July 1862. The Morrill Land-Grant College Act pro-vided for the donation of public lands to states and territo-ries for the "endowment, support, and maintenance of at least one college where the leading object shall be, without excluding other scientific and classical studies, and includ-ing military tactics, to teach such branches of learning as are related to agriculture and the mechanic arts, in such manner as the legislatures of the States may respectively prescribe, in order to promote the liberal and practical edu-cation of the industrial classes in the several pursuits and professions in life."[17] On 25 February 1863, the State of

Chemical Laboratory, begun 1869, opened 1871. Known also as Chem Fort and later as Physics and Electrical Engineering, this building was razed in 1955 to make room for the Library.

Top: **Armory, built 1885. Demolished 1939 to provide space for the Music Building.** *Above:* **Saint's Rest, men's boarding hall, built 1856, burned 1876.**

funds for land and buildings. On 12 February 1855, the State approved the establishment of the Agricultural College of the State of Michigan and provided funds for its campus.[20] John C. Holmes worked with a committee to select the 677-acre Burr farm in what is now East Lansing. In 1856 the State funded two buildings, which Holmes designed—the west wing of College Hall and a boarding hall later known as Saint's Rest.[21] The latter probably took its name from a popular nineteenth-century devotional guide, *The Saints' Everlasting Rest*, to suggest the importance of "rest" or meditation after a day of study and work.[22]

The first president of the Agricultural College of the State of Michigan was Joseph R. Williams who, according to Morrill, was one of the experts whose testimony was used to convince the U.S. Congress of the value of pledging land to establish colleges for the benefit of agriculture and the mechanical arts.[23] In 1857, Williams addressed the State Agricultural Society of New York, and months later he visited Washington, D.C., to urge passage of the Morrill Act. His belief in the importance of agricultural education was informed by his knowledge of European agricultural schools. He inferred that it would also be in the national interest of the United States to educate farmers in separate institutions.

With Williams as president, classes began on 14 May 1857. By 1861, Williams was a member of the Michigan Senate, and he had argued successfully to gain legislative approval for organizational reforms necessary to assure the school's continuance and for a name change to State Agricultural College, a name the college would keep until 1909.[24] In 1863 Michigan became the seventh state to accept the terms of the Morrill Land-Grant College Act, though by that time Williams was already deceased. He certainly would have been very pleased to know that this educational experiment in Michigan had influenced the passage of federal legislation that eventually would underwrite the establishment of more than sixty state-sponsored land-grant colleges and universities.

Michigan accepted the terms of this federal act and received an allocation of 240,000 acres of land from the public domain.[18] As this land was sold, the proceeds were to be used to endow the state agricultural college and its farms. The remaining land, in various parts of the state, was to be devoted to additional experimental farms.

Even before the Morrill Act was signed, the State of Michigan was committed to educating those who wanted to study scientific and practical agriculture and to lobbying members of the U.S. Congress for their legislative support. In 1849, at the request of the Michigan State Agricultural Society, Bela Hubbard, a Detroit farmer and geologist, drafted the proposal for a scientific agricultural college offering "an enlightened liberal education" for the farmer.[19] John C. Holmes, a Detroit businessperson and secretary of the Michigan State Agricultural Society, supported Hubbard's vision and lobbied the state legislature to establish a separate college of agriculture, rather than one appended to an existent institution, and to appropriate

Periods of Change

Each half century, divided here as 1855–1906, 1907–1945, and 1946–2002, brought important developments in the campus plan. As Michigan State matured, its acreage and the number of its buildings grew. Today, it has 5,239 contiguous acres with 2,100 developed acres and 3,139 acres of "experimental farms, research facilities and natural areas."[25] Geographical and architectural changes reflect a broadening of institutional mission. During each of these time periods, institutional name changes helped to focus Michigan State's identity.

In 1855 the school was called the Agricultural College of the State of Michigan, and then the name was changed to State Agricultural College in 1861. It became the Michigan Agricultural College in 1909, and then Michigan State College of Agriculture and Applied Science in 1925. In the most recent era, the school became Michigan State University of Agriculture and Applied Science in 1955 and, finally, in 1964, it became Michigan State University.

"Sacred space" in winter, Michigan State University Museum (*left*) and Beaumont Tower (*right*), 2001.

From an Oak Opening: The Campus Plan Emerges

1855–1906

While strolling amidst the trees and buildings of the West Circle Drive area, it becomes apparent that this quiet yet often traversed section of campus is special. It is the area where the earliest campus architecture, probably sited by John C. Holmes, once stood.[26] As West Circle Drive curves it delineates an open "sacred space," in which no buildings should ever be built; this area is anchored on the east by Linton Hall (1881), and on the west by Cowles House (1857).[27] These are the two oldest examples of extant campus architecture. The northern anchor is the MSU Union and the southern anchors are the Michigan State University Museum and Beaumont Tower.

When pedestrians head south from the MSU Union toward Beaumont Tower, they are enveloped by tree canopies that form a picturesque umbrella and are visually invited to ascend the knoll where the tower stands. From here, they can survey a random arrangement of oaks, conifers, other deciduous trees, and lawns that are now landscaped but that still recall the selection of this "oak opening" as the place where Michigan State University began.[28] This oak opening, a break in the densely forested area, was a desirable location because it required less clearing than many other possible sites and, fortunately, it possessed natural beauty. James Fenimore Cooper, the novelist of frontier life, described a Michigan forest in his 1848 book *The Oak Openings* as if it were this site: "The trees, with very few exceptions, were what is called the 'burr oak,' a small variety of a very extensive genus; and the spaces between them, always irregular, and often of singular beauty, have obtained the name of 'openings'; the two terms combined giving their appellation to this particular species of native forest, under the name of 'Oak Openings.'"[29] On the periphery of the oak opening, College Hall was erected in 1856 and collapsed in 1918—its wooden framework weakened with age. A decade later, Beaumont Tower arose on the same site in the Collegiate Gothic style. It commemorates the site of College Hall, the first campus building devoted to the study of scientific agriculture, and in its verticality, the tower symbolizes future scholastic aspirations.

In 1855, five years after the Grand River plank road extended from Lansing to present-day East Lansing, the Michigan legislature approved the establishment of an agricultural college and stipulated that the land could not exceed fifteen dollars an acre or a distance of ten miles from Lansing. Since cleared land cost more than fifteen dollars an acre, it was essential to find a piece of property with some clearing—hence the desirability of the Burr farm with its natural oak opening. This natural opening allowed College Hall and Saint's Rest to be erected more quickly in 1856 than had the land needed to be cleared entirely. Other reasons for the site selection included the proximity to Lansing and the need to use these 677 acres for experimental farming. There was considerable soil diversity and a variety of trees, including many hardwoods, "elm, white ash, swamp white oak, silver maple, basswood, shagbark hickory, and a small proportion of tulip, sycamore, butternut, white pine and tamarack."[30]

From the beginning, faculty and students from horticulture, botany, and related disciplines engaged in the taming of the campus grounds. In 1856, John C. Holmes was appointed professor in the Department of Horticulture with responsibilities for the preparation of "the grounds for the growing of ornamental trees, Fruit Trees, Shrubbery, and Vegetables. Experiments with the seeds of trees and vegetables, orcharding, vegetable gardening, Landscape gardening, etc."[31] In 1861 the school became the State Agricultural College. During that year, the State Board of Education approved the erection of the first bridge over the Red Cedar River, "near the center line of the farm,"[32] at what is now the intersection of Farm Lane and the river. In the 1860s George Thurber became professor of botany and horticulture and superintendent of gardens, orchards, and grounds. He planted many exotic trees. In the area

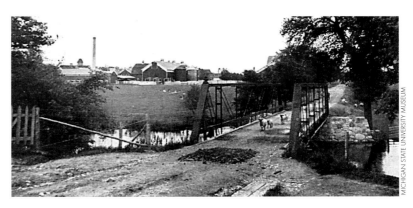

Top: **Farm Lane, early 1900s.** *Above:* **Williams Hall, begun 1869, opened 1870, burned 1919. Site of the current Michigan State University Museum.**

east of Cowles House, students fulfilled some of their required labor hours pulling stumps. In 1863 the first landscape gardening course was listed in the annual college catalog. In 1870 the scientist William James Beal became a lecturer in botany and horticulture, and he was responsible for many of the early campus plantings; the W. J. Beal Botanical Garden is named in honor of him. That same year Williams Hall, a dormitory, was completed. It stood between College Hall and Saint's Rest.

By the end of the 1860s there were twelve buildings: one classroom building (College Hall), a greenhouse, two barns, a farmhouse, a herdsman's house, a dormitory (the original Williams Hall), a boarding hall (Saint's Rest), and four faculty houses including Cowles House. Although all but Cowles House have long since disappeared, the sites of many of these buildings are occupied by extant buildings, and some of the same thoroughfares are still in use. The road just north of faculty house #4 (now Cowles House) and south of faculty houses 1, 2, and 3 (now Gilchrist, Yakeley, and Landon Halls) became Faculty Drive and then West Circle Drive. Eventually this road was extended to Michigan Avenue to become the Beal entrance, named for Professor Beal. This is the oldest road still extant on campus. By 1870 Farm Lane was a north-south road with a westerly jog. Later, this jog became part of East Circle Drive, just north of North Kedzie Hall, until it closed to through traffic in the late 1990s. In addition to Farm Lane, by 1870 two railroads already stretched across campus along courses similar to those of today.

During the 1870s the first campus plan emerged, the Committee on Buildings and College Property was created, and the number of campus visitors increased with the initiation of the Farmers' Institutes. The campus was becoming a more complex educational resource. In 1871 President Theophilus C. Abbot requested and received State Board of Agriculture approval to hire a landscape gardener. "Early in the spring [1872] the grounds were laid out by a competent landscape gardener. Locations were established for drives, walks, groups of trees, and several additional buildings."[33] Clearly, President Abbot wanted a cohesive plan integrating architecture and landscape. Adam Oliver, a landscape gardener from Kalamazoo, Michigan, provided the initial scheme for roads, walks, and building sites. His plan no longer exists, but the board's remarks do: "Resolved, that the plan submitted by Mr. Adam Oliver for

the improvement of the college grounds shall be completed by inking or painting the outlines of the river and ravines, and the walks and drives, and by marking upon it the trees and groups of trees existing upon the grounds."[34]

Oliver's main contribution was a fluid pattern of roads and paths, which is reflected in the first publication of a campus plan in *The Nineteenth Annual Catalogue of the Officers and Students of the State Agricultural College of Michigan* of 1875. This published plan reinforces the campus description that was included in the catalogs of 1869 and 1870. A portion of the 1875 campus description reads as follows: "There are walks, drives, rustic bridges, lawns, flower borders, and groves in pleasing variety. The buildings, mostly of brick, stand upon a slight eminence among the forest trees, which have been purposely retained."[35] Significantly, what is now West Circle Drive was influenced by Oliver's plan and emerges as a quasi-circular drive. The informal grouping of buildings in a park environment still speaks to us as a beautiful and humanly scaled place. Like other land-grant campuses, this informality was supposed to express "modest rural values" that contrasted with "the elitism and formality of . . . traditional colleges."[36]

In several of his annual reports to the State Board of Agriculture, President Abbot spoke of the campus plan and its development. The "college" and the "farm" were the terms many used to describe the area where buildings

MICHIGAN STATE UNIVERSITY ARCHIVES AND HISTORICAL COLLECTIONS

Rustic bridge near (W. J. Beal) Botanical Garden. Chemical Laboratory (*left*) **and original Wells Hall** (*right*) **in the background, late 1800s.**

"Michigan State Agricultural College," *Twenty-third Annual Catalog of the Officers and Students of the State Agricultural College of Michigan,* **frontispiece, 1879. Shows, left to right** *(clockwise),* **the President's House, a Faculty Row house, the farm foreman's house, and the Botanical Laboratory. The bird's eye view shows the humanly scaled early campus with a quasi-circular drive, later streamlined to become West Circle Drive. The view shows, from left to right, farm buildings, Williams Hall, College Hall, and the Chemical Laboratory. In the middleground are the original Wells Hall and greenhouses. In the distance, are the Red Cedar River and farm land.**

or farms were located respectively. Abbot offered a more cohesive perspective in his 1882 report. Here, he describes the grounds as a park, a *college park,* and even mentions the "rustic bridge" located near the (no-longer-extant) botanical laboratory and the (Farm Lane) bridge that leads to the "main part of the farm." He tells us that this rustic bridge was fashioned after one in New York City's Central Park. This is a significant reference. It offers evidence that he and other campus leaders probably knew of this exemplar of landscape architecture by Frederick Law Olmsted Sr. and Calvert Vaux. Later, in the early twentieth century, Olmsted's successor firm would serve as landscape architectural consultants to Michigan State. The following is Abbot's voice:

Directly east of the main entrance to the State Capitol is a wide avenue, which terminates three and a half miles distant, at the gate of the

grounds of the Michigan Agricultural College. These grounds are 676 acres in extent, and are separated into two parts by the Red Cedar River, a small stream whose source is thirty miles away. The college farm is mostly on the south side of the river, and the buildings are all in one large park of about 100 acres, on the north side. The college park has been laid out in the main by Mr. Adam Oliver, a landscape gardener of Kalamazoo, Mich. . . .

There are three entrances to grounds, but the west one [Beal Entrance], being nearest the city [Lansing], is the most used.

The drive from this entrance ascends a hill, and, leaving a pear and a cherry orchard on the left, keeps near the steep river bank on the right. At the top of the hill the drive divides, the left hand road passing by the president's house, a small astronomical laboratory, and seven dwelling houses for some of the officers of the College. The right hand drive follows the winding river bank, passes the apiary on the left and the new botanical laboratory, and crosses a ravine near the wild garden by a rustic bridge, modeled after one in New York Central Park.[37]

Writing in 1915, Professor Beal recognized the importance of Abbot's report in his *History of the Michigan Agricultural College*. Beal mentions the variety of trees and the "oak opening" of the early days. He uses the word "campus," which had not been used much previously, in relation to this site, and thereby reaffirms the concept of a campus as buildings set within a landscape. And finally, he quotes an alumnus and reminds us of the power of place while revealing his sensitivity to the aesthetic and educational significance of scenic surroundings. The setting is one with which we can still identify today.

The chief glory of a park or the surroundings of a home are trees and grass, and now on the campus of M.A.C. [Michigan Agricultural College] we have them in great profusion and luxuriance. . . .

A good many native trees of the original "oak opening" are still standing where they stood when the wild land was purchased for the use of the College, while large numbers of trees and shrubs, both native and exotic, have been planted. . . .

The fifty or more buildings are nicely distributed, with plenty of room for each. . . . We can justly claim the finest campus, all things considered, of any institution of learning in North America.

Now and then a person viewing our beautiful and extensive grounds deplores the fact, saying that it is a poor example to set our students, none of whom can ever hope to possess anything approaching it; but most people think the delightful surroundings cannot help exerting a healthful influence on the life of those who remain here for some time. In a recent address on "Our City's Breathing Places," Hon. C. W. Garfield, Class of 1870, says: "A child born into an environment of art, with lovely things to look

at from his earliest babyhood, will have his nature materially affected by the beautiful associations and will grow into a 'delicacy of texture,' if I may be allowed the expression, that can be imparted in no other way. Often a single picture upon the wall of the living room directs a career."

Any one with the least spark of love for the beautiful in nature, for the first time seeing the campus from the hill in the vicinity of the president's house [near Williams Hall], or on coming from the east along the highway [now Grand River Avenue], invariably makes use of one or more of the following: "This is grand, nice, inspiring, beautiful, magnificent, a lovely place"; and even one daily accustomed to the view, if he stops to think of it, will be found using some of these exclamations; while there can be no doubt that after an absence of a few weeks, months or years, the former student finds these views one of the chief attractions of the dear old College.[38]

In this same 1882 report, President Abbot noted that the Department of Horticulture would be responsible for the campus park. By 1884 Liberty Hyde Bailey, as the first professor of horticulture and landscape gardening and the superintendent of the Horticulture Department, was the person in charge. Professor Beal continued as the head of the Department of Botany. His contributions in the 1880s included numerous plantings across campus and in the botanical garden. Near campus, in 1887, he and Rolla C. Carpenter, another professor, platted the first subdivision in East Lansing called Collegeville, bounded by Michigan Avenue, Harrison Road, Oak Street, and Beal Street. As the campus grew, the surrounding area grew. Three years earlier, the first post office, "Agricultural College, Michigan," had opened on campus.

Bailey tells us in a 1885 report that the essential campus planning scheme was "picturesque"—a romantic delight in irregular and fluid natural arrangements rather than hierarchical patterns.[39] This approach to planning remained intact, as an academic and residential building program, to meet enrollment demands until the turn of the century. It included the series of classroom buildings that became known as Laboratory Row[40]—Eustace-Cole Hall (1888), Albert J. Cook Hall (1889), Old Botany (1892), Alfred K. Chittenden Hall (1901), Marshall Hall (1902), and Morrill Hall (1900), the first women's residence hall. Remarkably, they all still stand along the drive we now know as West Circle Drive. Across the drive, Linton Hall, without its later addition, already stood with its main entrance facing the oak opening or sacred space and what was then the main campus circular drive. Saint's Rest had burned in 1876. A two-by-two-and-a-half-foot stone marker embedded in the sidewalk between Linton Hall and the present-day Michigan State University Museum still marks the former northeast corner of the building. It reads as follows:

N.E. Corner
Saint's Rest
Built 1856
Burned Dec. 9 1876.

Williams Hall also faced the oak opening, standing west of the Saint's Rest site on the site of the present Michigan State University Museum, and east of College Hall, which, itself, stood on what would become the location for Beaumont Tower.

The campus was developing slowly and steadily. This is not to imply that these were the good old days of harmonic study and collegial cooperation. There were difficult moments that tested the tenacity and interest of presidents in assuring that the campus park remained a vital resource. Professor Beal, distressed by the unfortunate burning of the first botany laboratory, wanted the new Botany Building to be located in the center of campus. This would have disturbed what is now the oak opening or sacred space just west of Linton Hall. According to Madison Kuhn, who wrote the centennial history of Michigan State, "When the first load of brick was delivered . . . President Clute looked out from his office window in the Library-Museum [now Linton Hall] at this sudden invasion of the sacred circle." He then ordered that the brick be moved to the site where the building we now know as Old Botany was erected in 1892.[41] The open area, the oak opening or sacred space, which was integral to Oliver's plan, had been preserved!

Students identified with the campus. As Charles W. Garfield of the Class of 1870 predicted, they came to cherish its beauty and to leave their mark in the form of commemorative monuments. The Class of 1900 underwrote a class monument installed on the main campus circular drive that passed in front of the Library-Museum and

Administration Building (then Linton Hall) and then-extant Williams Hall. Though the drive was rerouted to its current location, the monument remains in its original location. On the front of the monument, "1900" is incised. This side was actually a trough for horses that once sauntered along the drive. On the rear of the monument, the pathway side, the phrase "Class of 1900" is incised. The fountain on this side, no longer operative, was once for the use of passersby.

By this time, the built environment had become too large for one person to handle. The board approved the

Class of 1900 fountain with a passerby taking a drink of water. Shows circular drive in front of the Library-Museum and Administration building entrance (present-day Linton Hall), early 1900s.

hiring of a superintendent for the construction and repair of college buildings, and the board secretary recommended "that the time has arrived when definite places should be decided upon for the new buildings needed."[42] In 1905 Thomas Gunson became the superintendent of grounds. This created a separation between the caring for the campus and any teaching department. In the same year, in recognition of the observation made by the board secretary, the board authorized President Snyder to hire Ossian Cole (O.C.) Simonds (1857–1931) or another landscape gardener to conduct a "careful survey of the College campus" and to offer "suggestions in reference to location of buildings and general improvements."[43] Simonds was chosen because he was well known nationally, he specialized in

Campus park and sacred space, State Agricultural College, 1902.

Midwestern commissions, and he was a friend of the afore-mentioned Charles W. Garfield, an alumnus and a member of the board 1887–99.

A reassessment of the grounds would provide guidelines for future development. By this time, the Père Marquette Railroad Company had built a spur from Trowbridge Road to a power plant on the north bank of the Red Cedar River southwest of where the John A. Hannah Administration Building now stands. The railway line was necessary but ill-placed. Across campus, both aesthetic and practical needs demanded reexamination.

Simonds believed in the interconnection between the perception of beauty and improved quality of life and the positive influence of college or university grounds on the lives of students.[44] For Michigan State, he offered numerous specific recommendations that the board approved and implemented in later years. Among these, the most important was his recommendation regarding the "sacred space." It had the most profound philosophical impact on subsequent planning for the entire campus.[45] By naming the oak opening the "sacred space," Simonds imbued it with spiritual reverence. It became something to be appreciated, preserved, and studied. With his sensitivity to beauty and ways of learning, Simonds's report influenced planning decisions for many other campus areas. A portion of his

report reads as follows: "I should regard all the ground included within the area, marked . . . as a sacred space from which all buildings must forever be excluded. This area contains beautifully rolling land, with a pleasing arrangement of groups of trees, many of which have developed into fine specimens. This area is, I am sure, that feature of the college which is most pleasantly and affectionately remembered by the students after they leave their Alma Mater, and I doubt if any of the instruction given has a greater effect upon their lives."[46] Simonds's spiritual analog is sympathetic to nineteenth-century pleas for conservation and to the piety of John Muir, the conservationist who established the Sierra Club in 1892 and called for the creation of national parks. Here, the sacred space is integral to a campus park.

Simonds was quick to note that although there were several campus entrances, the northern entrance to the campus (near Abbot Road) had become most popular due to the proximity of the streetcar line. Its campus terminus was near the corner of present-day Abbot Road and West Circle Drive, near Landon and Campbell Halls and the MSU Union. He even suggested that this line might be extended north of the Horticulture Building (now Eustace-Cole Hall) for close proximity to classroom buildings. It never was extended, but most of his other suggestions were implemented. The Library-Museum and Administration Building (now Linton Hall) was extended east, and the MSU Union and Agriculture Hall were erected respectively on or near the sites he preferred. The number of paths and roads was diminished, and one drive across the sacred space was eliminated. The main campus drive he recommended extending from what is now the Beal entrance and continuing "about the main campus" may have included the then-existent River Drive along the north bank of the Red Cedar River. He seemed to suggest that this drive, which ended near the present-day John A. Hannah Administration Building, should be extended to incorporate part of what is now West Circle Drive. All of these changes, he stressed, should include the qualities of the native landscape to form "pleasing outlooks and surroundings."

On campus, the superintendent for the construction and repair of college buildings reported to the board secretary daily and to the president directly. By 1902 Edwyn A. Bowd had been hired as the college architect to assess proposals and specifications and to produce his own designs. The board continued to develop grounds ordinances such as the 1905 policy that automobiles on campus were not to be driven faster than ten miles per hour or faster than five miles per hour on curves. Obviously, the eye of the college was turned toward the future, with the campus as an irreplaceable resource. President Snyder reported in 1906 that if Simonds's recommendations, particularly the preservation of the oak opening or sacred space, were followed, "the M.A.C. [Michigan Agricultural College] campus will go down to future generations as 'a thing of beauty and a joy forever.'"[47]

At the end of approximately a half century, 1855–1906, the built portion of the campus was north of the Red Cedar River, extending from its present western boundary to Farm Lane, close in its perimeter to Area 1 in this book. Glances at present-day Cowles House, Linton Hall, and the West Circle Drive Laboratory Row buildings allow us to re-experience the picturesque flavor of the early campus. East of Farm Lane were gardens, experimental farms, and an orchard; south of the Red Cedar River lay the rest of the farms and some athletic fields.

1907–1945

In 1907 the Michigan legislature chartered East Lansing. The municipality and the college grew side by side. During the next four decades Michigan State would engage in its own planning decisions to reaffirm its institutional commitment to the campus park. It would underwrite the sustained hiring of a landscape architect to develop a general campus plan with areas for prescribed uses and projected growth both north and south of the Red Cedar River. In 1909, as a sign of institutional maturity, the State Agricultural College became Michigan Agricultural College.

As funds for additional buildings became available, the issue of where to place this architecture became more urgent. Therefore, it is unsurprising that in 1908 the State Board of Agriculture decided that the president, the board secretary, and the college architect should decide where they should site the next building, Agriculture Hall. At 109,010 square feet, this would be the largest building constructed to date. They selected the general area Simonds had recommended. When this large academic building was complete, campus leaders had hopes for others. In 1913, the second Dairy Building, no longer extant, emerged just east of Agriculture Hall, at what is now the terminus of Farm Lane. That same year, the first phase of Giltner Hall, which is still in use, arose a half block east on what is now the south side of East Circle Drive. It was apparent that the expansion of the campus for academic buildings would be due east and that more specific plans were needed for precise building sites, landscape, and drives on both sides of the Red Cedar River. Even in 1908, Professor Robert Shaw, director of the Farm Department, wrote to President Snyder to request "that a river drive be . . . constructed this season, from the athletic bridge [near present-day "Sparty"] to the farm lane, on the south side of the Cedar River."[48] Without a fully developed plan, it was more difficult to respond to requests such as Shaw's.

In 1913 the board approved the formation of a committee consisting of Dean Robert Shaw, Professors Eustace and Kedzie, and board members Beaumont and Waterbury "to consider plans for the location of future buildings with authority to employ a landscape architect if necessary."[49] A month later, the committee was authorized to hire "Mr. Olmstead," which would actually be Frederick Law Olmsted Jr. (1870–1957) and John Charles Olmsted (1852–1920), of the firm Olmsted Brothers, Boston.[50]

The selection of this firm is significant because it reveals the strong Michigan State commitment to the development of the campus park as a place for buildings and nature. By hiring the Olmsted Brothers, campus leaders would receive professional advice from the leading landscape architectural firm in the United States—the successors to the designers of Central Park in New York City (1858–63, 1865–78), the World's Columbian Exposition in Chicago (1888–93), and, closer to home, Belle Isle Park in Detroit (1881–84).[51] In addition, they would benefit from the advice given by firm members who were the direct successors of Frederick Law Olmsted Sr. (1822–1903), the most well-known landscape architect of the nineteenth century and a professional whose commitment to social responsibility led him to a special interest in land-grant colleges.

Olmsted was so engaged in the topic that he wrote a treatise in 1866 entitled, *A Few Things to be Thought of before Proceeding to Plan Buildings for the National Agricultural Colleges*. The treatise was addressed to the Board of Trustees of the Massachusetts Agricultural College (now University of Massachusetts), but it was written with relevance for other land-grant institutions. Olmsted viewed the Morrill Act and the establishment of land-grant colleges "as evidence of a higher tendency of civilization."[52] Consequently, he thought campuses should be planned to accommodate and encourage the fulfillment of the goal of educating the "industrial classes" for their work and for their civic and family lives. He wrote, "You must embrace in your ground-plan arrangements for something more than oral instruction and practical demonstration in the science of agriculture, and for the practice of various rural arts. You must include arrangements designed to favorably affect the habits and inclinations of your students, and to qualify them for a wise and beneficent exercise of the rights and duties of citizens and of householders."[53]

Olmsted asked the question, "What can be done in the ground-plan of your college to bring farmers nearer to it?" i.e., to make them responsible for and responsive to their surroundings? Olmsted recommended that the campus be developed as an analog to a rural community, with the overall site divided into broad subdivisions according to use—horticulture, agriculture, etcetera. He favored having detached common buildings set back from the highway, as well as trees, shrubbery and turf, walks, a parade or drill-ground, and a ball or playground—all similar to a village common and "directly accessible from the public road."[54] Interestingly, his concept of a rural community is very sim-

ilar to the arrangement found at Michigan State at the time Olmsted's successor firm was hired. Olmsted Sr.'s belief in the role of an institution in developing civic pride and enlightenment had been shared by many Michigan State leaders since the time of its founding. Olmsted, like his contemporary Walt Whitman, wanted to foster the democratic public life. His park and boulevard designs were created in support of that ideal.

This is part of the professional heritage the Olmsted Brothers had at their command when the firm accepted the Michigan State contract in 1913. Work was begun, but by the 13 January 1915 board meeting, its report still had not been received. At the 17 March 1915 board meeting Professor Eustace reported that Mr. Olmsted had been ill and would respond soon.[55] At this board meeting, letters from Mr. T. G. [Glenn] Phillips, a landscape architect and planner from Detroit, were presented, and at the request of Mr. Beaumont they were copied and distributed to the board. It is probable that board members informally solicited these letters because, in the mid-1920s, Phillips would be hired to develop the campus plan further.

Two months passed, and then the 10 May 1915 report from the Olmsted Brothers arrived. In the report, the firm spoke positively about the success of the college in developing a "college spirit" of a sort that tends "to cling about the physical aspects of the college" and of its spacious and casual arrangement of buildings. The report continued, "While the architecture was not good, it was not aggressively bad; and it so happened that a fortunate combination of a pleasing topography, a soil and climate favorable to the growth of trees, a fair sprinkling of fine native trees to start with, and a long period of generally judicious planting and care, created what is undoubtedly one of the most beautiful examples, in some respects probably the very best example, of the type of landscape characteristic of the American college campus of the 19th Century."[56]

The Olmsted Brothers contended that the campus should not become a museum. Future plans would have to include more buildings for more students within walking distance of one another. It saw these needs as presenting a dilemma. To maintain feasible walking distances, the buildings would need to be closer together. These are "conditions which are unfortunately, wholly inconsistent with the beautiful landscape character of the old campus. . . . The problem . . . is whether it is practicable to have such a compact grouping of large working buildings as will be required . . . and still retain, apart from them, enough of the essential qualities of the old campus to be really worth while."[57]

A further recommendation was to leave what we now know as the oak opening or sacred space, the surrounding arrangement of buildings, and the parade ground (Walter Adams Field, just west of Cowles House and the Music Building) untouched. This seemed agreeable, and presumably even Simonds would have concurred. In a practical sense, by keeping all of the "working" buildings (academic and service structures) on one side of the oak opening, they would be easy to reach. Olmsted Brothers supported the idea of expanding south and east of the oak opening, incorporating most extant buildings, and maintaining spaces between buildings that were wider than city streets "to produce an impression radically different from that of streets,—that characteristic of the college 'quadrangle.' The spaces need not be precisely quadrangular to produce this effect . . . , but the kind of space which the term calls up to an American is a distinct type intermediate between the broad campus of an American small college and the typically urban grouping of nearly continuous building masses opening only upon courts and streets. Such typical college quadrangles in America are apt to have a width of 200 to 300 feet and a length considerably greater."[58]

Although the Olmsted Brothers state that the spaces did not have to be "precisely quadrangular," there was disbelief and concern over this aspect of the plan from the outset. Doubt must have been based on examining the written commentary and site plans and then forming pictures in the mind's eye. Site plans, however, are two-dimensional. They are not elevations and therefore cannot convey how buildings will look in three-dimensional space. The most intense opposition to quadrangles came in 1920 from the Chicago alumni group. After the demise of Williams Hall and College Hall, these alumni conducted a mail petition drive to obtain support to keep the circle open. They asked, "Do we want the Campus to retain its romantic character, or do we want it cut up into quadrangles?"[59] Those who considered the Olmsted Brothers proposal negatively must have assumed that quadrangles would inhabit the oak opening or that they would be completely antithetical to the surrounding circle drive area.

Actually, the Olmsted Brothers were trying to plan for Michigan State's transition from a small college to a larger institution. The firm was confronted with a built environment whose drives and building sites were much less defined than they are today. Its responsibility was to recommend ways to relate the built and the yet-unbuilt parts of campus cohesively. In its writing, Olmsted Brothers attended to institutional needs and concerns such as whether the college should provide more on-campus housing and actually offered some realistic suggestions for the grouping of extant and forthcoming buildings. It was correct in recommending that Williams Hall, on the site where the Michigan State University Museum now stands, be razed as soon as students could be relocated, and that College Hall, if it were "to burn up or tumble down," not be replaced unless a building of smaller or comparable size were erected. As it happened, College Hall collapsed in 1918, and Williams Hall burned the following year. John Beaumont, as a board member 1912–21, was integrally involved in the board's architectural and planning decisions. He must have read the Olmsted report and heeded its advice regarding College Hall.[60] Several years after it collapsed, he and his spouse donated the money to erect Beaumont Tower. The Olmsted Brothers would have been pleased.

With foresight, the Olmsted Brothers also recommended that after the antiquated Williams Hall was removed, a building, preferably a new library, be erected in its place facing northerly toward the oak opening and southerly toward the Engineering Building, now Olds Hall.[61] This became the site for the next library, which is now the Michigan State University Museum. Today, the museum and Olds Hall face each other as planned, although the grassy area the architects recommended does not exist. They had proposed a quadrangle, an expanse of grass surrounded by buildings. Instead, West Circle Drive is routed there. The Olmsted Brothers also suggested viable sites for future buildings. The Natural Science Building and additions to Giltner Hall were erected on two of these proposed sites. To solve the housing dilemma, the firm recommended building women's dormitories in the space between Morrill Hall and Farm Lane, which then terminated at Grand River Avenue. It also recommended building men's dormitories south of Cowles House. Although Michigan State did not build women's or men's dormitories on either site, these sites did become locations for other buildings: the Olin Memorial Health Center and Berkey Hall and, to the south of Cowles House, the Music Building and the Music Practice Building. Finally, in a successful effort to plan for expansion, the firm endorsed a site south of the Red Cedar River for what became the current football stadium.

The Olmsted Brothers, therefore, offered some perceptive thoughts to encourage efficient use of extant buildings and unused nearby sites, and it honored the picturesque nature of the oak opening. If its proposal had been executed in its entirety, however, the transition from this oak opening to the surrounding campus would probably have yielded calculated shifts in appearance, from one part of campus to another, rather than the fluid transition we know today. This is directly attributable to a change in the firm's aesthetics and conceptual base for planning—from romanticism and belief in the restorative powers of nature, preferred by Olmsted Sr. and other nineteenth-century thinkers, to belief in beauty expressed as system and harmony.[62] The firm's approach to landscape architecture became more pragmatic and efficient, influenced by the City Beautiful movement of the late nineteenth and early twentieth centuries.[63] Although all of the Olmsteds believed in the social value of public parks and thereby of campus parks, Olmsted Sr. designed these spaces for individuals, whereas the Olmsted Brothers designed them more abstractly, as examples of contemporary comprehensive planning.

The Olmsted Brothers envisioned the spatial development of the Michigan State campus according to a mixture of prevalent planning and stylistic norms of the day. From the Beaux-Arts planning tradition, so widely favored during the City Beautiful movement, it developed clear organizational patterns and axial plans using the aforementioned quadrangles, which brought to mind "collegiate ideals of intimacy and introspection" and the English university tradition of residential living and learning.[64] Less positively, these plans could also be construed to evoke a yearning for the "elitism of the past," a self-contained private enclave, disharmonious with the values of a land-grant institution.[65] Quadrangles were very popular for American campuses, and by the 1920s and 1930s, with the interest in period styles, they would be even more favored. There were other symbolic associations to consider, however, which the elder Olmsted had understood. There was the concept of the American campus as what Thomas Jefferson called an academical village. Olmsted Sr. liked the scale of a village for a campus conceived as a park. For such a campus he favored individual buildings, humanly

scaled and outwardly directed toward the community, or at least accessible to the surrounding community. There should be no enclosures, no high walls.

Despite mixed reactions, the Olmsted Brothers report was adopted in 1915 as "the permanent plan of the College campus," and it was decided that the College buildings "hereafter erected be located as near as may be in accordance with said general plan."[66] On various occasions, the board consulted the firm on the location of future buildings. On 6 February 1922, Frederick Law Olmsted Jr. visited the Michigan State campus to select sites.[67] In December the board agreed to consult Mr. Olmsted regarding the site for a new union building. This was the last mention in the board minutes of the Olmsted firm. The dissatisfaction with the firm must have grown to the point where the majority of the board did not view the 1915 plan as a suitable template for future growth. John Olmsted had died in 1920. Perhaps Frederick Jr., now the principal firm member, had become less interested. There was also the issue of geographical distance. The campus was going to become large enough to merit more frequent on-site visits and consultations by a landscape architect. Boston, Massachusetts, in the days before convenient commercial air travel, was a long way for an Olmsted firm member to travel on short notice. Someone closer would be better.

On 15 May 1923 the board moved to hire T. Glenn Phillips, a landscape architect and city planner from Detroit, as the consulting landscape architect "for the coming year." At the 26 June meeting the commitment was made final. Phillips would be required to visit the campus at least monthly to "confer with the . . . Board regarding location of buildings, general design and treatment of the Campus and all problems as may come before the Board that involve the present and future development of the College grounds."[68] Clearly, the board was interested in continuity. Hiring Phillips on an annual rather than a project-by-project basis would assure that continuity. Phillips was a logical choice. He had been under consideration by the board as a possible campus landscape architect at least since 1915. He was a member of the Class of 1902, and the first Michigan State graduate in landscape architecture. As an alumnus, he was loyal. With Phillips as the college landscape architect and Edwyn Bowd as the college architect, Michigan State now had the personnel who could work with the board to develop a built environment that would honor the natural resources of the campus park.

By November 1923 Phillips presented plans, which must have been preliminary, and they were approved.[69] In 1925 another institutional milestone occurred when Michigan Agricultural College became Michigan State College of Agriculture and Applied Science. Then, in 1926, to document the beginning of a new era, Phillips presented a general campus plan—a plan that provided the framework for all of his recommendations until 1945, the time of his death. His plan encompasses all of today's campus north of the Red Cedar River and part of the area south of the river—from Harrison Road to Bogue Street and from Michigan and Grand River Avenues to what is now South Shaw Lane. An initial glance at the plan reveals that his overall organizing principle was the informal or picturesque in contrast to the formal or symmetrical. Essentially, most American campuses fall into one of these categories or they feature aspects of both. The great advantage of an informal plan is its flexibility not only for building sites but also for its adaptability to different types of grounds without the need for much grading.[70] This flexibility was translated visually as a fluid arrangement of drives, buildings, and landscape echoing the winding of the Red Cedar River and the circle drive area. Phillips incorporated many of

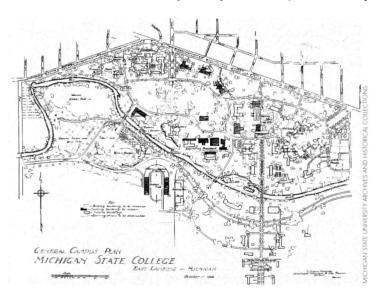

General Campus Plan, Michigan State College, by T. Glenn Phillips, 1926. Phillips eliminated some paths and drives to preserve the sacred space and create fluid, picturesque relationships between buildings and landscape along West Circle Drive and East Circle Drive. What is known as north campus today is actually the pre-1945 Michigan State campus.

the building sites and land uses already suggested by the Olmsted Brothers and others.

Phillips possessed a keen sense of how to accentuate certain areas and create visual linkages. One of his most significant recommendations was to simplify the circle drive area and visually expand the oak opening by eliminating the north-south route that ran from what is now the Music Practice Building site, past Cowles House, to Abbot Road. Simonds had recommended this earlier. Phillips also proposed moving the circular drive from the west to the east side of what is now Linton Hall. This change occurred by 1930.[71] He then created what is now East Circle Drive and suggested where to locate actual buildings and activity zones. Athletic fields and facilities would exist south of the river. Women's dormitories would arise west of Abbot Road and West Circle Drive, and other dormitories or fraternity houses would occupy the area near where Mason-Abbot and Snyder-Phillips stand today. The river crossings he showed are still in use. Phillips proposed closing the portion of what is now West Circle Drive that leads to the Beal entrance, probably to place more emphasis on the Abbot Road and the Bogue Street entrances. This change was not made. He allowed Red Cedar Road to run past the present-day Jack Breslin Student Events Center, all the way to Harrison Road, acknowledging that there are several campus entrances. He also supported the development of the boulevard adjacent to campus along Michigan and Grand River Avenues.

Before Phillips was retained, the board agreed in 1922 to cooperate with the citizens of Lansing and East Lansing, if its citizens decided to join the effort, to create these boulevards.[72] The timing was right for cooperation. This was the decade when East Lansing installed uniform lighting and paved such streets as Abbott, Albert, Hillcrest, M.A.C., and Oakhill. As evidence, these boulevards still exist today and represent an effort by Michigan State to work with its neighbors to interrelate campus and community. In this context, Phillips was able to succeed where the Olmsted Brothers did not, in extending the *ambience* of the oak opening or sacred space to the whole area north of the Red Cedar River and along its south bank as well. Nature and the built environment would remain intertwined. By the time of Phillips's death in 1945

Grand River Avenue, East Lansing, across from the MSU Union, 1945.

many of the spaces he designated years earlier for buildings were occupied and landscaped as he had planned.

From 1926 until 1940 many of the buildings in Areas 1 and 2 of this book were completed, including the Music Building; Michigan State University Museum; an addition to the MSU Union; Campbell, Williams, and Mayo Halls; Olin Memorial Health Center; the once extant Botany Greenhouses; North Kedzie; Auditorium; three additions to Giltner Hall; and Mason-Abbot. Jenison Field House and Demonstration Hall, in Area 3 of this book, arose in an area Phillips designated for athletic facilities.

From 1941 until 1945, as World War II raged, there was little construction across the United States. Building materials were scarce, and those that did exist were diverted to the war effort. At Michigan State, the situation was no different. Ironically, Phillips's role as landscape architect and planner ended not only at the close of the war but at a time that marked the end of an architectural and planning era in America—an era in which the "romantic landscaped suburb" and many residential campuses shared similar interests in intimacy, charm, and informal plans.[73] Certainly, in some post–World War II neighborhoods winding drives would be created to produce a picturesque effect, but most campuses would develop differently. Change was afoot. Formal Beaux-Arts schemes, favored for some campuses in

the early part of the century as a legacy of the City Beautiful movement, would lose their luster.[74] A more progressive approach to architecture and planning would continue to develop with a pragmatic and empirical demeanor, more receptive to change rather than to what was increasingly seen as a fondness for nostalgia. Campus life transformed as almost 10,000 army and air-corps personnel trained on campus from 1943 until 1945.[75] Simply put, the use of historical styles and either informal or Beaux-Arts planning yielded to the geometric empiricism of the International Style. Its more open-ended planning that frankly accepted growth and spatial adaptability over fixed, finite schemes seemed more relevant after World War II.[76]

At Michigan State, as on many other campuses in the United States and Europe, this change in planning would coincide directly with the post–World War II building boom. Spatial planning would become more regular than irregular. Drives would become straighter and less winding, although at Michigan State they would be accented with traffic circles to create a sense of fluid movement across campus. The overall effect would be simplicity, a directness of spatial use, suited to a new frankly geometric and less overtly symbolic architecture. Today's campus map reveals this change emphatically. With the Red Cedar River as the divider, it is easy to see the distinction between the pre-

1945 and post-1945 eras. Architecturally, the distinction is very obvious, too, because more than half of the buildings erected north of the river date from before 1940 and are historically styled.

At Michigan State and across the United States, there had been a long gestation period for architects and planners. In the 1920s, construction boomed. With the deepening of the Depression during the 1930s, there was little construction unless public campuses such as Michigan State received federal New Deal program funding. From 1935 until 1941, when he was secretary to the State Board of Agriculture, John A. Hannah was second in administrative command and was delegated the institutional responsibility of overseeing the campus park. As the person responsible for buildings and grounds, he had facilitated the self-liquidating building program begun by President Shaw in 1931 and seized the opportunity, later in the decade, to apply for federal Public Works Administration (PWA) and Works Progress Administration (WPA) funding. With the entry of the United States into World War II in 1941, reallocation of resources for strategic needs led to curtailment of construction, including campus construction, nationwide.

When the war ended, many ideas that had been on architects' drawing boards for more than a decade were ripe for picking. Clients, such as colleges and universities, wanted to build as soon as legislators, bank officers, and donors provided funds. Architects ready to work, burgeoning student enrollments fostered by the G.I. Bill of Rights, and a steady growth in the accessibility of building materials offered many colleges and universities an opportunity to grow quickly. At Michigan State, the incentive was more intense for two significant reasons. First, the college owned suitable land and, second, since 1941, it was fortunate enough to have a visionary president, John A. Hannah, who enjoyed the challenge of acquiring additional property.[77]

1946–2002

During this half century, the built environment of the Michigan State campus expanded considerably with renewed interest in the Red Cedar River as a picturesque link between north and south campus. The college added new programs and enlarged others, admitted more students, and became a university with regional, national, and international students and faculty. Significantly, every major development in the campus plan reflected the contributions of previous and contemporary presidents, faculty, board members, architects and landscape architects and, at times, students and alumni. In this time period the State

The Canoe Livery Service has been serving students since 1937. This view looks west along the Red Cedar River, 1991. After this photograph was taken, the Class of 1988 gift of a wooden deck for sunbathing and enjoying the Red Cedar Yacht Club was completed.

Board of Agriculture, known in 1959 and later as the Board of Trustees, adopted a new campus master plan and comprehensive zoning regulations to provide policy guidelines and a framework for future visions and decisions. These policies were not challenged until the late 1990s, when the 2020 Vision project began with the goal of drafting a revised campus master plan.

In 1946 President Hannah approved the creation of the joint position of campus landscape architect and head of the Department of Landscape Architecture. He appointed Harold Lautner to serve in this capacity. Lautner was a Michigan State alumnus and a landscape architect who in 1940–41 had gained experience working with a nationally recognized firm, the Olmsted Brothers. Lautner knew this was the same firm that, decades earlier, had provided campus planning recommendations at Michigan State's request. He also understood the history of the subsequent development of the campus under his predecessor, T. Glenn Phillips.

President Hannah explained that "the long range need is for someone to be located on the campus to be responsible for planning and development, including landscaping, and in my thinking it seems logical that this should be tied up with the teaching work in landscape."[78] With this statement Hannah revealed his strong belief in the ongoing significance of the campus park as a demonstration of the land-grant mission.

Years later it would become apparent that the campus had become too large and too complex for one person to assume the dual responsibilities of lead administrator for campus planning and head of an academic department. In the nineteenth century the responsibilities had been split. Now, after a number of different arrangements in the twentieth century, they were rejoined, only to be separated again in the 1960s with the establishment of the Division of Campus Park and Planning.[79]

In January 1946 the built environment began to change quickly. Earlier, toward the end of World War II, Hannah successfully negotiated with the federal government to obtain war surplus materials remaining from the demolition of cantonments and other war housing projects.[80] Given the scarcity of new building supplies, this federal surplus became the ideal material to reassemble and adapt to erect sorely needed temporary residences and classrooms. These buildings would serve the thousands of incoming veterans who, as students supported by G.I. Bill of Rights funding,

were ready to pursue their degrees. These "victory" structures arose on college farm or agricultural land.[81]

The newly created Campus Site Planning Office, under Lautner's direction, oversaw campus planning. Lautner was an ardent supporter of Hannah. His enthusiasm shows in the following passage: "No other university is known to me that equals Michigan State for its foresight, immediately after the war, in creating its own permanent campus planning office with the clear responsibility to answer the daily and long term needs for expanding its physical plant. Surely no institution carried out its plans more efficiently and with greater vigor. This was entirely due to a president who understood the building process and the professions that could make and carry out plans."[82] Whether Lautner's praise seems effusive or not, campus planning nationwide was bracing for postwar expansion, and Hannah had the prior experience he needed to act.[83] He was the person who visited campus construction sites early in the morning to witness daily developments and approve final changes. As the years passed, he developed an intimate knowledge of the campus built environment. When he became president in 1941 Hannah was ready to expand his influence on the campus plan. Before that occurred, however, the incoming veterans had to be served.

From the time the first federal surplus materials arrived, construction was constant. By 1947, new building complexes included Trailer Village, Quonset Village, Barracks Apartments, Faculty Village, and Red Cedar Village, as well as more than twenty temporary academic buildings.[84] Trailer Village filled the site of present-day University Village with 450 units. Due east, where the Jack Breslin Student Events Center now stands, was Quonset Village with 104 units housing 1,456 students. The 1,100 one- and two-bedroom Barracks Apartments, called "G.I. Ville,"[85] occupied the intramural field south of the Clarence L. Munn Ice Arena, where Cherry Lane Apartments, South Complex (Case, Wonders, Wilson, and Holden Halls), and Physical Plant now stand. Faculty Village had fifty single-family Quonset and other temporary structures. They filled the space that is now the Jack Breslin Student Events Center parking lot. Red Cedar Village, comprised of two prefabricated buildings, stood on the site of today's Emmons Hall within the Brody Complex. Temporary academic buildings, with an area of more than 200,000 square feet, contained classrooms and offices, and occupied the space where Wells Hall and the International Center stand today.

Above: **Seventy acres of post–World War II student and faculty housing, including Quonset Village and Faculty Apartments, ca. 1950.** *Right:* **Aerial view of campus showing the Red Cedar River as the link between pre- and post-1945 campus development, ca. 1940.**

In 1946, in honor of Robert Shaw, who was the eleventh president of Michigan State, 1928–41, the State Board of Agriculture approved the naming of the east-west road, south of the Red Cedar River, Shaw Lane. Today, East and West Shaw Lanes extend the width of the campus from Hagadorn Road to Harrison Road, although when Shaw Hall was built in 1950 the road extended east only as far as the building's easternmost facade. The axis formed by Farm Lane and East and West Shaw Lanes was to become one of the major nexus points in the overall campus plan. Even today, Farm Lane is the divider between east and west campus.

Beginning in 1946 campus designs also included plans for parking space. Prior to that time, given the residential nature of the campus, the cost of private car ownership, and wartime gas rationing, parking was an insignificant problem. In 1945, 360 acres were devoted to academic, athletic, and residential campus buildings and 500 parking spaces. By 1952 the number of developed acres had jumped to 628, and the number of parking spaces totaled 1,800.[86] Concurrently, the university updated its grounds ordinance and affirmed its commitment to the tree-planting program. As a characteristic annual example, the 1952 Report of the Campus Landscape Architect mentions that "279 rare ornamental evergreens, 18 unusual flowering trees, and 79 shade trees" were planted.[87] This botanical commitment affirmed the Michigan State tradition of developing and preserving the campus landscape. It also reflected the profound awareness on the part of Hannah, Lautner, and the State Board of Agriculture that the extent of the growth of the student population necessitated a rethinking of campus space utilization.

What Lautner called the "aesthetics of the river" became a vital concern in the late 1940s. On the site of today's John A. Hannah Administration Building, which would not be finished until 1969, stood the college steam power plant, coal bins, a spur railroad track, barns and sheds for the buildings and utilities and grounds maintenance departments, a cinder-covered road and, just south of Olds Hall, an old canning plant. It was becoming very apparent, as Phillips had suggested in earlier plans, that the Red Cedar River was no longer going to be the south end of the campus. This flood plain, from Harrison Road to Bogue Street, needed to be cleaned and landscaped "to exploit the natural beauty of the stream . . . in every way possible incorporating it into the campus scene to the north" and, in the future, to the south. The intent was to remove the railroad spur and to build updated utilitarian structures south of the river—well beyond its banks. An allocation for "sitework" became a component in the budget of every proposed building.[88] According to recent correspondence, "the rapids at the Hannah Administration Building were created by the construction of a dam across the river. This dam created a pool of water upstream from which water could be pumped. The water was used to cool . . . equipment and devices in the North Campus Power plant located in what is now the lawn of the Hannah Administration Building. The octagonal pump house or River Intake Station still exists, situated on the north side of the river, southeast of the computer center. The water is now used to irrigate Beal Gardens and several other campus greenspaces."[89]

With the railroad spur gone, highlighting the Red Cedar rapids became a complement to the south entrance of the John A. Hannah Administration Building. Ducks, encouraged by regular feeding, began inhabiting the grassy riverbanks. Concrete retaining walls defined spaces for people to congregate and enjoy the natural beauty.

Throughout campus, more than 750 trees and shrubs received identification labels for educational use. Milton Baron, assistant landscape architect, redesigned W. J. Beal Botanical Garden to enhance aesthetic appeal and highlight "plants indigenous or of economic value to Michigan."[90] He also redesigned the Horticulture Garden adjacent to what is now the Old Horticulture Building. His success in planning an "imaginative design" made it easy for the Architectural League of New York, a prestigious professional organization, to present an award on 18 March 1954 to Michigan State "for excellence in handling mass and space with relation to site and function and the integration of planting as part of the over-all composition."[91]

In 1953, Lautner mentioned that working plans for land use development and campus growth were in existence and exhibited defined park areas.[92] In 1955, in its centenary year, the campus encompassed 4,200 acres, and became a university—Michigan State University of Agriculture and Applied Science—and also received a Certificate of Merit from the Michigan Horticultural Society "in recognition of accomplishments achieved in the field of landscape gardening . . . some in the contemporary mode . . . in spite of the pressure for new building space, plaguing college campuses today."[93] In support of this institutional growth and maturity, Lautner describes the campus spaces south of the Red Cedar as "superblocks": "large generally rectangular blocks of land formed by a road pattern."[94] Although this may sound quite different from the winding paths Phillips offered in the 1920s for campus north of the river, Lautner allays any concerns with his description of the area: "These parklike interiors would be linked by pedestrian routes to peripheral landscape sectors, thereby contributing to an unfolding sensation of spaciousness."[95] In addition to affirming the institutional commitment to a campus park, his language also reveals the theoretical sources for many of his ideas.

Today, south of the Red Cedar River the campus park is still emphatically evident in this built environment with its landscape that accents traffic flow and provides visual anchors. Here, the scale is bolder than on north campus. Academic, athletic, residential, and service buildings are often larger and taller and positioned amidst an arrangement of divided roads and traffic circles, to create a sense of openness in a space that also clearly accommodates pedestrians, bicycles, and automobiles. This campus park reveals the planning theories of the influential Garden City movement whose architects, landscape architects, and urban planners such as the English reformer Ebenezer Howard espoused the creation of "the ideal living environment combining the advantages of both city and country."[96] Although Howard wrote in the late nineteenth century, his ideas influenced many architects and planners well into the 1950s. Howard directed his social agenda toward the improvement of the lives of city workers, but the relevance for those responsible for planned residential communities, including campuses, would become apparent as the twentieth century unfolded. Howard proposed a population of 32,000 as the optimal size for a garden city and included a surrounding aesthetic and productive greenbelt "as insulation against encroachment by outside development."[97] Among the many American architects and landscape architects who found Howard's ideas compelling were the notable Henry Wright and Clarence S. Stein. They were active in the Regional Planning Association of America in the 1920s and early 1930s and helped to disseminate the importance of planning self-sufficient communities. They followed their initial success at Sunnyside in Queens, New York, with the 1928–29 development of the enormously influential planned community of Radburn, New Jersey. Radburn appealed to those who would have future responsibilities for federal projects such as Greenbelt, Maryland, in 1935 and, after the wartime hiatus, for post-1945 planning including the design of college campuses.

If a campus is considered a community, the relevance of the Garden City concepts becomes clear: (1) plan neighborhoods that are large enough to make both the grouping of services and social interaction feasible; (2) group multiple dwellings around the edges of open areas and eliminate cross-traffic to accommodate shared parks and pedestrian paths; (3) cluster housing to free open space; (4) separate pedestrian and bicycle paths from major automobile thoroughfares; and (5) provide for the automobile without allowing "it free access to every corner" or the ability to "dictate patterns of human interaction."[98] When Lautner used words such as "superblocks" and phrases such as "peripheral landscape sectors" and spoke of the influence of Radburn, Greenbelt towns, and temporary war housing, he revealed that he had a firm grasp of the precedents for post-1945 planning and building.[99] He also realized then, as now, that the greatest challenge for campuses is to maintain a balance of quality-of-life issues—natural beauty, access to facilities, ease of use, and traffic patterns that allow for multiple ways of moving from one locale to another. Today, in an era when people have become increasingly accustomed to driving their own vehicles, this challenge on most college campuses is even more intense than it was in the 1950s.

By the end of 1957, roughly the end of the first post–World War II decade, the building boom was well under way. The demand for buildings was self-evident. In only six years, the first of the baby-boomers' children would be in college.[100] The number of students enrolled in degree programs nationwide and at Michigan State would double in the period 1951–62.[101] At Michigan State, among the new and expanded structures were academic, residential, administrative, athletic, and service buildings located across campus. Academic structures included the initial portion of the Michigan State University Library, Erickson Hall, Anthony Hall, and some Plant Science Greenhouses. The Brody Complex, part of Spartan Village and Cherry Lane Apartments, and Van Hoosen Hall became new residences, and the Student Services Building was the major administrative addition. The completion in 1948 of the upper deck of Macklin Stadium (now Spartan Stadium) offered enthusiastic football fans 27,250 more seats and marked the emergence of Michigan State as a major athletic competitor. In December 1948 Michigan State received its invitation to join the Western (Big Ten) Conference subject to certification. On 20 May 1949 membership became official; with it came national institutional visibility and an opportunity to compete for the Rose Bowl championship, which Michigan State won for the first time on 1 January 1954.[102]

In 1961 the university created the Division of Physical Plant Planning and Development to coordinate the work of the Department of Site Planning and Grounds Maintenance, the university architect, and the Department of Building and Utilities. Lautner became the administrative head directly responsible to President Hannah, rather than to the secretary to the Board of Trustees, for planning, construction, and maintenance. This reporting line indicates the importance Hannah placed on close presidential involvement in campus planning. Subsequently, in order to provide Lautner with time to address his new administrative responsibilities, Professor Milton Baron became the university landscape architect in 1962. Baron was an excellent choice. He had already experienced years of campus growth since his arrival at Michigan State in 1946 and through his service in a dual capacity as Assistant Landscape Architect and faculty member in the Department of Landscape Architecture.[103] By 1962 he was already a full professor of urban planning and landscape architecture and had designed the landscaping for most of the campus buildings erected since 1946.

W. J. Beal Botanical Garden, ca. 1990.

He had redesigned the former Horticulture Garden, south of the Student Services Building, as well as the W. J. Beal Botanical Garden, which he curated 1949–54. Widely respected on campus, Lautner credited Baron with "bringing to the campus-park the beauty and variety of a great wealth of plant materials. These acquisitions raised the University's collections to the status of an arboretum."[104] Given the campus growth, several professionals were needed to share in caring for the campus park, and Baron had became an integral contributor.

The 1962 report from the Division of Physical Plant Planning and Development to the board was especially important. It included a preliminary comprehensive campus plan showing the use of all university land south to Mount Hope Road to support the academic mission of the university. The board also learned that "366 new varieties of woody plants were acquired" for a "total of 4898 species and varieties on campus."[105] The following year, Milton Baron and George W. Parmelee received an award from the Michigan Horticultural Society for the beauty and educational value of Beal-Garfield Botanical Garden (now W. J. Beal Botanical Garden).[106] Dr. Parmelee served as the curator of the garden and of woody plants for many years.

Professional awards reminded people of the aesthetic appeal of the campus, yet some began to wonder whether it was possible to maintain a healthy balance between land-scape and the built environment as plans for new campus buildings received approval. In 1964 this became a vital question as Michigan State University of Agriculture and Applied Science became Michigan State University and the nationwide ecological movement, with its concern for protecting greenspace, gained momentum. That year, to protect birds, fish, and wildlife, the Board of Trustees enacted the initial wildlife ordinance to designate the campus as a sanctuary.[107] In 1965 President Hannah formed the Sanford Natural Area Faculty Committee. He asked its members to recommend ways to protect the Sanford Natural Area given the transformation of part of this site for the erection of McDonel Hall (1963), Holmes Hall (1965), and Owen Graduate Hall (1961, 1965). Today, as an outgrowth of this initial committee, the Campus Natural Areas Committee advises the administration on stewardship issues concerning natural areas and works to assure that these sites, almost thirty in number, are used and maintained properly.[108]

By 1966, as his annual report reveals, Lautner was the director of the Division of Campus Planning and Maintenance, a name change from the previous Division of Physical Plant Planning and Development. As the division title change indicates, there was a shift in emphasis toward a more visible recognition of the importance of *campus* planning. In that year, the division produced a significant document, a formal comprehensive report known as the Michigan State University Campus Development Plan (1966). In his cover letter to Hannah, Lautner states the following:

> There are no planning proposals offered here that essentially have not been incorporated on the large scale model map or other exhibits and studies shown in your office over the years. What this presentation does, in a summary way, is to compile the parts of the master development plan with a short explanation or graphic basis for them.
>
> Planning, as you know, is as much a continuing daily process as it is the production of a set of finished drawings at a given time. However, I would recommend that the following plans be considered and adopted in principle by the State Board of Trustees [Board of Trustees] recognizing that planning is not static but that the basic concepts in the plans for expansion and the preservation of the open

landscaped quality of the campus be acknowledged and retained.[109]

The "intent" of the Campus Development Plan was to "establish a functional framework of various land uses that will satisfy future needs," "determine systems of vehicular and pedestrian circulation," and "formulate general guidelines for the preservation of open space."[110] To implement these goals, the report called for strong ongoing support of a planning office to recommend "specific locations for all structures and to plan and coordinate landscape architectural work for each site" and direct "the maintenance of the arboretum park-like grounds."[111] This 1966 Campus Development Plan is actually a refined presentation of ideas that were in gestation for decades. In the plan, Lautner speaks as if he knows what Hannah wants and is careful to avoid lofty prose. Practically, if the institution wants to continue to have a campus park as a demonstration of the land-grant philosophy, then it must support the planning office and encourage long-range thinking. A map of projected growth patterns shows a remarkable similarity to the campus as it exists today with north and south campus academic areas surrounded by housing areas.[112] The major topics in this concise yet prescient report remain vital issues today: regional context, land acquisition, growth patterns, mass transportation, general land use, projections of student population size, parkways, parking, walkways, open space, and future development. For example, the report mentions "obstacles to a free north-south traffic pattern"[113] created by the laying of the Grand Trunk Western Railway (now Canadian National Railway) and the Chesapeake and Ohio Railway (now the CSX Railroad) across college property in the 1870s and suggests that Bogue Street could be placed under the Grand Trunk line to create an unimpeded path without a grade crossing. This did not occur. In 1999 the Board of Trustees approved the solicitation of bids for pedestrian passages to provide unimpeded access for students, under the Canadian National Railway, to the parking lots south of Fee Hall and Holden Hall. Additionally, given the need for ready access to campus from Trowbridge Road, in 1999 the Board of Trustees approved the building of a link from Trowbridge Road to south campus. This new Trowbridge entrance opened in Fall 2001. By eliminating the portion of Red Cedar Road that would have paralleled Trowbridge Road and providing landscaping, campus greenspace is reconfig-

ured, yet preserved. Making decisions about change and growth are difficult. They reflect the delicacy of the deliberations that must occur if long-term and immediate needs are to be met and if the campus *park* is to thrive.[114]

Beal Pinetum, white pine plantation planted in 1896 by Professor William J. Beal.

The Campus Development Plan suggested parking areas and ramps, including those that exist today or are being considered for future development. The plan spoke of the need for mass transit and shuttle service to parking lots—both of which now exist and are being developed more extensively.

The plan's discussion of open space is most interesting. Admittedly, there is less open space than there was thirty years ago, but the campus is still anchored by three large preserves: the Red Cedar Natural Area along Kalamazoo Street, the Beal Pinetum and the Sanford Natural Area stretching from Hagadorn Road to Bogue Street, and the Clarence E. Lewis Arboretum and the Baker Woodlot (and Rachana Rajendra Neo-Tropical Migrant Bird Sanctuary) between Bogue Street and Farm Lane along Service Road. The plan suggests that "space may be preserved in two ways": (1) use "setback lines from the travelled ways" to "create visual order and harmony . . . and to allow for adequate utility easements, tree plantings and traffic movements," and (2) designate "open areas either free of buildings or where architectural activity is discouraged."[115]

At this point in the report, a critical question is raised: What criteria will be used to determine how space is pre-

Clarence E. Lewis Arboretum, 2002.

served and which areas are to be designated as open? The report offers seven criteria that are as vital today as they were in the 1960s. These spaces are determined

- by *history and tradition* which respects certain areas and demands their preservation;
- from *scenic values* either natural or man-made which would be destroyed by structural encroachments;
- by respecting *flood zones* along the river where water storage areas are necessary for proper control of high water and to minimize property damage along the waterway;
- with knowledge of the needs for both *active and passive recreation*,—play-fields for organized sports for active recreation and spaces that provide meandering walks, shade, views and solitude for passive recreation;
- where specific areas are used for *educational purposes* as outdoor laboratories—Beal-Garfield Botanic Garden, Sleepy Hollow, Sanford Natural Area all provide readily accessible classroom aids;
- from existing and proposed *major pedestrian routes* for a growing number of students and their mass movements from one part of campus to another, these walkways must be respected and their continuity maintained;
- where *surface parking* occurs, either as a final solution or an interim land use and where pedestrian enjoyment is limited, paving nevertheless reserves space which ultimately can become parklike when the needs demand.[116]

These seven criteria are reasonable and are sensitive to tradition and to the future. They reflect the hard work of the staff in studying more than fifty planning documents from public, private, domestic, and international colleges and universities. The staff also had to sift through numerous reports on parking and traffic. Given the national figures of more than three million new students enrolled in institutions of higher learning in the United States in 1939–60, it is not surprising that these planning issues demanded constant administrative attention.[117]

By the mid-1960s Lautner knew his own retirement was in sight and that Hannah was nearing the latter years of his presidency. In August 1964 he wrote to Hannah acknowledging Hannah's interest in preserving the Circle Drive Area. There was an urgency in his voice, a desire to complete unfinished work, to have certain policies in place. He wanted assurance that there would continue to be an office with the prime responsibility "for the campus plan, all site and landscape work and maintenance outside of buildings and structures and, most important, that will be administratively responsible to either the President's or perhaps the Secretary's Office [Secretary to the Board of Trustees]. You have said there would be no administrative change in this area while you were President, but like I think you are, I am concerned by what may happen after your influence is gone." He went on to say, "I don't think our administrative direction, submission of budget personnel control and work programs should ever be subject to the judgment of a department whose main concern is with building maintenance, underground utilities and steam plants."[118] The landscape architect-planner and the university president, who had worked together for so many years, were about to have their wish realized.

On 18 April 1968 the Board of Trustees delegated authority to the Division of Campus Park and Planning for the administration of the Michigan State University Zoning Ordinance with the understanding that final approval for site changes would rest with the president and the Board of Trustees.[119] The Division of Campus Planning and Maintenance became the Division of Campus Park and Planning and was ready to use this new set of zoning regulations as an "integral part of the 'Comprehensive Campus Plan,'" or what was actually the 1966 Campus Development Plan.[120] This zoning ordinance, one of the first for a major university, was developed to "preserve the campus environment of spaciousness and landscape, promote order and unity, and minimize congestion."[121]

It is no surprise that the board approved this zoning ordinance. Many of its guidelines were already evidenced in the incredible amount of building from the previous decade. The years 1958–67 witnessed the doubling of the built environment with the erection of the east wing of the Library; Kedzie Hall–South; Bessey Hall; Parking Ramp No. 2; the north gallery, east wing, and Sculpture Annex of the Kresge Art Center; Baker Hall; Psychology Research; and the groundbreaking for the John A. Hannah Administration Building. South campus now displayed six more units in Cherry Lane Apartments, Wonders Hall, Case Hall, Wilson Hall, Holden Hall, Physical Plant, Grounds Maintenance, Urban Planning and Landscape Architecture–Instructional Media Center, the original wings of the present Engineering Building, Food Science, Packaging Laboratory, Natural Resources, Wells Hall, International Center, Plant Science Greenhouses, Pesticide Research Center (now Center for Integrative Plant Systems), part of Plant Biology Laboratories, Biochemistry, Chemistry, part of the Cyclotron, Abrams Planetarium, Parking Ramp No. 1, the Eppley Center (now part of the Business College Complex), Owen Graduate Hall, McDonel Hall, Holmes Hall, Akers Hall, Hubbard Hall, Fee Hall (originally Fee Residence Hall), Conrad Hall, the first portion of the Veterinary Medical Center, and some buildings no longer extant such as the Biological Research Center, which was razed to make way for the Biomedical-Physical Sciences building. Along Harrison Road, most of the Spartan Village Complex arose, along with the Manly Miles Building, University Housing, Food Stores, Cooling Tower 65, and the first phase of the T. B. Simon Power Plant.

By the end of the 1960s most space on the north campus was developed as it appears today and the south campus emerged as a place that also had major academic and residential buildings. In sum, the built environment doubled in that decade in ways reflective of programmatic innovations. For example, several residence halls such as Case Hall were designed to became innovative living-learning environments with classes taught on site. A 1957 graduate would have been stunned to witness the extent of the development ten years later. In 1957 Michigan State was an average-sized state university, and by 1967 it had become one of the largest in the country.

As 1968 unfolded, the ambience on many campuses nationwide changed dramatically as the Vietnam conflict became a daily topic of campus conversation and, later, protest. Large open spaces and buildings became rallying places for teach-ins and sit-ins.[122] At Michigan State, in addition to the change in campus mood, an era of university leadership ended when, in 1969, John A. Hannah completed his twenty-eighth year as president. Professor Walter Adams, from the Department of Economics, became interim president and used his popularity with faculty and students to temper demonstrations and guide the university through these turbulent times. In 1970 Dr. Clifton R. Wharton assumed the permanent position of fourteenth president, signaling the beginning of a new administrative era. He was the first African American to serve as the president of a public university in the United States. At the same time, Milton Baron succeeded Harold Lautner and became the director of the Division of Campus Park and Planning. As this new generation of campus leaders set to work, they made recommendations to the Board of Trustees regarding future buildings and the campus park within the parameters of the Campus Development Plan and the Zoning Ordinance. Michigan State's plan differed from those of other universities in that it allowed flexibility within designated areas to accommodate unforeseen needs, maintain greenspace, and expand circulation paths. The subsequent directors of the Division of Campus Park and Planning, first Thomas Kehler, and then Jeffrey R. Kacos, continued to use the plan and zoning ordinance to inform their recommendations for campus park improvements.

The 1970s witnessed high inflation, more stable university enrollments nationally, and overall less capital outlay for new campus buildings. At Michigan State, after the extensive development of a variety of residential complexes, the next most immediate needs called for additional academic, athletic, and service buildings. Although much less construction occurred than during the 1960s, the new buildings and additions fit within the Campus Development Plan to serve expanded programmatic and service needs. Munn Ice Arena was the major new athletic facility of this decade. The Herbert J. Oyer Speech Hearing Clinic, Life Sciences, the Clinical Center, and the additions to Wells Hall, Physics-Astronomy, and the Plant Science Greenhouses were the academic upgrades. Finally, in order to serve administrative and service needs, the

Public Safety building, MSU Laundry, Regional Chilled Water Plant No. 1, Stephen S. Nisbet Building, Salvage Yard, and Spartan Village School opened along with an addition to the T. B. Simon Power Plant.

Although the 1980s began with severe statewide economic constraints, the decade witnessed the erection or updating of several major Michigan State facilities for expanding institutional needs. The renovation and expansion of the Kellogg Center affirmed the importance of this facility as a place for continuing education and conferences. Major athletic and recreational construction addressed the need for all-weather sports and recreation facilities—namely, the Hugh "Duffy" Daugherty Football Building, the Indoor Tennis Facility, and the initial work on the Intramural Recreative Sports–East (IM East). The Jack Breslin Student Events Center opened to feature events that had outgrown Jenison Field House. Similarly, the completion of the Clifton and Dolores Wharton Center for Performing Arts provided performing arts space, in size and in kind, that was not available in the Auditorium. The completion of the technologically innovative Communication Arts and Sciences building and the groundbreaking for the Jack Breslin Student Events Center eliminated the need for the last group of Quonset huts dating from the 1940s. They were razed. The Cyclotron, Packaging Laboratory, Plant Biology Laboratories, Regional Chilled Water Plant No. 1, T. B. Simon Power Plant, and Clinical Center received additions. The Research Complex–Engineering arose as a utilitarian design adaptable for changing needs. Subsequently, diagonally southwest of the Clifton and Dolores Wharton Center for Performing Arts, Plant and Soil Sciences appeared, complementing the Wharton Center in scale, abstractness, and color and signaling a new era in campus architecture.

Even before the completion of Plant and Soil Sciences, the fate of the Soil Science Building, Old Horticulture, and the Horticulture Garden needed to be decided. Soil Science, originally the college dairy, stood at the northernmost end of Farm Lane between Agriculture Hall and Berkey Hall. Although it had some notable architectural traits, Soil Science was sorely in need of repair. The university decided to raze it. Concurrently, it committed to the development of the new Horticulture Demonstration Gardens, adjacent to the new Plant and Soil Sciences building, the renovation of Old Horticulture, and the adaptive re-use of the Horticulture Gardens. These signifi-

cant decisions recalled prior commitments to preservation. As a prime example, Cowles House, the oldest building on campus, received a major renovation in 1950 and significant improvements in subsequent decades. This is incontrovertible since the residence is designated as the home of the current Michigan State president. Other older buildings, however, are not designated for such a clear use and, because the university is continually faced with the construction of new academic buildings, a vital question is posed: What should we do with those buildings that are structurally sound and/or historically significant but beyond the prime of their original use?

Rose Arbor, Horticulture Demonstration Gardens, Plant Biology Laboratories in the background, 1990s.

A look at cities, towns, and individual homes across the United States reveals that this question has been asked many times since Congress authorized the Historic Preservation Act of 1966. Campus leaders, like municipal officials and individual homeowners, have had to ask hard questions about what to preserve and what to remove from the built environment. It is not possible to keep everything. But what should be kept, renovated, adapted, and/or reused? What are the economic and the symbolic costs? At Michigan State, from the late 1980s to the millennium, it is very apparent that campus leaders have grappled with finding answers to these questions.

During the 1990s, while new construction flourished, campus leaders also devoted serious attention to the issue of constructing additions and renovations to serve programmatic directions, comply with health and safety codes and, at times, preserve aspects of Michigan State's history. The Cyclotron, Veterinary Medical Center, Public Safety building, Cooling Tower 65, T. B. Simon Power Plant, and the Regional Chilled Water Plant No. 1 all received needed additions. Then, as a sign of adaptive reuse, several architectural projects resulted in the joining of extant buildings or the linking of new and extant buildings. Among the most extensive renovations were the linkage of two separate classroom blocks to form one large Bessey Hall, the incorporation of the Hugh "Duffy" Daugherty Football Building into the new Clara Bell Smith Student Athlete Academic Center, the attachment of the new Kellogg Parking Ramp to the Kellogg Center, and the connection of the new North Business Building with the Eppley Center to form the Business College Complex. The addition to the Engineering Building enlarged it considerably. Several years later, the entire Engineering Building and its easterly and freshly renovated neighbor, Anthony Hall, became one complex. The success of the Old Horticulture renovation led to the historically inspired additions to Marshall Hall, Linton Hall, and Agriculture Hall, and extensive renovations to Mason-Abbot and Eustace Hall, to become Eustace-Cole Hall.

All of these developments are indicative of a nationwide change in philosophical attitude. Although the prevalent attitude is still to build anew, there is a growing interest in adaptive reuse and renovation for both historical and economic reasons. Michigan State University, other educational institutions, and the United States are maturing at a time when the world population is expanding exponentially. As the population and the marketplace become increasingly global, the finite nature of land becomes more apparent. For universities, there is little additional land to purchase, and it is often impossible to annex new land. Expansion must occur in other ways. One way is through reuse of existent structures. This does not require additional land, and it enables an institution to forge ahead with innovation while it preserves those elements that symbolically recall its growth and enhance its future success.

The challenge is enormous. Recall the time at Michigan State more than a century ago, when there was a temptation to build a botany building just west of Linton Hall in the "sacred space" of West Circle Drive. Recall the thoughts of extending a road north of the railroad tracks clear across campus from Trowbridge to Hagadorn Roads. Recall the continuous pleas for more parking. Then ask, "Is it still feasible for the campus of a land-grant university to be a demonstration model for others?" The answer is "yes."

As the well-respected planner Richard P. Dober stated with foresight several decades ago, the continual expansion of "higher education will eventually yield good clues as to how to control the urban environment outside the campus."[123] In order to accomplish this end, however, campus leaders must engage in long-range planning and in the development of incremental solutions to problems. All needs cannot be met at once.

Unlike Europe and parts of Asia, the United States did not develop a national plan for the development of colleges and universities, because individual states are mandated to oversee higher education. As a public institution with a responsibility to educate the citizenry of its state, the land-grant university must continue to be a role model both in how a campus looks and how it works. A campus plan is an "instrument by which the campus administration can make good decisions . . . [It] should reflect the institution's point of view on land-use development, incorporate the widest range of opinions as to how the institution should grow, but restrict such opinions to reasonable alternatives. Plans should aid the architect in successfully completing . . . [a] commission, give design form to the entire campus, serve as symbol for friends and alumni to support emotionally and financially. Plans must be practical and plans must be imaginative."[124] And synoptically, the challenge is to be practical and imaginative because "For the first time in four centuries, Americans may be unable to sprawl at will, to walk away from a fouled urban [campus] nest. Tend to deferred maintenance, make do with less, and reuse inventively will become our domestic . . . [incantation]. Expect a golden age of ingenious retrofitting but also much painful debate about what cities [campuses] should do and be in a built-out postindustrial information nation."[125]

We cannot keep everything the same. When Michigan State became a college it began in an "oak opening," an area where some of the plentiful trees were already cut. The campus was small and its surroundings were rural. As the campus grew in size and population, so did the nearby community. Collegeville became East Lansing. Roads changed from dirt to gravel to asphalt. The city's population grew. The surrounding towns became the Greater Lansing Area while the context for Michigan State changed from rural to suburban. It will eventually be fully urban. Should the campus plan stay the same? Should the campus still be a park? Will this campus and others become tourist sites? To a certain extent many campuses fulfill this role already. They are often places for reminiscence, places where, for lack of funds, time has stood still. But this is not enough. Primarily, campuses are places of intellectual inquiry and social interaction. The responsibility for the future is to prove that a campus such as Michigan State can continue to be a place to study, work, reflect, and join together in an inviting natural and built environment. A campus should be an enduring example of how we live on the land and the relationship, in microcosm, of society to nature.

People often pay large sums of money to vacation in micro-worlds of perfection—resort cities or natural areas. Resorts are places with "no industry and high median incomes, . . . places . . . where the messy parts of planning for 2050" are absent.[126] Campuses can be living role models with an emphasis on the integration of greenspace and pedestrian-friendly access to classrooms and facilities with readily available public and private transportation. Resort areas are often "walkable"; they are scaled for human use. This is what people crave—ways to feel part of an environment. Campuses can achieve this kind of ambience. Overall, Michigan State University already has made great strides toward this achievement.

A campus is a public resource. More than a hundred years ago, Olmsted wrote about the democratic importance of public space. This kind of space must be preserved. Consider New York City without Central Park, its massive greenspace accessible from all parts of Manhattan. The loss of that greenspace in one of the world's largest cities would lessen the quality of life for many and would render the city less desirable culturally. Foresight made this public space available at a time when the city's population was a fraction of its present size.

Likewise, at Michigan State, leaders must continue to exhibit foresight to preserve and improve the campus park and its built environment as an educational resource. In 2001 the Board of Trustees approved the revised campus master plan and 1968 Zoning Ordinance based on an intensive and extensive initiative called "2020 Vision: A Community Concept for the MSU Campus." For this initiative, the Division of Campus Park and Planning invited campus and community members to offer suggestions and to comment about the goal of sustaining "a campus that ensures the future success of faculty, staff and students, while accommodating the new ways that they'll be teach-ing, learning, and conducting research, . . . remains true to Michigan State University's heritage, . . . [and] facilitates the mission of the University."[127] The revised master plan and ordinance will guide future decision making regarding the campus park and its built environment.

Today, there are students at Michigan State from urban areas who, before they arrived on campus, had never been close to a duck or a chipmunk or had never heard water run over a river's rapids as the Red Cedar does just south of the John A. Hannah Administration Building. Conversely, there are students from rural or suburban areas who had never lived in a high-rise multiple dwelling or used public transportation prior to their freshman year. The Michigan State campus population reflects the range of contemporary human experience. These students are brought together by a common interest in education. The campus should speak to these students in ways that will invite them to grow as individuals and learn to work together for the common good—for a world with a balance of the natural and the built environment.

The campus park of Michigan State University possesses indicators of its past and signals to its future. It will not be the same fifty years from now. It will not even be the same next year. Hopefully, it will continue to grow and preserve elements integral to its mission as an institution where students become equipped to face challenges and enjoy the rewards of life in a global culture.

Visual Culture: Ways of Seeing the Michigan State University Campus

Style

Once upon a time, two professors were walking south across the Farm Lane Bridge on their way to the International Center for lunch. A student walked toward them in a hurry and asked for directions to the Computer Center. One of the professors answered, "turn left and walk along the river past this International Style Building (Bessey Hall) and the parking ramp. The next building, a Collegiate Gothic one, will be the Computer Center." The student said thank you and went on his way. Then, the otherwise silent professor said to the one who had given directions, "Do you really think the student will recognize a Collegiate Gothic building when he sees it?" The professor who had given the directions stopped, thought, and then exclaimed, "Oh! I don't know, the way we view our world does indeed become our reality!"

This incident occurred several years ago at Michigan State University and provides food for thought. Although the way people view their world does indeed become their reality, the language they use to convey meanings about what they see can also lead others to different *ways of seeing*.[128] When a speaker describes a building as Collegiate Gothic, a listener might conjure up certain kinds of visual and symbolic associations that would be absent were the building described as dark and foreboding, ornate and old-fashioned, or simply as brick and limestone.

Art historians have long used stylistic labels to classify visual types systemically in the same way scientists label natural organisms by genus and species. In recent decades, some art historians and art critics have questioned this use of stylistic labels and descriptions. They argue that a focus on style will limit the possibility of new meaning being ascribed to or derived from particular works of art and architecture. These historians or critics want to reduce the usefulness of stylistic labels and descriptions to a triviality; they hope to weaken their role as expedients that can direct viewers to important aspects of art works. Style remains one path to follow toward understanding art works or buildings; it is a taxonomic way of seeing.

What else is style? It is "constant form,"[129] a consistent arrangement of shapes and volumes that comprise an object or a building. Individually, these shapes and volumes may be simple or complex. What constitutes their style, their constancy, is their reappearance together. Gothic brings to mind pointed arches, ribbed vaults, and decorative finials. Romanesque recalls round arches and heavy construction. International Style refers to implied volumes, unadorned geometric form, and flat walls and roofs. On the Michigan State University campus there are examples of these and other styles prevalent in American architecture.

Users

Being a user of a building is a kinesthetic way of seeing it. The user sees differently from the spectator. As potential users, students, if asked, could objectively identify a particular building as the one in which their class will be held. At that moment, perhaps unconsciously to them, the building is "a space awaiting events." Then, as these students enter, the building actually becomes "an event in itself"[130]—an experience, pleasant or unpleasant, that is integral to their lives. Sometimes unknowingly, and sometimes with full comprehension, they respond to the building—its lighting, architectural detail, scale, upkeep, smell, and color as they walk to class. Once inside the classroom, they may select a seat in the back or front row as they momentarily think about liking or not liking this class, in part because the space sends certain messages. Perhaps it feels too rigid or too informal.

After a few days of attending class, one of the behavioral lessons these students may learn is to arrive early enough to move a chair closer to the window or, perhaps, to where there is enough space to sit and balance a coffee container or stash a backpack out of the way of fellow classmates. As these students use the building they become contributors to its history—to a change in its colloquial name, the wear and tear on its steps, or the arrangement of its furniture. These students, as building users, personalize the environment, create ownership of a place, and become agents in the transformation of this architecture and space over time.[131]

There are several places on the Michigan State University campus where people have regularly walked across grass to shorten their walk from one building to another. As months and years have passed, their steps created dirt paths, which eventually were paved in recognition of the preferred passageways. In these instances, users influenced the university to change the space. Likewise, for decades, many students covertly brought soft drinks and snacks into the Library. The university recognized this fact and established a fourth-floor snack bar. But its location proved to be inconvenient so the university rearranged the first-floor space to create an actual place to eat, read, and use computers, and aptly named it the Cyber-Café. Again, users acted as agents for change. Users possess a kinesthetic way of seeing.

Discourse

There is another way to gain visual, physical, or conceptual access to a building or a complex of buildings and landscape on campus. Thinking of them as an arrangement of signs and signifiers, as a work to be understood, offers a textual way of seeing. "Reading" the text (a building) can be enjoyable and fruitful, especially if the goal is to understand as much as possible while acknowledging that meaning keeps changing. As with the re-reading of a novel, fixed interpretations are not real because individual buildings, the campus itself, and those who view and use them keep changing as time passes.

What matters is how to participate in a "conversation" with a building or the campus and how to equip ourselves to engage in this discourse.[132] When people view, use, and think about their surroundings, the process of coming to know these surroundings can be a fascinating way to uncover new meanings. Receptivity to new ways of seeing is the key.

Take the example of the Music Building. Let's suppose you had never seen this building. You find yourself overhearing a conversation at a luncheon held on campus for retirees.[133] At one of the tables, former music faculty members are reminiscing about "the old days." They recall teaching in the Music Building, built in 1940, and describe

it as a modern building—as the best and most beautiful one on campus. They like its uncluttered exterior design and the views outside through the large windows of the Hart Recital Hall. Now, look at the Music Building. It still features an uncluttered exterior although it does not seem modern. But its overall proportions, Art Deco reliefs, and contrasting brick and limestone render it truly characteristic of its day. These different ways of engaging in discourse, of reading the text, reveal that although the building structure is essentially the same, aspects of its architectural meaning have changed.

Aesthetics

To understand buildings and their surroundings well, consider certain aesthetic characteristics. Scale, size, site, variety, texture, color, and consistency provide visual ways of seeing.

We react to the scale and size of a building in response to neighboring buildings and to other buildings we can recall. Buildings and landscape elements have to be in view or in our memory for us to understand scale and size. Buildings do not make sense in isolation. On the Michigan State University campus, look at Agriculture Hall. From afar, it appears to be a large building because Cook Hall, to its north, is much smaller in height and width, and North Kedzie, to its south, also has less height and bulk. With this visual analysis as a given, the next question is, What else besides its sheer height, width, and bulk makes Agriculture Hall impressive? Its scale is remarkable. The columns that support its front facade are huge. Its doorways seem unusually large, although at the time Agriculture Hall was completed, this scale was the norm for many public buildings. When people enter the front doors, after seeing the huge columns, they feel small and insignificant, which makes the building seem powerful. The creation of this effect was probably a conscious design decision intended to affirm the authority of Michigan State as a place to study agriculture.

Next, there is the issue of its site. Agriculture Hall is located across the street from the John A. Hannah Administration Building. When people exit from Agriculture Hall via its front or south doors, often their eyes are drawn across the street to the esplanade, that flat open stretch of grass, in front of the John A. Hannah Administration Building. Conversely, when people exit from the Administration Building by descending its front steps, they are invited to gaze at the esplanade that leads their eyes to Agriculture Hall. This is no accident. Michigan State University began as an institution for the study of scientific agriculture. Via the site placement, the importance of the link between the College of Agriculture and the university is reinforced both ways. Similarly, at another land-grant institution, Iowa State University, the university's administration building, Beardshear Hall, stands across the "great lawn" from Curtiss Hall, which houses the College of Agriculture.

Scale and site change over time. When the Clifton and Dolores Wharton Center for the Performing Arts opened in 1982, it seemed visually bigger than it does now because the surrounding spaces were less developed. Today, to its southwest and northwest respectively, stand Plant and Soil Sciences and Michigan State University–Detroit College of Law. All three buildings are similar in their height, bold abstract form, and dark-brown brick. By bike, by car, and on foot, it is easy to feel this constancy of scale.

Likewise, for those traveling west from Hagadorn Road along East Shaw Lane, the impact of the large scale of the Michigan State University–Detroit College of Law emphatically sends a message of importance. Positioning the building at the end of this long vista provides the viewer with time to grasp the building's front facade. This planning makes it possible to hold the attention of passers-by. Similarly, in winter, when heading west along Dormitory Road from Bogue Street, the front entrance of the Physics and Astronomy Building appears in view from a distance through the trees. Undoubtedly, the scale and site of these two buildings are distinctively different. The Michigan State University–Detroit College of Law is bigger, the approach along East Shaw Lane is longer, and the trees that accent the view are set back from the street. Physics and Astronomy is smaller, Dormitory Road is narrower, and there are more trees nearby. Yet in both instances, passersby become aware of the building's front facade from a distance and, conceptually, they bridge the gap between where they are and where they are heading.

Subtle attention to scale and a balance of open and occupied space are characteristics that make a university campus work. Sometimes, without knowing what will be razed, renovated, extended, or built next, it may be difficult to understand why certain buildings take the shape they do and why certain geographical areas are filled or not filled with buildings. The Michigan State University cam-

pus park will always be a work-in-progress. It should continue to be a successful design because overall it includes a sensitivity to building placement and landscaping and the way in which occupants will approach and use buildings and grounds. Witness the unfolding of vistas and the complementary transitions between buildings and open or landscaped space during a walk along the Red Cedar River, a drive or walk north along Farm Lane from Mount Hope Road, along Kalamazoo Street past the Jack Breslin Student Events Center, or in either direction along Wilson Road or Service Road from Farm Lane to Hagadorn Road.

Variety within order is desirable. Everyone has had the experience of walking in a department store and revisiting the same section needlessly or exiting from the wrong interstate ramp because the visual markings were not clear. A campus is no different. Its space needs to be arranged so possible vehicular and pedestrian paths are apparent. A glance ahead provides time to decide which way to go and an understanding of how nearby and distant space relate. If people can see a variety of structures in the distance, they also need the sense of order visual clues or markers provide to enable them to relate one place to another. Campus planners provide these clues, as landscape or space, so these linkages can occur. Sometimes, they also have to include explicit markers such as traffic lights or signage.

In addition to site planning, other visual markers on the Michigan State campus are texture and color. Witness the textural changes from smooth brick, aluminum, and expansive glass to unadorned concrete and the contrast of a smooth lawn with the irregularity of ornamental evergreens or a group of crabapple trees. View the color changes from gray and tan to dark brown and earthen tones. See the lively polychromy of the Kresge Art Center and the Owen Graduate Hall and the vivid blue on some exterior sections of the Engineering Building. On the facades of Bessey Hall and several north and south campus buildings, notice the varying shades of green and green-gray used for spandrels, the space between the top of one window and the sill of the window above it. Think about whether or not this frequent and subtle use of green and green-gray is meant to contrast with the relatively neutral tones of aluminum, brick, or concrete to create a subtle architectural analog for Michigan State's colors—green and white.[134] Given the frequency of the use of green for campus buildings, especially those erected after 1950, this color choice seems intentional. For north campus examples, see the south facade of IM Recreative Sports Circle (IM Circle), Bessey Hall, Brody Hall, and the north facade of the Kresge Art Center. For south campus examples, see Erickson Hall, the original portion of the Engineering Building, and Plant Biology Laboratories. Across campus, looking from one building to another, green may become green-gray, and in other instances, gray or taupe or even black. Depending on sunlight and shadows, the shift from one hue to another is often subtle, yielding visual unity. In other instances, the use of green is bold, as the light green tile spandrels of the Engineering Building and the "Spartan Green"[135] tiles of the Jack Breslin Student Events Center reveal.

Consistency helps assure visual legibility. The group of classroom buildings on West Circle Drive, fondly known as Laboratory Row, is as remarkable as a group for its scale and color as it is for its recollection of late nineteenth and early twentieth century American architectural styles. Complexes of residence halls become comprehensible when they share the same constant form or style. The West Circle and East Circle Complexes in their Collegiate Gothic style collectively recall a pre–World War II notion of scholastic life. The ambitiously large Brody Complex and the South and East Complexes are understandable because they are similar in their form, scale, and International Style.

The prolific use of Collegiate Gothic before 1945 and the predominant use of International Style for several decades thereafter provides visual constancy in many parts of a changing Michigan State campus environment. A glance at many other colleges and universities nationwide reveals similar stylistic choices, although some stylistic interpretations may be more or less formal. In the Midwest, Indiana University, Bloomington, is one of several Big Ten universities that has many examples of both Collegiate Gothic and International Style.

For those who will live in these spaces during the twenty-first century, the messages these buildings send will not be the same. Some will enjoy the idea that those who lived here before them once considered these buildings contemporary, while others will long for the latest in architectural design. Students have to be inventive to make their rooms in a Collegiate Gothic or an International Style residence hall accommodate computers, printers, scanners, and other belongings. Those who designed these rooms thought of a student as someone who brought only clothes and perhaps a manual typewriter to campus. It does take creativity to make these rooms useable for the contemporary student, but perhaps it takes no more creativity than it required for a student in the 1920s to live in a dormitory built in the 1880s.

History

History offers a temporal way of seeing. Each building has its own history, which includes its purpose, occupants, role within the university, name, and architects. In some instances, a building's purpose has not changed since the day it opened. After all, the Abrams Planetarium has always been a planetarium, Erickson Hall has always been the home of the College of Education, and the Packaging Laboratory has always housed the School of Packaging.

Other buildings have had different purposes and, therefore, different occupants. A walk through Linton Hall provides a hint of a bygone day. In its first floor hall, notice the projecting counter edges along the north wall. These were once the customer windows of the Office of the Registrar, the place where students used to stand in line to order a transcript or check their enrollment status. The Michigan State University Museum was once the library. Fee Hall used to be a residence hall designed with living-learning environments; it is now a classroom and administrative building and houses offices, including those for the Colleges of Human Medicine and Osteopathic Medicine. Likewise, Old Horticulture, once the home of the Department of Horticulture, now houses the Department of Romance and Classical Languages.

The gender of the occupants of campus buildings affects their use. Although women enrolled at Michigan State as early as 1870,[136] their early numbers were small. They studied many of the same subjects as men—Latin, French, mathematics, astronomy, history, and music. They lived in a section of the first Williams Hall or, if they were from a faculty family, on Faculty Row, and they commuted from Lansing or nearby farms. As the decades progressed, demand for domestic science or home economics, the so-called women's curriculum, increased. Legislators, educators, members of the Grange, and parents began to realize the social and economic importance of this new course of study. Michigan State already had a course in scientific agriculture and engineering. As a land-grant institution, it should have a scientific course in home economics, too.

Part of the delay in establishing this curriculum was the lack of residential space for women; for decades, admissions committees denied some women admission because there was no place for them to live.

Although Michigan State admitted some women earlier than many other public and private institutions, the priority was to assign residential space to males. Whether the delay, in the form of intermittent admissions, was due to preference or simply space, finally, in 1896, the Women's Course began. This was seventeen years after Eva Diann Coryell became the first woman graduate of Michigan State.[137] With this new curriculum, a larger number of women, from several different states, applied. To accommodate these new admits, the first Abbot Hall, located near where the Music Practice Building now stands, became a female, not a male, dormitory equipped as a "laboratory for cooking, sewing, and calisthenics."[138] Men received new on-campus residential assignments, or they moved off campus. Home economics became an academic strength of Michigan State and women enrolled specifically for this program. Myrtle Craig, the first African American to graduate from State Agricultural College, earned her Bachelor of Science in Home Economics in 1907.

The first Abbot Hall provided only a temporary home for this new curriculum. In 1900, the Women's Building, now known as Morrill Hall, opened with offices, classrooms, a cooking laboratory, music and reception rooms, and bedrooms for 120 women. It was a hard-won fight, but the legislature agreed to appropriate $95,000 for this brick structure. Whether or not legislators or university leaders realized it, the decision to build this residence hall for women was part of a national trend to encourage the education of women in a secure environment. At this time, "Colleges and universities successfully convinced middle-class families that their daughters could remain safely feminine even when exposed to higher education away from the protection of home. In part the schools did this by building dormitories on campus and by regulating boardinghouses."[139] It was now possible to feel confident about sending a daughter to Michigan State. As an alumnus exclaimed a decade earlier, it was simply *the* thing to do to support the school. "And so, to give the State's fair school the honor that is due, You'd better send your sons out there, and send your daughters too."[140]

Years later, after the erection of the Human Ecology building and the completion of most of the West Circle Complex, Morrill Hall became a classroom building. Today, it houses the Department of English, the Department of History, the Department of Religious Studies, and offices for the Center for Integrative Studies in the Arts and Humanities and the College of Human Ecology.

The admission of veterans after World War II made a

Former pond, north side of Women's Building, now known as Morrill Hall, early 1900s.

college education widely available to the middle class. It may seem difficult to understand today, but there were some who feared this influx would "dilute . . . quality" and "diminish the status of degrees."[141] This kind of class bias is a useful example of fear of the unknown and was unsupported by the performance of these students.[142] At Michigan State, the increased number of new students, or building occupants, made it necessary to look afresh at how and where to teach and how and where to house students.

As new academic programs emerged to serve a changing student population, the need for specialized facilities increased. As one example, when it was built in the 1920s, Kedzie Hall was a state-of-the-art chemistry building. By the late 1940s, it was outdated, although it remained the home of that department until the current Chemistry Building opened in 1963. Likewise, the Quonset huts and trailers that housed veterans and their growing families spurred the development of University Village, Cherry Lane, and Spartan Village.

In the early 1950s, as Michigan State College of Agriculture and Applied Science aspired to become a university, it also moved toward the development of a strong commitment to international education. Faculty went off campus to teach, conduct research, and provide technical assistance while students from around the world began to enroll on the East Lansing campus. To encourage cross-cultural exchange among domestic and international students, the university opened the International Center in 1964 in what was to become a new geographical center for the campus. Seven years earlier, in 1957, in recognition of the growth of the student population, Student Services opened to provide offices for student counseling and career resources and a place for many student organizations to call home. The fact that these buildings were constructed to serve these purposes for the *entire* student population reflects the institutional commitment to broadening the academic and sociocultural experiences of *all* students. Rather than assigning temporary quarters or makeshift space, the allocation of new resources for international education and student services buildings affirmed their role within the university and the importance and integrality of these activities to campus life.

College and university campuses reflect institutional mission, priorities, and the kind of institutional authority they want to portray and convey. A research university should look different from a liberal arts college. It requires a built environment that is more extensive in its allocation of space for laboratories; it may require farms, performance and demonstration spaces, and specialized facilities such as a cyclotron; it may also require study collections of scientific and cultural materials. If a university's institutional role includes a commitment to serve a large number of students from different backgrounds, it must have a range of types of living, learning, and recreational spaces. John Hannah, the twelfth president of Michigan State, spoke of the campus as a demonstration model for its students and for the public. He continues to be correct. One of the major challenges facing higher education today is the urgency of "fostering a lasting public understanding of the societal values that universities and colleges supply the nation."[143] One of the effective ways to meet this challenge is for a university to show, via its campus, how the production of knowledge benefits both today's students and our society.

In the second half of the twentieth century, federal funding of university-based research "made federal support a defining feature of higher education." Universities became "the principal locus of basic research in the United States." To house research facilities, the number of campus buildings dedicated to this purpose, funded by state and private dollars, grew extensively. Michigan State became one of the prominent players in this arena and was invited to join a consortium of major research universities, the American Association of Universities (AAU). "Federal sponsorship of research . . . help[ed] extend the lines of development begun in the nineteenth century with the Morrill Act and the largely Germanic model of universities organized for the pursuit of research."[144]

In addition to funding research, the federal government also continued to fund the G.I. Bill of Rights for veterans and a range of student-aid packages with the premise that "a nation that invests in the college educations of its young is in fact investing in itself."[145] Fostering research and serving students are dual needs the federal government recognizes as roles for universities. For Michigan State, this federal involvement is a latter-day reminder of the role the federal government played a century and a half ago when it authorized the Morrill Act enabling the State of Michigan to form its own land-grant institution. Michigan State University's mission remains unchanged. The education of its citizenry and the production of knowledge to equip this citizenry for the future remain vital goals.

Names of buildings send messages. From the day a building is dedicated, its name may remain the same, but the meaning of the building may change. The Auditorium is still the Auditorium, but it is no longer the only large performing arts facility on campus. For those who regularly attended concerts there, its meaning is different than for those who work or study there today. Now, there is also the Clifton and Dolores Wharton Center for Performing Arts. As generations pass, people's historical knowledge changes. Some may already be unsure why the center was named for the Whartons. From 1970 until 1978, Clifton Wharton was the fourteenth president of Michigan State University and, as mentioned previously, the first African American president of a public university in the United States. Dolores Wharton, his spouse, was well established as a nationally known arts advocate. Together, they served as strong advocates for campus arts and for Michigan State's first cultural capital campaign.

Whether or not one knows the name of a building may affect the association a person brings to it. When people are not familiar with a building, the name becomes a tool. Like the title of a book, it is one of the signs they use to determine whether or not they want or need to enter a building or, perhaps, to return to it.

At Michigan State, a building's name often reveals its use. This seems logical, although sometimes, when a building's use remains essentially the same for a long period of time, the original name may be misleading given current social practice. For example, the building that contains the administrative offices for University Housing used to be called Married Housing, reflecting an earlier assumption that the only people who should or would want to live in this housing are married. Some campus buildings used to reflect the gender of the majority of users. As gender barriers collapsed, the Women's IM Building became IM Circle, the Men's IM became IM West, and IM East opened with a geographical rather than a gender-based name. Without these name changes, the accessibility of these facilities could appear to be limited by gender.

In some instances, a building is reassigned from one academic or support unit to another, and a name change seems important to distinguish this reassignment and to avoid having two buildings with the same name. The Computer Center used to be the Engineering Building. When engineering moved to its new quarters in 1962, the original building's use changed. Today, above its entrances,

incised in limestone, are the words, "Computer Center." They were placed there after sandblasting obliterated the original "Electrical Engineering" lettering.

In other examples, the name of the building remains as a descriptor of its original use. Above the Chittenden Hall entry, the word "Forestry" is still prominent in bold relief. Given the age and size of this building, which was built in 1901, it is certainly improbable that the study of forestry could occur in this space today. Perhaps that is why the doorway title seems quaint rather than real. Markers that remind us of the past help us to distinguish the present more clearly. As an especially interesting example, look at Beaumont Tower, the Power Plant–Shaw Lane tower, and the T. B. Simon Power Plant tower—three sentinels linking north, central, and south campus. Beaumont Tower reminds us of the university's academic beginnings, and the two towers tell what is practically needed to make it function. The Power Plant–Shaw Lane tower, just south of Spartan Stadium, is no longer used, but with its "MSC" initials, it stands as a beacon to remind us of when Michigan State was a college. From this tower, a glance north reveals Beaumont Tower and a glance south reveals the Simon Power Plant tower, representing, in a sense, another stage in the life of Michigan State—on its exterior are the initials "MSU," standing for Michigan State University. In an earlier day, before its demolition in the 1960s, there was a Michigan Agricultural College, or "MAC" tower near where the John A. Hannah Administration Building stands today.

Some buildings feature the names of those whom Michigan State University chooses to honor. These honorific building names include those of faculty, staff, students, and alumni; presidents and members of the Board of Trustees; public figures important in the life of the State of Michigan and Michigan State University; individual or institutional donors, and combinations thereof. The person's achievement may have a direct connection to the purpose of a particular building or the connection may relate more generally to the university. The G. Malcolm Trout Food Science and Human Nutrition building is named for Professor Trout, who invented the process of milk homogenization. Linton Hall, which once housed the Office of the Registrar, is named for a former registrar, Robert S. Linton. Faculty Apartments are named for students who, as alumni, died during World War II. Mayo Hall recalls Mary Mayo, a leader in the Michigan Grange, who worked in support of education for rural women and helped establish domestic science courses at Michigan State. Hubbard Hall carries the name of Bela Hubbard, the Detroit farmer and geologist who in 1849 developed a proposal for a state agricultural college at the request of the Michigan State Agricultural Society. An institutional donor, the S. S. Kresge Foundation, funded the Kresge Art Center. An individual donor, alumnus, and a professional basketball star, Steven D. Smith, funded the Clara Bell Smith Student Athlete Academic Center, named in honor of his mother. Beaumont Tower is named for alumnus, donor, and member of the State Board of Agriculture (now Board of Trustees), John Beaumont. Approximately half of the campus buildings display men's or husband-wife names, and twelve have solely women's names.[146] All of these people have contributed in important and different ways to the development of Michigan State University.

Conversely, some campus spaces that rank high in people's minds as important and beautiful are unnamed. The most significant example here is the rapids area of the Red Cedar River just south of the John A. Hannah Administration Building. Featured in university publications and on its electronic home page, the beauty of sparkling water, the resident duck population, and surrounding trees is exceptional and unique among college campuses. It is, by far, the most frequently visited area on campus.

Another popular area is the field between the Auditorium and the Red Cedar River. At the crest of the slope sits "The Rock," the Class of 1873 boulder. Its craggy surfaces feature spontaneously and brightly painted slogans and symbols often proclaiming an upcoming event. With its wide expanse, this area is a perfect site for outdoor concerts and other student gatherings. Nearby, down the slope, the Department of Theatre stages Summer Circle Theatre annually. Yet the area has no name.

Nestled amidst the trees is another grassy area, known informally as "frog hollow." It is north of the Red Cedar River, just across the street, west of the IM Circle. Here, on hot summer evenings, people once met for concerts. In the 1990s, small performing arts groups, as part of the Festival of Michigan Folklife, continued the tradition. It has no official name. Perhaps, for these areas, meeting at the "ducks," the "rapids," or "frog hollow" is sufficiently definitive. Sometimes, people feel they can call a place their own when someone has not already given it an offi-

Top: **Red Cedar rapids and duck feeding area, looking toward the John A. Hannah Administration Building, 2002.** *Above:* **"The Rock," Class of 1873 Rock, an ever-changing billboard, looking south toward the Red Cedar River, 2002.**

cial name. The way we use space keeps evolving.

After this look at the purpose, occupants, role within the university, and names of campus buildings and spaces, the missing piece is information about their architects. During the lifetime of Michigan State University, the practice of architecture in the United States has changed considerably. Architectural firms with a single principal and a few assistants have become large corporate organizations. Although a single person may be listed as the architect on any given building, the building concept is often formed by the work of many architects. The work of related professionals, such as engineers and landscape architects, shapes other aspects of the overall design. For the buildings on the Michigan State campus, the story is the same.

As architectural firms became larger and the firm principals began to emulate corporate structuring, they divided work by specialty. This division of labor provided a way to enhance design efficiency and maintain administrative and "ultimate design" control.[147] Firms became confident they could provide the service the client wanted. Likewise, if the client wanted a number of buildings with similar purposes, it was wise to rehire the same firm or to establish a contractual relationship for a certain period of time. This explains why there are relatively few firms responsible for the buildings we experience today at Michigan State.

As architectural firms grew, some focused their attention on the development of expertise and, hopefully, a good reputation for the design of certain building types. This explains why some architectural firms received certain contracts. They possessed the skill needed to design for a specific building function. In 1924, Pond and Pond, a nationally recognized firm, won the commission for the MSU Union, most likely because it had already designed other union buildings on campuses such as the University of Michigan.

The commissioning of building contracts at Michigan State reflects these national developments in the architectural profession. When a campus building was the size of a house, it was feasible for a single architect to be the prime professional. As building needs became more complex, firms became larger. A firm's name might include the names of the lead architects or, as with a law firm, the name may remain long after the original participants retire, to assure the visibility of the firm's professional presence.

The list of architects for the buildings on campus reveals that a construction firm or the campus Physical Plant is responsible for certain buildings. Often, these are utilitarian structures or additions to extant buildings. This choice of a builder rather than an architect also reflects twentieth-century practice. Developers, not architects, design the majority of buildings in the United States. Here, the word *architect* is used to include any professional involved in building design.

At Michigan State, when the buildings were small, not much larger than a house, a single architect could be the lead professional. But even for the oldest extant buildings on campus—Cowles House, Linton Hall, Eustace-Cole

Hall, Cook Hall, and Old Botany—builders usually worked with the architects. Each of these buildings was designed by a different architect. Edwyn Bowd, a Lansing architect, designed Old Botany in 1892. During the next decade, as Michigan State affirmed its commitment to campus planning, it decided to hire a university architect and chose Bowd. He proceeded to design Marshall Hall, an addition to Old Botany, Agriculture Hall, the 1913 portion of Giltner Hall, IM Recreative Sports Circle, Spartan Stadium, and other buildings. At this time the campus architect actually designed campus buildings. Over time this practice would change, and the university architect eventually served as a consultant, an enforcer of campus architectural policy, and as a liaison with the firm hired for a particular commission. As the complexity of architectural needs accelerated and as the funding sources became more varied, it became both important and practical to hire different architects and their firms to address a growing range of architectural needs.

Bowd continued as the campus architect after he joined with Orlie Munson to form Bowd-Munson. Until 1940 this firm designed the majority of campus buildings, many of which are Collegiate Gothic. The Munson firm, successor to Bowd-Munson, continued, until 1957, to design numerous campus buildings in several styles, including Spartan Stadium additions, Jenison Field House, Berkey Hall, and Faculty Apartments. Other firms also received commissions. The Ralph Calder firm designed Williams Hall in 1937 and, subsequently, Olin Memorial Health Center, the Library, the Music Building, the Paolucci Building, Landon Hall, other residence halls, and many of the buildings that date from the 1950s and 1960s. Manson and Carver and their successors focused on residential design for Michigan State and designed University Village, Cherry Lane, Spartan Village, and Van Hoosen Hall.

Since the early 1970s, no single architectural firm has been predominant. This reflects the complexity of contemporary building designs, more diverse ways for securing architectural funding, and the overall tendency of Michigan State and other universities to work with a range of corporate providers. Just as most campuses contract for food and other services, they also contract for architectural commissions. The days of one firm designing a majority of campus buildings in a specified period of time are over. Campus needs change. Specialists in restoration might be needed for a commission such as Eustace-Cole Hall and different specialists would be called upon for scientific laboratory design in Biomedical-Physical Sciences. This change has interesting implications for the future. With a range of architectural firms eligible to bid for commissions, the diversification of the architectural vocabulary for new buildings may expand. As always, too, the ways in which people see, use, and experience the campus will affect the built environment of the future.

Conclusion

If culture is "all aspects of the way in which a society relates to and makes sense of the world,"[148] then visual culture is the exploration of these ways through visual phenomena such as the built environment and the landscape. Michigan State University's visual culture is integral to its commitment to the stewardship of its campus park; it becomes comprehensible through the use of exploratory tools—style, users, discourse, aesthetics, and history.

Visitors like the interweaving of campus landscape and buildings. Sometimes they remark that it is unusual that there is no main entrance, no single building that outshines the rest, and no international architectural stars who left buildings as monuments to their individual creativity. The answer is simple and direct. As a large public university with a complex mission to produce, teach, and disseminate knowledge, access, not exclusivity, is paramount. The campus should be accessible from many entrances, buildings should complement one another, and no area should outshine the rest. Even the Trowbridge Road extension, which opened as a campus entrance on 21 August 2001, bears similarities to some campus entrances. It has a brick and limestone marker, incised with "Michigan State University," like the Bogue Street entrance; it provides boulevard access, like the Abbot entrance; it features a curved roadway, like the Beal entrance; and like all of them, it includes trees to mark space.

The campus is an environmental metaphor for the common good. It is the interstices that hold everything together. Its parts, while of high quality, should not demand inordinate attention. Each contributes uniquely to the whole.

The strength of Michigan State University comes from its people.
Its people built and use its buildings.
These buildings offer paths to knowing the university . . . ways of seeing.

The Campus as Areas to Explore
Buildings, Places, Spaces

Area One: West Circle Drive

The West Circle Drive area is the site of the original built environment of the Michigan State University campus park. Its Abbot entrance bears the name of Theophilus C. Abbot, the third president of Michigan State, who served in 1862–84.

What makes the West Circle Drive area remarkable is its preservation as a campus park, historical and serene, although it is traversed every day by hundreds of students, faculty, staff, and visitors. Almost a century ago, Ossian Simonds, a nationally known landscape architect, described this area, surrounded by West Circle Drive, as a "sacred space," because it is the "oak opening," the place where Michigan State University began in 1855.

Unique among college campuses today, this beautiful, picturesque space retains its nineteenth-century character. It borders downtown East Lansing and includes academic and residential buildings, historical markers, and outdoor sculptures all set amidst trees, shrubs, and lawns. Notable natural areas are the Beal Plantation, at Michigan Avenue and Grand River Avenue, with oaks dating from the eighteenth century, and the W. J. Beal Botanical Garden, established in 1873, the oldest continuously operated botanical garden in the United States.

By 1928 all of the buildings that exist today along West Circle Drive from Agriculture Hall to the MSU Union already stood. In their scale and styles, they provide a glimpse of the development of American architecture from the late nineteenth to the early twentieth centuries. During the late 1930s and through the 1940s, the West Circle Complex of residence halls (Campbell, Gilchrist, Landon, Mayo, Williams, and Yakeley) and the Music Building opened their doors. Then, in the 1960s, the Music Practice Building and the Library arose to complete the complement of buildings we know today.

West of the Music Building is Walter Adams Field, a lawn framed by mature trees. This greenspace is a frequent site for informal student athletic games, practices and pep rallies of the Michigan State University Marching Band, and special public outreach events.

Easiest access: From the Beal entrance, off Michigan Avenue, head east; from the Abbot entrance, Grand River Avenue at Abbot Road, head south.

Boundaries: Michigan Avenue, Grand River Avenue, east edge of West Circle Drive, and the Red Cedar River.

Predominant historical style, name, or theme: Revivalist styles. The "sacred space," an academic village.

Date of oldest extant building in this area: 1857, Cowles House (original portion).

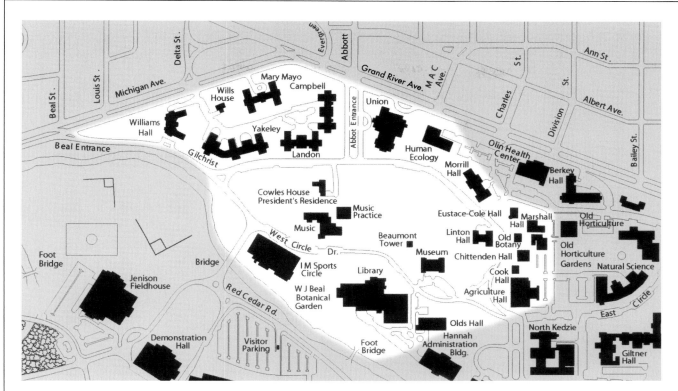

Selected Historical Sites or Markers, Public Art, and Natural Areas

1900 Fountain, between the Michigan State University Museum and Linton Hall

When the Class of 1900 donated this white sandstone fountain, its location was along the perimeter of West Circle Drive. To obtain water, horses used the trough on the drive (north) side of the fountain. Its face reads, "1900." Passersby used the spigot on its footpath (south) side, where the phrase "Class of 1900" is incised.

Beal Plantation, east of Mayo Hall, in the West Circle Complex

In 1874 Professor William J. Beal planted oak trees here to complement those already standing. The oldest oak, a swamp white oak, is close to Mayo Hall. Mark Nixon wrote the following in the spring 2001 issue of *MSU Today*:

"Before there was a Michigan State University—heck, before there was a State of Michigan—I stood tall, lording over the land.

"I'm the granddaddy of trees hereabouts. Not exactly older than dirt, but you can honestly say Ben Franklin and I were contemporaries. . . .

"I was a grown-up when the Agricultural College of the State of Michigan was founded in 1855. Some of my limbs were thick as fence posts by the time R. E. Olds and Henry Ford started tinkering in their garages . . . .

"My closest neighbors are the oaks planted from acorns by W. J. Beal, the university's famous botanist. That was in 1874. Young whelps is what they are. Babes in the woods."

Botanical Laboratory, commemorative ground marker, just east of the Intramural Recreative Sports–Circle (IM Circle)

The marker reads: "NE COR. / Botanical Lab / Built 1879 / Burned 3/20/1890."

Children Reading, terra cotta sculpture, outside the north entrance of Williams Hall, ca. 1938, Clivia Calder Morrison

Turquoise glaze accentuates these simple yet graceful girls who, perhaps, one day will live in Williams Hall, a residence hall originally for women. The artist, Clivia Calder Morrison, produced this work as part of the Works Progress Administration/Federal Art Project.

THOMAS KACHADURIAN

Children Reading, by Clivia Calder Morrison, north entrance, Williams Residence Hall.

Fountain, on the terrace of Mayo Hall, in the West Circle Complex

This fountain stands in an octagonal pool on the terrace of Mayo Hall. It was a gift from Nelson S. Mayo, son of Mary Bryant Mayo (1845–1903).

Half-way Stone, fragment outside the southwest corner of the MSU Union

Also known as the "split rock," this fragment was part of a larger stone that marked the halfway point between campus and downtown Lansing, at Kipling Boulevard and Michigan Avenue, and the end of the trolley line. Students stopped at this stone to rest. In 1924, in anticipation of the widening of Michigan Avenue, pieces of the rock were dispersed, with one fragment being delivered to campus. Long after his college days, Frank Hodgman, Class of 1862, wrote:

When half the toilsome way was passed, we rested by the stone

Within whose cleft a cherry pit had taken root and grown;

Eventually, the cherry tree grew large enough to split the rock, thus making it possible to call it "split rock" and, later, to disperse its pieces to different locations.

Michigan State College, relief, Abbot Road entrance, Samuel Cashwan

The Class of 1938 and Michigan State's agricultural heritage are commemorated with this relief. Samuel Cashwan, who also produced the sculpture *Three Musicians* that stands outside the Music Building, used an Art Deco vocabulary here to depict a young man leaning on a horse and a seated woman holding a sheaf of wheat. The curved base, often covered with vegetation, provides a stable foundation for this relief, funded by the Class of 1938 and the Works Progress Administration/Federal Art Project.

Saint's Rest, sidewalk marker, between the Michigan State University Museum and Linton Hall

This marker, two feet by two-and-a-half feet, recalls the first residence hall on campus, Saint's Rest. The marker's lettering is faint but it reads as follows:

N.E. Corner
Saint's Rest
Built 1856
Burned Dec. 9, 1876

Three Musicians, cast concrete sculpture, outside the Music Building, Samuel Cashwan

With their bold energy and intertwined, angular contours, these three musicians—a bass player, a drummer, and a saxophonist—recall Cubism and convey the vibrancy of the sounds that preoccupy them. Originally, the sculpture stood on the east side of the Band Shell that once existed on the site of Bessey Hall. The Class of 1939 gave this sculpture and another similar one as a class gift.

World War I, stone marker, just west of Williams Hall

Amidst a stand of red oak trees, a large stone boulder bears a bronze plaque. It reads:

In memory of the men of the Michigan Agricultural College who gave their lives in the Great War this grove is planted.
June 11, 1919.

The thirty-six names listed are those of men who were members of classes from 1894 until 1920.

W. J. Beal Botanical Garden, 1873

Professor William J. Beal designed the original format for the oldest continuously operated botanical garden in the United States. He initially collected plants native to Michigan. Today, this display garden contains more than 5,000 species from around the world that may be observed via a self-directed tour. The garden's nineteenth-century rustic setting, complemented by a pond, winding paths, and the nearby Red Cedar River, is still evident. Frederick Law Olmsted, the nationally prominent nineteenth-century American landscape architect, would have been pleased with this place for reflection and learning because he stressed the importance of aesthetics in the design of land-grant colleges to encourage responsiveness to one's surroundings. At one time, this garden was named the Beal-Garfield Botanical Garden to recognize the contributions of Charles W. Garfield, M.S. (Class of 1870), who served as garden supervisor during the period when Professor Beal began to plant along the Red Cedar River ravine. The garden is listed on the State Register of Historic Sites.

Nearby, across West Circle Drive, just south of what is now Beaumont Tower, Dr. Beal buried twenty pint bottles, commonly known as "Beal jars," each with 1,000 seeds from twenty different plant species, to test seed germination. As the years passed and jars were dug from the ground, several species grew.

The commemorative plaque reads:

W. J. Beal Centennial 1873–1973
Michigan State University

W. J. Beal Botanical Garden
Professor William James Beal, Scientist and Teacher, started this garden in 1873 with 140 grasses and cloves. Other useful plants were added until at Dr. Beal's retirement in 1910, the collection included 2,100 species. Dr. Beal saw the garden as an educational tool in the development of observational talent in both students and visitors. His emphasis on a naturalistic design with both native and exotic plants has endured from its original inception. This outdoor laboratory has expanded to 6 acres and over 5,000 species and on its centennial is acknowledged as the oldest of North American botanical gardens.

Walter Adams Field

On the east edge of the field a plaque, mounted on a rock, reads:

Walter Adams (1922–1998), master teacher and one of the foremost antitrust economists of his generation, served from April 1, 1969, until January 1, 1970, as 13th President of Michigan State University. Prolific author and frequent witness before Congressional Committees, Adams joined the faculty in 1947, retiring in 1993 as Distinguished University Professor and Professor of Economics. . . . As president, he guided the University at the height of the student protests associated with the Vietnam War and the Civil Rights Movement.

He was an honorary member of the Spartan marching band.

On autumn Saturdays, he led the band from this field to Spartan Stadium. May those who visit Adams Field forever cherish the memory of a scholar who embodied the values and traditions of Michigan State University with dignity, humor and love.

In 1999 the Board of Trustees approved the rededication of this field, informally known to some as Landon Field and, even earlier, as the Old Drill Field.

Intramural Recreative Sports–Circle (IM Circle)

Bowd, 1916
Calder, 1958

This symmetrical Beaux-Arts Classical design is urbane and exudes confidence. Strong vertical rhythms of projecting piers and arched windows complement prominent, horizontal bands of brick and limestone. The exceptionally beautiful details of the front entrance include festoons, comprised of garlands and wreaths, and a cartouche or ornamental tablet featuring the script letters "MAC" for Michigan Agricultural College. While the original building dates from the time of the City Beautiful movement and reflects an interest in civic pride, the International Style addition along the south facade offers a reserved geometric vocabulary.

IM Circle was originally the Women's Gymnasium. Later, its name became the Women's IM to distinguish it from the Men's IM, which is now known as the Intramural Recreative Sports–West or IM West. The IM Circle contains sports gyms, two swimming pools, sauna, steam, and weight rooms, and a private sunbathing area. It is one of several campus locations for intramural and special-events athletic programming. Occasionally, in earlier years, the building was the site of public meetings and large campus events. In 1923 commencement ceremonies occurred on the second floor.

Music Building
Calder, 1940
Calder, 1956

As a Public Works Administration project, this brick building embodies the exterior design simplicity that emerged in the 1930s. A prominent hipped roof caps the rambling floor plan. Limestone trim visually links the different sections of the building. While the overall massing appears to be a spare interpretation of Collegiate Gothic, the relatively large and metal-framed windows allude to future stylistic developments.

Subtle decorative details are Art Deco. They include streamlined limestone reliefs that enframe the southwest entrance as symbols of dance and performance and introduce the viewer to the world of music within the building. Samuel Cashwan, who supervised the Michigan sculpture program for the Works Progress Administration, produced these reliefs to make art a part of people's lives.

In the courtyard, Cashwan's Cubist *Three Musicians* "perform." This cast-concrete sculpture includes a bass player, drummer, and saxophonist. It was one of a pair of sculptures that flanked the Art Deco Band Shell of 1938, which once occupied the grounds where Bessey Hall now stands.

***Three Musicians* by Samuel Cashwan, ca. 1940. This sculpture is from a pair of sculptures the Class of 1939 gave to flank the stage of the former Band Shell, which was dedicated in 1938 as a Class of 1937 gift.**

GARY BOYNTON

Music Practice Building

Calder, 1968

This tall, International Style design stands unadorned amidst the trees on the periphery of the oak opening. Its brick and concrete exterior complements its "partner" across the courtyard, the Music Building. Prominent concrete projecting piers heighten the overall square plan and, on a sunny day, transform the facades into a dramatic interplay of light and dark verticals.

The Music Practice Building is best seen from West Circle Drive by looking north across the lush grotto, known as Sleepy Hollow, where concerts are performed in warm weather. Until the early twentieth century, a wooden wagon bridge crossed this grotto or ravine, most likely in the same way West Circle Drive does today. In Sleepy Hollow, an extension of the W. J. Beal Botanical Garden, the special growth requirements of acid soil plants are met. In the 1850s, clay was dug here to make the brick for the first campus building, College Hall. Several decades ago, students gathered here to burn freshman caps and senior textbooks.

When classes are in session, it is possible to walk on this part of campus and hear a variety of musical sounds before it is possible to actually see either the Music Practice Building or the Music Building through the trees.

Library

Calder, 1955   *Calder, 1967*
Physical Plant, 1964   *Calder, 1995*

Precise linearity, open-ended internal spaces, and refined geometric patterning are attributes of this fine example of brick-and-glass International Style architecture. The visual lightness of the steel-cage construction is especially evident at night when the bands of windows truly appear as transparent openings. The projecting pavilion that forms the north-facade stairwell is actually a glass box—a hallmark of the International Style. A walk up or down the stairwell's cantilevered stairs, the "floating" steps, provides an opportunity to see the space between these steps and the exterior curtain wall and to experience the openness of International Style design. Users of this stairwell also have lovely views of trees, landscaping, and the fountain facing West Circle Drive. Green-tinted glass, green spandrels, and aluminum trim all reflect light and help to integrate this asymmetrical plan with its site. Marble, granite, and stainless steel are other featured building materials. During the warm months, the fountain, a gift of the Class of 1968, provides additional beauty.

The East Wing of 1967 employs the same simple geometric vocabulary, but here transparency alternates with opacity as large swaths of brick cover most of the facade and accept narrow vertical window openings as accents. The 1995 addition expanded the fourth floor of the original building with sensitivity to the overall design, so that today the different stages of building construction are barely discernible.

The Library houses an expanding research collection of more than 4,500,000 volumes, the G. Robert Vincent Voice Library, and Special Collections in cooperation with fourteen branch libraries. Social customs come and go, but the library remains a center of student life. In 1999, the Cyber-Café, whose name reflects the involvement of the Michigan State University Libraries with new technologies, opened on the first floor to provide users with computer access as well as beverages and snacks.

On a wall near the reference area is a Works Progress Administration mural by Henry Bernstein. Bernstein produced the mural, titled *America's First Agricultural College*, for the East Lansing Post Office. It is on loan from the United States Post Office.

Beaumont Tower

Donaldson-Meier, 1928

In its verticality and detailing, this brick and limestone Collegiate Gothic monument asserts the traditional ideals of scholarship and aspiration toward high standards. It recalls English, French, and other European church towers with the extension of one spire to a greater height (104 feet) than the others. Lancet windows, crenelations, and random limestone detailing are other Collegiate Gothic traits.

Lee Lawrie conceived the tower's Art Deco relief, *The Sower*, which carries the Biblical inscription, "Whatsoever a man soweth." He was a nationally known sculptor of the 1920s who had amassed a considerable reputation for his civic and ecclesiastical sculpture. Previously, he had used the sower image for other commissions such as the Nebraska State Capitol in Lincoln, Nebraska. Here, the sower is a symbol of the growth and dissemination of knowledge that underscores the land-grant heritage. In the upper-left-hand corner of the relief, an owl wisely oversees the sower's activity while perched on a medallion showing College Hall and carrying the inscription "1857 Michigan State College of Agriculture and Applied Science." Fred Pfeiffer and Son did the actual carving.

Beaumont Tower stands on the edge of the "sacred space," the area where the initial Michigan State University buildings once stood. This is also the actual site of the northeast corner of College Hall (dedicated 1857), believed to be the first building in the United States erected for the teaching of scientific agriculture, and known to be the first home of the Michigan State University Museum. John W. and Alice Beaumont of

Detroit donated the bell tower to express the "gratitude and loyalty" Mr. Beaumont felt as an alumnus of the Class of 1882. From 1912 until 1921, when he served as a member of the State Board of Agriculture (now Board of Trustees), Beaumont assumed responsibility for directing the plans to renovate College Hall. After it collapsed in 1918, he offered his own money to erect the tower.

In addition to serving as a timepiece for decades, Beaumont Tower has become a prominent university symbol and a landmark for many formal and informal gatherings, including meetings of the Tower Guard and Mortar Board honor societies, student demonstrations, and carillon concerts. In 1996 the carillon renovation was completed. The carillon now has forty-nine bells, with ten dating from 1928 and thirteen from 1935. Today, every fifteen minutes the Westminster Quarters strike to remind us of Michigan State and the strength to be found in the pursuit of knowledge.

Michigan State University Museum
Bowd-Munson, 1927
Calder, 1957

Gently pointed arches, projecting piers, and limestone window surrounds are strong Collegiate Gothic traits. They complement Beaumont Tower, which is one year older and stands just a few hundred feet west. The museum's symmetrical plan is accented with two projecting pavilions at either end. The central hallway, impressively dressed in polished Tennessee Napoleon marble, extends between the north and the south entrances and leads respectively to the "sacred space" and to West Circle Drive. Decades ago, when West Circle Drive was smaller, it ran on the north side of the building, past what was known then as the front entrance. The more abstract piers of the west facade are surprisingly expressive and, with the contrast of the recessed windows, affirm their stolidity.

Bowd-Munson designed the original building as a library to replace the space the library had occupied since 1881 in the Library-Museum (now Linton Hall). Then, in the mid-1950s, the library collections were transferred to the new library, across West Circle Drive. Renovations followed to prepare this space for museum collections, including the extension of the top floor to enclose more space. The band of windows along the top of the south facade defines this area. With their tripartite arrangement, these windows affirm the rhythm established by the original projecting piers located below.

Today, the Michigan State University Museum houses documented research collections in anthropology, history, paleontology, zoology, and folk culture as foci for scholarly study and extensive educational-outreach programming.

THOMAS KACHADURIAN

Olds Hall

Bowd, 1916

The Ransom E. Olds Hall of Engineering is a Neo-Classical design with a pronounced white, bracketed cornice and attic story. The tripartite division of the wall elevation into the components of a classical column lends a sense of historical tradition and visual stability. The column base is the ground story, the shaft is made up of the intermediate floors, and the capital is the attic story. Two projecting end pavilions affirm the symmetry of the front facade. The front entrance features a bold, bracketed, two-story, segmental arch. Below, a cornice and a patterned transom accent the entry doors. Rows of windows display segmental arches with limestone keystones, sills, and diamond shapes in their spandrels to create a lively pattern of light and dark across the facades.

On 5 March 1916 a fire raged and destroyed the previous Engineering Hall (1907) and the workshops (1885). Ransom E. Olds, the famous automaker from Lansing,

Michigan, was persuaded to donate $100,000 for a fireproof general engineering building and three workshops. The State of Michigan legislature could not garner the votes to allocate funds for rebuilding because there was sentiment, at the time, to absorb the Michigan Agricultural College's engineering program into the engineering program at the University of Michigan. On 28 April 1916, Olds told the State Board of Agriculture, "I have great faith in the Michigan Agricultural College and see no reason why it should not become one of the foremost colleges in the United States." At the 1 June 1917 dedication, many commented favorably about the location of the buildings in a prominent position "facing the campus" on what is now West Circle Drive. Today, the shops are gone and the main building, identical to the original 1907 design, houses different academic and administrative units.

GARY BOYNTON

Agriculture Hall

Bowd, 1909
Physical Plant, 1991
Architects Four, 1999

"Ag Hall" sits imposingly atop a landscaped knoll. Four gargantuan, poured-concrete, Tuscan columns assure the monumentality of this Neo-Classical design. The three-story gallery, balustrade, and decorative brackets that support the entrance lintel are all notable characteristics. A prominent cornice, attic coursing, and limestone base all form horizontal bands to reaffirm the building's girth.

At the time of its construction, Agriculture Hall was the largest and most noticeable building on campus. Its internal concrete supports rendered it more fireproof than other campus buildings. Stylistically, it continued the Neo-Classical vocabulary seen earlier in nearby Morrill Hall (1900), but immediately it began serving as a symbol of a modern land-grant college and of contemporary approaches to agricultural research. It occupies space formerly used for a cattle barn, and at one time it included a livestock-judging pavilion at the rear with a gallery for observers. Farm mechanics, animal husbandry, agronomy, and soil

chemistry were some of the subjects taught in this building. Today, it continues to be home to the College of Agriculture and Natural Resources, houses some of its programs, and is listed on the State Register of Historic Sites.

In October 2000, the 27,000-square-foot east-wing annex was formally dedicated. Its exterior blends stylistically with the main building while providing up-to-date offices for 4-H Youth Development, the Department of Agriculture Economics, and MSU Extension. Particularly notable is the atrium, furnished by the Class of 1949, which links the annex and the original building. This impressive interior space features a triptych mural, *ANR Past, Present and Future*, on its west wall. Robert "Bob" Brent, a university artist, created this mural, four feet high and twenty-one feet long, to honor Lynn "Bus" Robertson, who worked for forty years at Michigan State in crop and soil sciences and extension.

Albert J. Cook Hall

Samuel Johnson, 1889

Cook Hall is stylistically eclectic and made of brick and Lake Superior sandstone. It includes general Romanesque Revival characteristics such as the round-headed windows above its front entrance and the Richardsonian arched entry with recessed entry doors. Relieving arches, simple roof bracketing, and stone sills are other interesting details.

Cook Hall was the first agricultural laboratory on campus. It is one of five domestically scaled designs for what became known along West Circle Drive as Laboratory Row. This group also includes Chittenden Hall, Old Botany, Marshall Hall, and Eustace-Cole Hall, an unusually intact grouping of late-nineteenth-century architecture, characteristic of what once existed on many other land-grant college campuses. The entire group is listed on the State Register of Historic Sites.

When Agriculture Hall opened in 1909, this building became "Entomology," as the incised lettering above its entrance indicates. After 1948, the date of the completion of the Natural Science building, entomology moved there. In 1969 this building assumed a new name, Cook Hall. It honors Albert J. Cook (Class of 1862), who, after study at Harvard University, returned here as an instructor in mathematics. Later, he became a professor of zoology and entomology and one of the leading economic entomologists in the United States. He also served as the first curator of the museum.

GARY BOYNTON

Alfred K. Chittenden Hall

George Lohman, 1901

Chittenden Hall is an eclectic design with a unique Neo-Classical entrance. It displays Doric pilasters, a sunburst brick entryway arch, and an entablature containing a frieze with letters that say "Forestry." To recall trees and forestation, the carved and cast "strokes and serifs" of the letters are represented as tree trunks and limbs. Round-headed second-story windows reiterate the shape of the entryway arch. Standard first-story sash windows recall the rectilinearity of the entablature. The result is a reserved brick and sandstone design.

This was the first campus building designed for dairy operations. In 1900, a few months before the building's 1901 dedication, it received the college's commercial oper-

ation from the basement of the first agriculture laboratory, Cook Hall. In 1913, after the dairy moved to a new building at the north terminus of Farm Lane, the frieze inscription had to be changed to remove the "dairy" signifier. It became Forestry to identify a new academic occupant, the Department of Forestry, which would reside here until 1966.

In 1969 the building acquired a new name, Chittenden Hall, to honor the outstanding achievement in forestry of Professor Alfred K. Chittenden, who directed the academic forestry programs 1914–30, conducted research on reforestation and maple sugar, and developed a nursery on campus. The building is listed on the State Register of Historic Sites.

GARY BOYNTON

Old Botany

Bowd, 1892
Bowd, 1908

The Queen Anne style, with its fondness for irregularity, is evident in the asymmetrical facades and in the variety of the gables, chimneys, and windows. There are round-headed windows, standard sash windows with relieving arches and, on the north side, an exceptionally large stairwell glass with a segmental arch. This eclectic design displays heavy massing and a bold entry arch, both of which are reflective of the Richardsonian Romanesque, a very popular style of the day. Lake Superior sandstone, Michigan fieldstone, and unusual brickwork add textural variety inventively.

MICHIGAN STATE UNIVERSITY ARCHIVES AND HISTORICAL COLLECTIONS

Botanical Laboratory, built 1879, burned 1890. This building was designed by Watson and Arnold of Lansing.

The first botanical laboratory was a Gothic-frame structure that housed Professor W. J. Beal's botanical museum. Unfortunately, it burned in March 1890. For this building, the second botany laboratory, there was an impressive cornerstone-laying ceremony and dedication on 22 June 1892. The cornerstone inscription, "Botany A.D. 1892," is still prominent. Look for it just left of the building entrance; sometimes ivy covers it. A complementary addition arose in 1908. Today, this entire building is known as Old Botany and is listed on the State Register of Historic Sites.

Marshall Hall

Bowd, 1902
Physical Plant, 1991

Although Marshall Hall is stylistically eclectic, the Richardsonian Romanesque inspiration is evident in its hipped roof with cross gables, cavernous arched entrance, and decorated gables. The entryway arch springs from heavy Michigan fieldstone piers and has prominent brick and limestone archivolts. The first-floor paired sash windows have brick hoodmolds with limestone stops to add decorative interest. Inside, the Gothic-inspired wooden staircase banister is intact. Marshall Hall is positioned slightly east of the other members of Laboratory Row and, therefore, slightly farther from West Circle Drive, but in scale, color, and style its membership in this group is unmistakable. The 1991 addition of a seminar room has large round-headed windows that tastefully recall those of the original building, which is listed on the State Register of Historic Sites.

In 1903 this building was known as Bacteriology and was one of the first structures erected in the United States solely for research and teaching in this field. Dr. Charles E. Marshall served here as assistant professor and head of the Department of Bacteriology and Farm Hygiene 1900–02 and professor and head of the Department of Bacteriology and Hygiene 1902–12. He is the person for whom Marshall Hall was later named. As a brilliant researcher, he also edited the journal *Microbiology* and initiated the production of hog cholera serum for distribution in the state of Michigan.

Eustace-Cole Hall

William D. Appleyard, 1888
Architects Four, 1998

Stylistically, Eustace-Cole Hall is eclectic yet impressive in its direct, bold massing. Its prominent shingled front gable and blended stair tower and its deep window reveals speak of the Shingle Style. Its conical tower roof, emphatic arched entry, and use of brick, ashlar, and Indiana limestone recall the Richardsonian Romanesque. The overall asymmetry and the inclusion of a tower are characteristic of both styles. Simple sash windows predominate.

Originally, three sash windows with pivot windows above them occupied the front facade. Now there are sets of four. At one time, the shingling was multicolored, the tower had a turret, and a greenhouse stood attached to the south facade. This is the fifth building in Laboratory Row and is a recognizable member of the group in view of its scale, textures, and arched entrance.

Initially, Eustace Hall was the Horticultural Laboratory. Professor Liberty Hyde Bailey conceived the building as

the first distinct horticultural laboratory in the United States. In 1961 the building was renamed for Professor Harry J. Eustace, who was an alumnus (Class of 1901) and head of the Department of Horticulture 1908–19. The building was home to Liberal Arts in 1927–37, Philosophy and Psychology in 1937–44, and "Basic" or University College beginning in 1944. Since 1969 it has been the home of the Honors College.

In 1998 the Board of Trustees approved a name change to Eustace-Cole Hall, in honor of two alumni, Jeffrey and Kathryn Cole, who donated funds for the building's extensive renovation. It is listed on the State Register of Historic Sites. Jeffrey Cole was a Social Science–Pre-Law major and member of the Honors College who graduated with High Honor in 1970. Kathryn Cole graduated with a Master of Business Administration in 1990.

Robert S. Linton Hall

Marsh-Arnold; Appleyard (supervising architect), 1881
Munson, 1947
FTC&H, 1996

The original High Victorian Romanesque T-shaped design has a central lantern tower, rich moldings, prominent dormers, and stringcourses. Orange brick, buff Indiana limestone, Michigan fieldstone, granite, and wood enhance strong surface rhythms and reflect Victorian taste. Above the arched entryway are the words "Library-Museum" and another arch, which contains two windows with trefoil arches and delicate, floral incising surrounding the building's date, "1881."

The West Circle entrance leads to the 1947 Collegiate Gothic addition and displays an oak tympanum. The tympanum's relief depicts the historic Michigan State University seal including College Hall. This seal derives from an 1869 State Board of Agriculture authorization for a woodcut to be used to print the frontispiece of the college academic catalog. In 1876, an unidentified student created a drawing for this woodcut and, in turn, for what became the Linton Hall relief. In 1996 Linton Hall became accessible with the completion of a second addition executed to blend with the Collegiate Gothic style. The entire building is listed on the State Register of Historic Sites.

Linton Hall is the second oldest extant building on campus. It arose in 1881 as the Library-Museum, facing the open "sacred space" and the predecessor of West Circle Drive. Nearby, to its south, is the Class of 1900 gift of a horse trough and drinking fountain, which helps to define this historic area. Horses used to drink from the north side of this stone monument as they sauntered along West Circle Drive in front of what are now Linton Hall and the Michigan State University Museum.

Since its earliest days, the Library-Museum (Linton

Hall) also served as the administration building, including the president's office. In 1927, with the completion of a new library (now the Michigan State University Museum), the library holdings moved to this new facility and, for a few years, the president's office moved there, too. In the 1930s the Office of the President returned to the second floor of Linton Hall, to what is now the Office of the Dean, College of Arts and Letters. In 1969 the administrative offices and the Office of the President moved to the new John A. Hannah Administration Building. Overnight, Linton became "Old Administration." In that same year, Linton Hall acquired its present name in honor of Robert S. Linton, an alumnus of the Class of 1916 who worked for many years in this building as registrar. Today, the Graduate School and the College of Arts and Letters have offices here.

In 2001, reflecting on his own days as a Michigan State student and on President John Hannah's achievements, President M. Peter McPherson described Linton as "the place from which Hannah built the school."

Morrill Hall

Pratt-Koepka, 1900

This large Neo-Classical building displays a white pediment and cornice on its central pavilion and entry. In their whiteness, these architectural features contrast with the brick and Lake Superior red-sandstone exterior. Tuscan columns and unadorned piers sit atop the high porch. At one time, a balustrade added decorative detail to this entry porch and the entire roof. Originally, the design called for a symmetrical facade with north and south projecting pavilions. To avoid overspending the state appropriation, the north pavilion was never added. Trees were planted to hide this visual imbalance.

At first, Morrill Hall was known as the Women's Building. Madison Kuhn, in his 1955 history of Michigan State, notes that male students called it the "Coop." Designed for the teaching of domestic science, it contained offices, classrooms, a cooking laboratory, music rooms, and "living rooms" (bedrooms and sitting rooms) for 120 women. During the nineteenth century, as colleges and universities increased their commitment to educating women, the need for appropriate facilities to support new or revised curricula and to house female students grew. According to Mary Evans, president of Lake Erie College, who spoke at the 25 October 1900 dedication ceremonies, "The times were ripe for it . . . , the first in the world upon

Students in front of Morrill Hall, ca. 1950s.

such a scale, for the housing of an ideal of Household Science."

In 1937, as women students moved to the new West Circle Complex of residence halls, the building was remodeled solely as classroom, laboratory, and office space and the name "Morrill Hall" was affirmed. Justin S. Morrill introduced the bill that became the Morrill Act of 1862, as signed by President Abraham Lincoln, which gave land to each state to support colleges that would teach "agriculture and the mechanic arts . . . to promote . . . liberal and practical education." Many land-grant colleges and universities have a building named in honor of Morrill.

Among past and present users of Morrill Hall space are the Department of English, Department of History, Department of Philosophy, Department of Religious Studies, Center for Integrative Studies in the Arts and Humanities, and programs in the College of Human Ecology.

GARY BOYNTON

Human Ecology

Bowd, 1924
Bowd-Munson, 1937
Physical Plant, 1980

The steep roof, prominent cross gable, pier buttresses, and random limestone trim characterize this Collegiate Gothic design. The main entrance is notable for its dual segmental arches crowned by a larger arch, tripartite window with limestone medallions, and castellations. The ubiquitous metal-framed awning windows with pivot panels are characteristic of the 1920s and 1930s. These windows, like the readable L-shaped plan, seem modern in contrast to the otherwise historically inspired design.

Home Economics was the original name for this building. It was one of several substantial new classrooms and research buildings erected between the world wars to pro-vide facilities for specialized training that was not possible in older facilities. This building replaced the Women's Building (now Morrill Hall) as the site for instruction in home economics. In 1935, two years before the Home Economics building opened, the Division of Home Economics, which was founded in 1909, reorganized as four departments: Foods and Nutrition, Home Management and Child Development, Institutional Administration, and Textiles, Clothing and Related Arts. Subsequently it became the School of Home Economics, the College of Home Economics, and then the College of Human Ecology.

MSU Union

Pond and Pond, 1924   *Mayotte, Crouse, Dhaen, 1980*
Bowd-Munson, 1936   *Ralph Calder Associates, 1997*
Calder, 1949

The Michigan State University Memorial Union is Collegiate Gothic. Numerous cross gables, prominent limestone door surrounds, and semi-hexagonal two-story bay windows are strong stylistic traits. Subsequent brick and limestone additions offer complementary stylistic interpretations. These include a well-integrated access ramp and, as replacements for drafty Gothic wood tracery, unadorned thermal windows. At the south porch entrance, the Art Deco relief by Samuel Cashwan speaks heroically of the Greek mythological figure Prometheus, who brought fire and creativity to humankind. Light illuminates and inspires, from left to right, music, drama, sculpture, research, engineering, and agriculture.

The Union has four entrances to assure ready access to campus and to the city of East Lansing, thereby linking "town" and "gown" and helping to enhance the entrance at Abbot Road, which is a boulevard. Beginning in 1905, campus leaders called for a social and community center for students, faculty, alumni, and friends. The Class of 1915 pledged funds. Alumni endorsed the idea of converting College Hall to this purpose, but it collapsed in 1918. After World War I, at Michigan State and on many college and university campuses, the desire to commemorate alumni who died in the war became intense. Faculty, students, alumni, and friends pledged funds for the Michigan Agricultural College Union Memorial Building to serve as a campus community center and to honor alumni. The college selected the well-known Chicago architectural firm, Pond and Pond, for the commission because it had considerable experience designing unions, notably for Purdue University and the University of Michigan. In 1923, during "excavation week," students, faculty, and alumni voluntarily worked in four-hour shifts

to dig and remove 3,000 cubic yards of dirt to create space for the foundation and the basement. When the Union opened on 12 June 1925, the M.A.C. Association owned the building. In 1936 the college assumed ownership when it secured $150,000 in Works Progress Administration funds to finish the original building and add the east wing. Subsequent class gifts provided funds for accessibility remodeling and for the purchase of many of the art works that grace its halls. The Union continues to be the home of the Michigan State University Alumni Association; its 1990s renovations help to assure that it will continue to be a place where campus organizations meet and special community events occur.

In 1991 the Kresge Art Museum accepted a mural by Michigan artist Edgar Louis Yeager depicting Thomas Edison's workshop and the invention of the light bulb and placed it on long-term loan on the first floor of the Union. Originally, this 1937 mural hung in the Public Lighting Commission Building in Detroit, where it was integral to the decoration of a large room. In what is now the first-floor women's lounge, Pewabic tiles shine iridescently to form the fireplace surround. On the second floor, boldly carved wood reliefs by Professor Leonard Jungwirth adorn the wall outside the ballroom. *Diana and the Chase* (1947–48), approximately six by eight feet, features fluid forms. *Paul Bunyan Legend* (1947–48) is actually four separate reliefs, roughly textured, with dimensions of three to six feet.

The original President's House, built as part of Faculty Row in 1873 and designed by E. E. Meyers, Detroit, stood on the site of present-day Gilchrist Hall.

Cowles House

J. J. Scott, 1857
Calder, 1950

Alice B. Cowles House is the oldest extant building on campus. J. J. Scott of Toledo, Ohio, constructed this "farm cottage" as one of four houses for faculty and their families known as Faculty Row. The other three houses stood north on the other side of West Circle Drive. Today, what remains of the original structure are parts of the stone foundation and two exterior walls whose bricks probably were made from Red Cedar River clay. The original eclectic design had slightly projecting eaves. Its front-facing gable and full-height pilasters suggest the Italianate, its corbel gable and corbel course recall the Romanesque Revival, and the roundel affirms the influence of both styles. Renovations and additions integrate the house with the landscaping and maintain a modest, domestic scale in keeping with the democratic focus of a land-grant institution. The picturesque garden south of the house features a graceful bronze sculpture, *Young Girl and Fawn*, 1946, by John Hope, who was a staff artist at Michigan State 1942–62.

The first resident was the college's first president, Joseph R. Williams, who lived here during his term, 1857–59. Theophilus C. Abbot, the third president, was the next presidential occupant from 1862 until 1874; in 1874 he moved to the new President's House that once stood on the site of present-day Gilchrist Hall. Subsequent residents included Professor William James Beal, who stayed for thirty-nine years; Professor and Dean Ernst Bessey; and Herman Halladay, secretary to the State Board of Agriculture (now Board of Trustees) and secretary to the college. At one time, the house was used for the Department of Education and as a residence for women students. Since 1941, the beginning of the presidency of John A. Hannah, Cowles House has been the official presidential residence and an important site for many university receptions and social functions. In 1950, the estate of Michigan State alumnus Frederick Cowles Jenison provided the funding for extensive building renovations. The home became Cowles House in honor of Alice B. Cowles, the mother of Jenison. It is worth noting that Mrs. Cowles's father, Albert E. Cowles, was a member of the first group of students to enroll in 1857 at the Agriculture College of the State of Michigan. Cowles House is listed on the State Register of Historic Sites.

West Circle Complex

The West Circle Complex of six residence halls, originally for women, stands amidst ample trees between the Beal and the Abbot Road entrances. The complex is a visually cohesive unit executed in the Tudor style that draws on late medieval English (Gothic) examples and their Renaissance detailing. It is this Renaissance detailing that distinguishes this style from the more prevalent campus use of Collegiate Gothic. The West Circle Complex is reminiscent, in its quaintness, of the English country-house tradition. High-pitched gabled roofs and metal casement windows, often grouped in rows of three or more, are typical. Refined attention to precisely detailed brickwork, slate roofs, terra cotta, and metal trim recall the Arts and Crafts movement and its love of materials.

Given their consistent use, until recently, as residence halls for women, it is appropriate that each building is named in honor of a woman who made an important contribution to the history of Michigan State University. Campbell Hall is named for Louise H. Campbell, who was a state home demonstration leader from 1920 until 1930, an acting dean of home economics from 1922 until 1923, and the organizer of the first Farm Women's Week in 1928. Gilchrist Hall honors Maude Gilchrist who became dean of the Women's Department in 1901 and then served as dean of the Division of Home Economics from 1909 until 1913. Landon Hall derives its name from Linda Eoline Landon, who served as head librarian from 1891 until 1932. Mayo Hall commemorates Mary Bryant Mayo, a Grange leader, who appealed for the establishment of domestic-science courses for women and the funding of a women's building at Michigan State. Williams Hall bears the name of Sarah Langdon Williams, the spouse of Joseph R. Williams, the first president of Michigan State, 1857–59. Sarah Williams prepared and served meals to students in the first dormitory, Saint's Rest. Yakeley Hall recalls Elida Yakeley, the first registrar.

Campbell Hall

Malcomson, Calder, Hammond, 1939
Calder, 1969

Campbell Hall stands near the corner of Abbot Road and Grand River Avenue. Its symmetrical plan features a short central pavilion and longer projecting pavilions at either end. A formal garden with paths and benches extends this sense of order to the building's exterior. Simple round-headed entry doors with cut stone quoin-like detailing offer aesthetic appeal. Public Works Administration funds underwrote the completion of this hall designed for 250 women.

THOMAS KACHADURIAN

Gilchrist Hall
Calder, 1948

Gilchrist Hall is located on the site of the former President's House (1873), amidst horse chestnut and other varieties of trees, and faces West Circle Drive. It is linked with Yakeley Hall to form a large rambling plan. Gilchrist is stylistically the same as Yakeley. The quality of its detailing is notable. The dining room, now known as the "Pub," features oak flooring and stained glass windows with red, orange, green, yellow, rose, and clear glass. Plaster animals, oak leaves, owls, squirrels, acorns, and flowers form the crown molding of the walls. The first-floor lounge displays a photograph of Maude Gilchrist. The West Circle Drive or south entry doors have leaded glass insets.

GARY BOYNTON

Landon Hall
Calder, 1947
Calder, 1969

Landon Hall is slightly smaller than Campbell Hall but possesses the same symmetry. It stands just west of the cor-

ner of Abbot Road and West Circle Drive and displays beautiful patterned brickwork and prominent chimneys, window arcades, oriel windows, and a large semi-hexagonal window bay. In the cafeteria there are glazed terra cotta reliefs showing figures feeding chickens, carrying fish, picking grapes, or playing instruments. The artist of the reliefs is Professor Leonard Jungwirth, who also produced *The Spartan* (otherwise known as "Sparty"). In the lounge a photograph of Linda Eoline Landon hangs over the fireplace.

GARY BOYNTON

Mayo Hall
Malcomson, Trout, Higgenbotham, 1931

Mayo Hall has a large T-shaped design and can be approached from Michigan Avenue or along numerous other paths. The long view from West Circle Drive, framed by Landon Hall and Yakeley Hall, is particularly impressive because it sets the building at the end of an expanse of lawn reminiscent of a manor house. Decorative brickwork and prominent chimneys complement the restrained rhythm of the roof gables and the expanses of multi-paned windows. An outdoor fountain in an octagonal pool, centrally located on the front terrace, provides additional aesthetic interest. It was a gift from Nelson S. Mayo, son of Mary Bryant Mayo. Inside, an oil portrait of Mary Bryant Mayo (1845–1903) hangs in the east lounge on the oak paneling above the fireplace.

Williams Hall
Calder, 1937

Williams Hall stands west of the other residence halls in the West Circle Complex. A U-shaped plan allows for access from Michigan Avenue and West Circle Drive. Its south entrance is quintessentially Tudor; the door surround is incised with Gothic lettering that reads "Sarah Langdon Williams Hall" and topped with an oriel window and narrow casement windows. The inscription over the southeast entrance reads, "Every day in thy life is a leaf in thy history," and over the northeast entrance, it says, "Our life is what our thoughts make it." Above these inscriptions are decorative shields that read "MSC" and "1937" to honor Michigan State College and the date of Williams Hall. The large Michigan Avenue staired entrance includes a fish-head fountain spout and, above, on the parapet of the stair landing a turquoise terra cotta sculpture, *Children Reading*. Clivia Calder Morrison produced this work, circa 1938, as part of the Works Progress Administration/Federal Art Project. The three children are stylized yet representational and gracefully sit—absorbed in their reading. The figures are female, which is appropriate for a women's residence hall. Art historians agree that they are a symbol of education. Inside, a photograph of Sarah Langdon Williams (1822–1902) hangs over the lounge fireplace.

Yakeley Hall
Calder, 1948

Yakeley Residence Hall links with Gilchrist Hall. Its main facade stretches along West Circle Drive, separated from the sidewalk by a parapet, terrace, and cozy garden space. Prominent gables alternate with dormers that punctuate the slate roof. Brickwork in complex patterns such as herringbone and leaded glass in the entrance doors are among the high-quality decorative details. In its west lounge, a photograph of Elida Yakeley hangs over the fireplace. In the dining room are six simply contoured figures, in relief, depicting women working at an industrial machine, tending children, or carving. Opposite are men preparing food, tasting soup, or butchering poultry. The reliefs bear the signature of "Rudy 46" who prepared the molds for casting.

H. Merrill Wills House

Bowd-Munson, 1927

Wills House is a fine example of the Colonial Revival. This was the dominant style for domestic architecture in the United States during the first half of the twentieth century. The main hipped roof of this two-story brick building has a second, smaller, hipped roof on its west side that covers the two-story side porch. The south or front facade features a large Palladian window atop the main entrance. A cornice, four pilasters, and sidelights frame the paneled entry door. The roofline cornice has dentils that run continuously around the entire building. Its rear section, designed for the U.S. Weather Bureau as a weather observation post, is squarish, flat-roofed, and includes a cupola for sky observation.

In the 1940s, Michigan State received this house as a gift. It is located at 257 Michigan Avenue between Mayo Hall and Williams Hall and was the home of H. Merrill Wills, a meteorologist. Professor Madison Kuhn, on 14 May 1969, wrote the following of Merrill Wills: "Each morning he relayed the forecasts that came out of Chicago, assembled returns from Michigan stations, and issued each afternoon his own predictions for the state. By that work, by teaching courses in meteorology, and by working with many of the faculty he continued a tradition begun by Dr. Robert C. Kedzie, chemist, who in 1863 began to publish what became the oldest series of continuous weather observations in the state."

Area Two: East Circle Drive, Auditorium, Physics, and Dormitory Roads

The East Circle Drive area extending to Bogue Street emerged as the second major area of the campus to acquire academic and residential buildings and to occupy the remaining property north of the Red Cedar River. The story of its site development is interesting. Although the dates of the extant buildings range from the initial construction of Giltner Hall in 1913 to the opening of the John A. Hannah Administration Building in 1969, there were a number of buildings, long since burned or razed, that once occupied some of the same sites. For example, engineering shops and a power plant used to stand just east and south of Olds Hall in the location of the John A. Hannah Administration Building and its grass esplanade. Also, the East Circle Complex grounds used to be a large orchard. The area's Bogue Street boundary bears the name of Ernest Everett Bogue, professor of forestry and chair of forestry in 1902–07.

T. Glenn Phillips, hired initially in 1923 as a consulting landscape architect, was retained permanently in 1926, and in that same year, he presented his general campus plan, which focused attention on the natural beauty of the Red Cedar River and its suitability as a site for buildings. The Electrical Engineering Building, now known as the Computer Center, was the first building erected with its front door facing the river. Farther east along the river, just south of the Auditorium, large ornamental evergreen plantings also complement the river's banks.

What emerged was a picturesque arrangement of buildings, gardens, lawns, and streets rather than a hieratic, formal plan. There was and is a sense of planning purposefulness. The northern border of this area is Grand River Avenue. At the east boundary is the East Circle Complex, with Mason-Abbot and Snyder-Phillips, both originally designed for men as a complement to the West Circle Complex with its residence halls for women. The rest of the area contains academic and administrative buildings bordered to the south by the Red Cedar River.

Stylistically, the predominant use of Collegiate Gothic and the

Easiest access: From the Collingwood entrance, off Grand River Avenue, head south; from Bogue Street, head west on Dormitory Road; from Farm Lane, head east or west on Auditorium Road.

Boundaries: Grand River Avenue, Bogue Street, the Red Cedar River, the greenspace in front of the Administration Building, the parking areas at the terminus of Farm Lane and the parking area west of the Olin Memorial Health Center.

Predominant historical style, name or theme: Collegiate Gothic and International Style. The academic village becomes an academic park.

Date of oldest extant building in this area: 1913, Giltner Hall (original building).

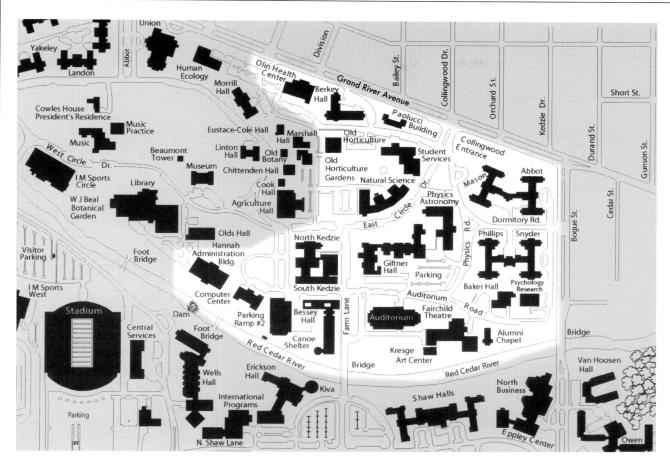

International Style parallels architectural developments on countless other American campuses and in the United States during these decades. Beyond this area is south campus and the post-1945 campus development that left period styles largely behind and more fully sought the modernism of the International Style, Brutalism, High Tech, and postmodernism.

Selected Historical Sites or Markers, Public Art, and Natural Areas

Band Shell marker, just west of Bessey Hall and north of the Red Cedar River walk

A large rock with a bronze plaque commemorates the place where the Band Shell stood before ground was broken for Bessey Hall. The plaque reads, "A Band Shell erected here was the gift of the Class of 1937. For 22 years, this structure was a center of cultural activities

for thousands of students in whose memories it will live forever. This marker commemorates part of our history."

Canoe Livery Service, south of Bessey Hall, on the north bank of the Red Cedar River

From Memorial Day through Labor Day, on Fridays, Saturdays, and Sundays, students and the public can rent canoes to use on the Red Cedar River within the limits of the MSU campus. The Class of 1988 provided funds for the construction of a wooden deck where people can sit and enjoy the river's beauty. A bronze plaque commemorates this gift and recalls that for a time, in the 1980s, this livery service was known informally as the Red Cedar Yacht Club. The plaque reads: "Red Cedar Yacht Club. Gift of the Class of 1988." The Class of 1937 funded the original livery service at this site.

Class of 1873 Rock, boulder standing just south of the Auditorium, near Farm Lane

This boulder, now known as "The Rock," came from the "delta" area, the triangular expanse of land that converges at the intersection of Michigan Avenue and Grand River Avenue in East Lansing. Students from the Class of 1873 hauled it, by ox teams, to the "sacred space," just south of Beaumont Tower, in that year as a gift. In 1986 the university moved it to its present location, where it continues to serve as an ever-changing billboard.

Master Benchmark, sidewalk in front of Olds Hall

This is the master benchmark for Michigan State University. Its bronze marker reads, "Master Benchmark 1934. U.S. Coast Guard and Geodetic Survey and Michigan State College." Campus Park and Planning records indicate that the benchmark is at elevation 844.224' above sea level. Latitude is N 42° 43' 50.19789" and longitude is W 84° 28' 54.34666". According to Jeffrey R. Kacos, director, Campus Park and Planning, "the benchmark is used as a reference point in the creation of other campus benchmarks. In turn, these benchmarks are the basis for accuracy when we hire land surveyors to create topographic maps of sections of the campus."

Old Horticulture Garden, 1939, 1991

Flanked by the Old Horticulture building, the Student Services building, and the Natural Sciences building, this greenscape was formerly the site of the Department of Horticulture's display gardens. In the late 1980s, the new Horticulture Demonstration Gardens were opened adjacent to the Plant and Soil Sciences building west of Bogue Street. During 1991 and 1992, an updated irrigation system, brick pavers, and new shade trees were added.

To the west of the Old Horticulture Garden and behind the Old Horticulture building, the Botany Greenhouses, 1930, once stood. Collections included the popular Butterfly House that is now located in Plant and Soil Sciences.

"S" marker, in front of the John A. Hannah Administration Building

A bronze block "S," a symbol of "State" and thereby of Michigan State University, is embedded in the concrete. It is a gift of the Class of 1978.

Stockman Sesquicentennial marker, traffic island south of Agriculture Hall

The marker reads:

1837–1987

A Sesquicentennial Marker

Dedicated in honor of the contribution of Michigan women to this state's progress 1837–1987. Placed by the Michigan Women's Studies Association and the Directors of the Michigan Women's Hall of Fame. HISTORIC WOMEN of MICHIGAN. DORA HALL STOCKMAN (1872–1948). First woman to hold elective office in Michigan when in 1919 she was elected to the State Board of Agriculture. She was the first woman in the United States to be on the Board of Control [Board of Trustees] of a Land-Grant Institution, Michigan Agricultural College. Elected to Michigan House of Representatives in 1938, she introduced legislation for the Michigan Medical Insurance program, which became Blue Cross/Blue Shield.

Taft marker, at the corner of East Circle Drive and the Collingwood entrance

A rock with a bronze plaque states, "On this spot May 24, 1889 Professor Levi R. Taft. First in Michigan. A pioneer in America. Began the control of orchard diseases by spraying." This location and the land directly east, where Mason-Abbot now stands, formed a large orchard.

Untitled, undated, by Melvin Leiserowitz on the north side of the Kresge Art Center

Professor Leiserowitz, of the Department of Art and Art History, produced this Minimalist sculpture in Cor-ten steel to focus on the power of elemental geometric form.

Olin Memorial Health Center

Calder, 1939, 1956, 1969

Gabled end pavilions, a gabled entryway porch, prominent chimneys, and a projecting bay window all recall the Collegiate Gothic. Here, however, the bulky massing, textural variety, and limestone trim are less detailed than in the West Circle Complex. With its stylized Art Deco entryway, this Public Works Administration building presents a more modern form.

The entryway displays an Art Deco program of a dozen reliefs. The artist is Samuel Cashwan, the same Michigan artist who produced the School of Music reliefs and sculpture. Here, the reliefs symbolize the healing arts. In the entablature, the building's name is anchored on the left by Panacea, a Greco-Roman mythological remedy for all diseases, and on the right by Hygeia, the Greek goddess of health. Each pilaster displays five reliefs with themes from modern medicine. In descending order, on the left, they are "Medical Magic," "Diagnosis," "Anatomy,"

"Physiology," and "Vaccination." On the right, they are "Herbs," "Microscope," "Anesthesia," "X-Ray," and "Chemistry."

The Olin Memorial Health Center, originally known as the Olin Memorial Hospital, is named in memory of Richard Milo Olin, M.D. (1875–1938), who served as the first full-time college physician and health service director from 1925 until his death. He planned this facility as a hospital outfitted with sixty beds, surgical, diagnostic and therapeutic facilities, a laboratory, an outpatient clinic, and a pharmacy, but he died prior to its completion. Olin practiced health care in the former president's home on Faculty Row (West Circle Drive) where Gilchrist Hall now stands. The first health care facility was opened in 1894 in a seven-room home located where the MSU Union now stands. Today, the Olin Memorial Health Center serves ambulatory clients with basic health care needs.

Berkey Hall

Munson, 1947

Berkey Hall is a quintessential example of the Collegiate Gothic, proudly displaying parapeted cross gables, eave dormers, lively patterns of brick and limestone, and a slate roof. The south (main) entrance is especially notable for its limestone, segmental arch set within a twin-towered cross gable. At the time of its construction Berkey Hall, with its L-shaped floor plan encompassing 126,895 square feet, was the largest classroom building yet to be built at Michigan State. In 1994 Freeman/Smith completed a major interior renovation.

William H. Berkey, for whom the building is named, was a member and chair of the State Board of Agriculture (now Board of Trustees) in the 1940s and was instrumental in Michigan State's procurement of low-interest loans in anticipation of the post–World War II demand for academic and residential campus buildings. Today, the offices of the Dean of the College of Social Science are among the campus units housed in this building.

THOMAS KACHADURIAN

Old Horticulture

Bowd-Munson, 1924
Physical Plant, 1963
Freeman/Smith, 1991

This symmetrical, three-story, brick Collegiate Gothic classroom building displays prominent parapeted cross gables accented with finials and Indiana limestone trim. The central, gabled entrance is framed with pilasters and occasional unadorned heraldic shields.

In 1923, the State of Michigan appropriated $400,000 to erect the Horticulture Building (39,996 square feet). President David Friday, who served from 1921 until 1923, convinced the legislature of the need to strengthen the Department of Horticulture at a time of expanding markets

for perishable fruits and vegetables. This was the department's home until it moved to the new Plant and Soil Sciences Building erected in 1986. At that time, the Horticulture Building was renamed Old Horticulture.

Since its renovation for adaptive reuse in the early 1990s the building has been the home of the Department of Romance and Classical Languages. In addition to classrooms, offices, and a modernized auditorium, it houses the Language Learning Center.

Paolucci Building
Calder, 1947

Hipped roofs, cross gables, brick facades, and metal casement windows are all evidence of the late Collegiate Gothic, but the overall effect is different. The limestone belt course creates a horizontal sleekness and makes the Paolucci Building one of several stylistically transitional buildings from the late 1940s. It is historically inspired and yet, with its abandonment of surface adornment, it also foresees what would become a campus favorite, the International Style.

Residential in scale and reminiscent of a garden apartment, the Paolucci Building originally was the Home Management Building for students in the School of Home Economics, known by 1955 as the College of Home Economics, and by 1970 as the College of Human Ecology. Its U-shaped plan formed four separate apartments, each with its own entrance.

In 1989 the building became the Paolucci Building in honor of Beatrice Paolucci who, as a professor of family resource management from 1956 until 1983 developed an international reputation for her role in leading Michigan State in the advancement of the ecological basis of home economics.

DERRICK TURNER

Student Services

Calder, 1957

The flat roof, windows set flush with the curtain walls, and the absence of ornamentation make the Student Services building a successful International Style design characteristic of the 1950s. Green enameled spandrels emphatically span the facades and accentuate their flatness. The north (front) entrance features a yellow, enameled, cantilevered entrance canopy—a leitmotif of this style. Inside, marble and cedar offer rich floor and wall surfaces. A glance outward reveals the Old Horticulture Gardens. From these gardens, the view of the south facades clearly shows the building's overall L-shaped plan.

Just inside the north entrance, a bronze bust of the Reverend Martin Luther King Jr. (1929–68), titled "*I Have a Dream,*" sits atop a pedestal. Students from the Wonders Hall Black Caucus commissioned this sculpture by Nancy Leiserowitz, which was dedicated on 10 May 1988. Several months later, on 27 October 1988, a committee commemorating Dr. King planted an oak tree on the building's south side and dedicated it to Michigan State University. Its marker reads: "United As One We Shall Overcome." By 2002 the tree had grown two stories high. Both the sculpture and the tree serve as reminders of Dr. King's commitment to the advancement of human rights. The Office of Financial Aid, offices for the Vice President for Student Affairs and Services, many student organizations, and major governing groups are in this building.

GARY BOYNTON

Natural Science
Munson, 1948

At 257,690 square feet, the Natural Science building is an unusually expansive Collegiate Gothic design, featuring a southern facade that stretches along East Circle Drive to form a 430-foot long arc. This arc is reaffirmed in the building's plan, which has a central curved hallway. Three pavilions project from this hallway to form a highly complex north facade. Celebrated stylistic traits include prominent parapeted gables, projecting dormers and piers, extensive limestone trim, segmentally arched entrances, and blind Gothic arcading. The truly exceptional features of the building, however, are the scale and complexity of the detailing and the overall plan, with a ground floor and four additional stories. Wooden quatrefoils and floriated crown molding are among the interesting Gothic interior details.

In a booklet, "The Natural Science Building at Michigan State College," printed in 1950, Professor Lloyd C. Emmons, dean of the then-existent School of Science and Arts, stated that this is "one of the nation's largest buildings devoted to study and research in the natural sciences. It answers a long-standing need for space and facilities on the East Lansing, campus." Originally, it was the home of the Departments of Botany, Entomology, Geology and Geography, Zoology, and two Basic College departments, Biological Science and Natural Science, as well as the Office of the Dean of the School of Science and Arts. Today, its classrooms, lecture halls, laboratories, offices, and auditorium serve many units, including the College of Natural Science.

Kedzie Hall–North

GARY BOYNTON

Kedzie Hall

North *Malcomson and Higgenbotham, 1927*
South *Harley-Ellington, 1966*

This finely detailed classroom building is a consummate example of the Collegiate Gothic. Most notable is the main (north) entrance and lobby. Its tall, streamlined arch is remarkable. With its height and fluidity, the arch blends the archivolt and supporting columns into one continuous form and thereby unites entry doors and windows. Floriated detailing is historically inspired, but the overall simplicity of the arch transcends dry historical copying. Interweaving period style with an abstract treatment of form was a frequent characteristic of American architecture of the 1920s. Prominent examples include Eliel Saarinen's competition design for the Chicago Tribune Building, 1922, and Albert Kahn's Fisher Building, 1929, in Detroit. The architects, from the Detroit firm of Malcomson and Higgenbotham, surely would have known these contemporary examples.

Inside the lobby, passersby are symbolically transported. Dim lighting, metalwork, and the gray stone walls recall the inspired world of medieval scholasticism. This ambience provides an intermediary experience preceding entry into unadorned laboratories and classrooms beyond the lobby. Lancet windows, oak paneling, and polychromed Pewabic tilework enhance the overall mood. Especially notable are heraldic shields, which contain luminescent Pewabic tesserae. Outside, these shields are set within circular medallions to accent the facades, and on sunny days their tesserae reflect light.

Although the date above the main (north) entrance is "A.D. 1926," the Kedzie Chemical Laboratory was actually completed a year later. As early as 1913, and even with two additions, the old chemical laboratory, erected between 1869 and 1871, was outdated. When this new

Kedzie Hall–South

facility opened, faculty praised the large lecture spaces and the laboratories scaled to accommodate small classes—both arranged within an H-shaped plan.

Now known as North Kedzie, this portion of the two-building complex was originally named "Kedzie Chemical Laboratory" in honor of Robert Clark Kedzie (1823–1902), M.D., D.Sc., LL.D., who taught chemistry at Michigan State from 1863 until 1902. Known as an outstanding teacher, Kedzie was also instrumental in the development of the beet sugar industry in Michigan and the promotion of legislation to establish a state food and dairy commission. Among his extensive public service responsibilities were his presidencies of the Michigan State Board of Health from 1877 until 1881, the Michigan Medical Society in 1874, the American Public Health Association in 1882, and the Association of Agricultural Colleges and

Experiment Stations in 1899. Professor Kedzie had three sons who became Michigan State alumni. One of them, Frank S. Kedzie, became a professor of chemistry, like his father, and then, from 1915 until 1921, president of Michigan State.

South Kedzie includes a five-story office-classroom block, a row of three large lecture halls, an intimate courtyard, and passageways contiguous with North Kedzie. This International Style addition is more boldly scaled than North Kedzie. Its exterior offers emphatic contrasts of brick planes and limestone trim. Other details such as rusticated piers and recessed metal spandrels create rhythms and patterns to complement the original design. In the courtyard, the rock garden includes igneous, metamorphic, and sedimentary rock.

John A. Hannah Administration Building
Calder, 1968

The John A. Hannah Administration Building is a stylistic hybrid. Its marble and travertine entrance lobby includes floor-to-ceiling glass walls to provide an openness characteristic of the International Style. The building also subscribes to the Brutalist aesthetic, used often for modernist architecture in the 1960s and 1970s, in which structural form and materials are starkly presented. On its exterior, the strength of reinforced concrete is especially apparent in large, textured ground-floor buttresses and huge, smooth piers that support the upper stories.

Physically and metaphorically, the Hannah Administration Building is imposing in scale and size and sits impressively along the north bank of the Red Cedar River. Its south entrance faces the picturesque setting of the river's rapids. Its north (front) entrance faces a large landscaped esplanade, with a view of Agriculture Hall, the home of the College of Agriculture and Natural Resources.

Interestingly, the Hannah Administration Building also relates well to its other neighbor, Olds Hall, for they both have a tri-partite elevation including a sloped base.

John A. Hannah, 1902–91, to whom this building is dedicated, served as president of Michigan State University longer than any other person—from 1 July 1941 until 1 April 1969. He requested that the letters spelling his name and, thereby, the building's name, not be affixed until after he retired. For many years, until the move in early 1969, his office was on the second floor of the oldest academic building on campus, now known as Linton Hall (1881). Just inside the north entrance is a bronze bust of John A. Hannah, by the artist Nancy Leiserowitz of Mason, Michigan. It is a gift of the Class of 1980. Outside, the bronze "S" embedded in the sidewalk is a Class of 1978 gift and the flagpoles are from the Class of 1982.

GARY BOYNTON

Computer Center

Munson, 1948

The steep gabled roof, dormers, pier buttresses, and contrasting limestone and brick facades identify the Computer Center as Collegiate Gothic. On the south facade is the main entrance, which faces the Red Cedar River. This placement serves as a prime example of the commitment on campus in the 1940s to relate buildings more directly to the river's beauty. The relief over the main entrance reads "1947," although the building opened the following year. "Computer Science" lettering over each entrance once read "Electrical Engineering." From 1948 until the opening of the Engineering Building on South Shaw Lane in 1962, this was the Electrical Engineering Building.

In 1948 Michigan State College had 16,000 students, 2,000 of whom were in the School of Engineering. Professor Ira Baccus, head of the Department of Electrical Engineering, was quoted in a 15 March 1949 press release as saying these facilities were "comparable to any school of this kind in the Mid-West." Innovative facilities included laboratories, shops, classrooms, offices and, atop the tower, a television antenna.

The Computer Center was designed by the same architectural group, the Munson firm, as Berkey Hall (1947) and Natural Science (1948) and is very similar stylistically to these contemporary counterparts.

Bessey Hall
Calder, 1961
McNamee, Porter, Seely, 1994

The International Style traits of flat roofs, curtain walls, and an essentialist geometric vocabulary are prominent in both the classroom and office wings. A refined use of brick, glass, aluminum, and stainless steel enhance the simplicity of the unadorned surfaces. The cantilevered entrance canopy and the green, slate spandrels of the classroom wing are particularly notable. The 1994 addition is a very successful renovation. It transforms the original space between the two wings into a multistoried classroom and office space that blends well and links the earlier buildings to form one large structure.

Scaled appropriately for its Farm Lane location, Bessey Hall was erected in 1961 near the site of the razed Band Shell. Its namesake, Ernst A. Bessey (1877–1957), was an internationally known scientist, a professor of botany and

Band Shell, dedicated in 1938, seen here in 1955.

mycology, head of the Department of Botany and, from 1930 until 1944, the first dean of the Graduate School.

GARY BOYNTON

Auditorium
(and Fairchild Theater)
Munson, 1940

An aura of historical authenticity surrounds this imposing Collegiate Gothic building. It continues to serve as an important venue for a variety of cultural and academic events. Those passing the auditorium entrance on Farm Lane are visually invited to walk along the curved drive and ascend the steps. Atop these steps are three identical entry portals whose limestone spandrels are decorated with compact, yet fluid images of comedy, tragedy, musical instruments, and vines. Above the portals is an intricate arrangement of Gothic tracery woven into a fine web including lancet windows and reliefs. Inside the lobby, oak paneling, chandeliers, black and white marble flooring and, most impressively, three murals by Charles Pollock, a former faculty member in the Department of Art and Art History, are reminiscent of an earlier era. The murals continue to inspire with their vibrant, heroic images of the role of freedom in the advancement of civilization. Executed in casein in a figurative style reminiscent of the American painter Thomas Hart Benton and other 1930s muralists their titles are *Proclamation of Emancipation* (1943), *We Assure Freedom to the Free* (1944), and *The Modern Man I Sing* (1944).

DERRICK TURNER

The seating in the Auditorium and Fairchild Theater is unique in that the two theaters face opposite sides of the same proscenium stage. This arrangement eliminates the need for duplicate technical equipment and lighting, although it makes it difficult to hold simultaneous performances. In the auditorium, the shallow balcony forms a U-shape that runs the full length of the three interior walls, with the stage occupying the fourth wall. In the oak-paneled theater, the graduated seating arrangement faces the stage directly.

In 1938 the Public Works Administration allocated more than $500,000 toward the final cost of $1,025,000. As early as the days of Jonathan L. Snyder, who was president from 1896 until 1915, campus leaders asked the State Board of Agriculture (now Board of Trustees) and the legislature for a large auditorium to accommodate academic and cultural activities. Prior to the completion of this building, Demonstration Hall was the site for large campus gatherings. Fairchild Theater derives its name from George T. Fairchild, who was a professor of English literature from 1866 until 1879.

Giltner Hall

Bowd, 1913   *Bowd-Munson, 1940*   *Calder, 1968*
Bowd-Munson, 1931   *Munson, 1947*
Bowd-Munson, 1938   *Munson, 1952*

The north (main) entrance of this Collegiate Gothic design faces an entrance to the Natural Science Building, as if to link the academic pursuits that occur on either side of East Circle Drive. A grass esplanade, lined with trees, draws those who might enter Giltner Hall to its oak entry doors and tympanum filled with carvings of ferns. Interesting details include the heraldic shields in the spandrels and especially those shields that contain images of books, which serve as scholarly reminders of the building's purpose.

In 1913 the Veterinary Clinic, a surgery and animal clinic building for the School of Veterinary Medicine, arose in the Collegiate Gothic style at the southeast corner of Farm Lane and East Circle Drive. In 1931 a separate Collegiate Gothic building for the Department of Anatomy and the Department of Animal Pathology arose just east of the 1913 structure. Public Works Administration funds of 1938 made it possible to complete a second addition to the clinic. By 1952, the date of the fifth addition, the expanded veterinary clinic and its Departments of Anatomy, Physiology, Bacteriology and Public Health, Surgery and Medicine, and Animal Pathology joined to form one building, Giltner Hall. Its resultant rambling plan, covering five acres, reflects these developmental stages and is well suited to the parcel of land on which it stands.

Ward Giltner (1882–1950) joined the Department of Bacteriology in 1908 and became its head in 1912. He was the dean of Veterinary Medicine from 1923 until 1947, when he retired. He introduced a new curriculum to train medical technologists, was instrumental in improving the veterinary curriculum to include more arts and sciences courses, and served as a member of the faculty committee that developed the Basic College curriculum required of all students beginning in fall 1944.

Physics-Astronomy

Calder, 1949   *Physical Plant, 1973*

Physical Plant, 1955   *Sedgewick-Seller, 1976*

This is a stylistically transitional building, part Collegiate Gothic and part International Style. Its overall proportions, projecting entry pavilion, and brick trimmed with limestone recall many of its Collegiate Gothic neighbors, but there are no gables, roof dormers, or Gothic detailing. The hipped roof of the central pavilion reinforces the symmetry of the main facade, which is discernible from quite a distance east along Dormitory Road. Relatively large expanses of glass, no decoration except the incised, figurative carvings, and the partial use of flat roofs suggest the International Style which, soon after the completion of this building in 1949, replaced the Collegiate Gothic as the predominant campus mode. A look to the south, to the

Kresge Art Center of 1958, designed by the same architectural firm, reveals the mature International Style.

Until the Department of Mathematics moved to its present location in Wells Hall, this building was the Physics-Mathematics Building. In the early 1980s, when astronomy became part of physics to form the Department of Physics and Astronomy, the exterior limestone lettering on the building became "Physics and Astronomy."

Thirteen incised carvings depict famous mathematicians and scientists to enframe the main (east) entrance doors. Ample entrance steps provide a pleasant waiting area from which to view these images. Carl L. Schmitz (1900–1967), a New York artist who taught at Michigan

Famous mathematicians and scientists by Carl L. Schmitz, entryway relief, Physics-Astronomy, ca. 1949.

State in the late 1940s, produced the casts that Bruno Mankowski and other stone masons used as models for these carvings. The academic figurative style of the carvings is appropriate for their didactic purpose. The outer nine subjects include known historical figures and generic figure types. In the lower left, Galileo experiments with his pendulum. In the background is the Tower of Pisa from which he purportedly observed the speed of falling objects. Above, Sir Isaac Newton watches a falling apple to test gravity. Across the entryway are five scenes. They show men demonstrating basic laws of physics using a lever, a pulley, a gear, a screw, and an inclined plane. To the right, Benjamin Franklin flies a kite to study electricity. Below him, Hans Christian Oersted demonstrates the magnetic effect of an electric current. The four inner reliefs begin with Archimedes, on the lower left, who discovered the principle of buoyancy. Here, he realizes that the crown of the ancient king Hieron is displaced by an equal amount of water. Above Archimedes, Christiaan Huygens looks through a telescope. He is famous for discovering Saturn's rings. On the inner lower right, Gottfried Wilhelm von Leibnitz and Sir Isaac Newton, both of whom independently invented differential calculus, stand. Above them, Michael Faraday, the discoverer of electromagnetic induction, observes the passage of electric current.

There are four other exterior carvings at different entryways. The southeast carving features Wilhelm Konrad Roentgen, the discoverer of x-rays, and William Crookes, who studied cathode rays. The southwest carving shows Guglielmo Marconi, known for the transmission of longwave radio signals, and James Clerk Maxwell, known for his fundamental contributions to electromagnetic theory. The north carving presents Albert Michelson, known for his accurate measurement of the speed of light and precision optical instruments, and Hermann von Helmholtz, whose acoustical research inspired the development of audio speakers. And finally, the northeast carving offers Albert Einstein, famous for his theory of relativity, and Ernest Lawrence, the inventor of the cyclotron.

East Circle Complex

On the former site of an orchard, the East Circle Complex of four residence halls stands between the Collingwood and the Bogue Street entrances. Dormitory Road runs east-west between Mason-Abbot and Snyder-Phillips. The complex is a visually cohesive unit executed in the Collegiate Gothic. Slate roofs, cross gables, oriel windows, and roof dormers are some of the most telling stylistic characteristics. Fine oak paneling, tile, Gothic or classically detailed fireplaces, and metalwork are among the interior attributes.

These residence halls, originally designed for male students, were to serve as the residential complement to the West Circle Complex (1931–48) for women. Before they existed, the only other dormitory for male students was the previous Wells Hall, a 1907 facility that by the late 1930s was sorely outdated. It stood just west of Olds Hall on the site of the present Michigan State University Library.

During World War II, women lived in Abbot Hall and Mason Hall. Over the years, either men or women have occupied the rooms in the East Circle Complex or, with alternating floor assignments, both have been occupants. Each building is named for a man who made an important contribution to the advancement of education in the state of Michigan or to the development of Michigan State

University. Abbot Hall is named in honor of Theophilus Capen Abbot, professor of English, logic, and mental philosophy and president of Michigan State for more than two decades, from 1862 until 1884. Mason Hall honors Stevens T. Mason, who became secretary of the territory of Michigan in 1831, acting territorial governor in 1834, and governor in 1835, the year the people of Michigan ratified their constitution. During his governorship, Mason worked diligently to achieve statehood for Michigan, which finally occurred in 1837. He also helped to establish the system of free public schools in Michigan, the University of Michigan, and a number of banks, while also encouraging the development of canals and railroads.

Phillips Hall recalls T. Glenn Phillips, Class of 1902, who as a landscape architect developed the general campus plan of 1926 that preserved the original "oak opening," expanded the circle drives fluidly, and integrated landscape with architecture to affirm the campus park. Snyder Hall is named for the seventh president of Michigan State, Jonathan L. Snyder, who served from 1896 until 1915 during a time of institutional growth and name change from State Agricultural College to Michigan Agricultural College.

THOMAS KACHADURIAN

THOMAS KACHADURIAN

Mason-Abbot

Abbot Hall
Bowd-Munson, 1938

Abbot Hall, although dated 1938, actually opened the following year. Cross gables, random limestone window surrounds, and semi-hexagonal limestone multi-story bay windows are among the many Collegiate Gothic traits. Like its partner, Mason Hall, Abbot has an I-shaped plan and was designed to be more than a place to sleep. It included amenities such as a game room, laundry room, valet room, trunk room, basement snack shop, and lounges. During the construction of Abbot Hall, a shared service area containing the kitchen, bakery, food storage, and other related facilities was created to link the two buildings and thereby form a complex. It took another twenty years, however, with some minor remodeling in late 1958, for residents to be able to walk from one hall to the next using the basement corridor. Abbot Hall was one of several Public Works Administration projects of this time period.

Mason Hall
Bowd-Munson, 1938

Mason Hall has a steep slate roof, prominent roof dormers, emphatic limestone courses, and a main entry with a segmental arch topped with an oriel window. This Collegiate Gothic building's I-shaped plan is connected to Abbot Hall to form a large H. Mason Hall was funded via the sale of bonds paid entirely from hall revenues.

Snyder-Phillips

Phillips Hall
Munson, 1947

Phillips Hall stands west of Snyder Hall, with which it is linked to form a large H plan. A stepped cross gable highlights the main entrance. The entryway is flanked by limestone pier buttresses and crowned with a segmental arch and a decorated oriel window. The Gothic inscription carved on the segmental arch of the entryway reads, "T. Glenn Phillips Hall."

Snyder Hall
Munson, 1947

Stylistically identical to its architectural partner, Snyder Hall displays the same approachable residential scale and careful attention to detailing of the Collegiate Gothic. The view looking west provides a clear sense of the building's I-shaped plan, cross gables, limestone coursing, and continuous dormers. Today, in addition to serving as a residence hall, Snyder Hall also contains offices and laboratories related to the Department of Psychology.

Psychology Research
Calder, 1965

The 1960s interest in the Brutalist aesthetic flavors the use of materials in this International Style design. Bold concrete posts; a wide, boxed, overhang; and windows set flush with the exterior wall mark this building as International Style. Textural variety reveals the Brutalist interest in showing the role different materials play in a building's construction. Red-brick curtain walls, tinted glass, green-metal spandrels, and a fieldstone base and parapet each fulfill their assigned roles. Surrounding evergreen and deciduous trees complement the essentialist geometric vocabulary.

The Psychology Research Building includes laboratories for behavioral neuroscience, vision research, cognitive processes, social psychology, developmental psychology, and industrial/organizational psychology.

Baker Hall

Eberle Smith, 1967

Although the simple, geometric form of Baker Hall recalls the International Style, the strong, external expression of inner structure, using different materials and textures, affirms a Brutalist influence. Recessed windows and their composite-stone spandrels define one layer, brick mullions define the next layer, and brick piers and unadorned wall surfaces accentuate the outermost layer—to form powerful, dark and light, surface rhythms. The southeast-corner stairwell is distinguished by windows set flush with the exterior wall. A cantilevered, steel entrance canopy denotes the west (main) entrance of this office, classroom, and laboratory building.

This building honors Ray Stannard Baker (1870–1946), an alumnus who became a nationally known author. He wrote adventure novels under the pseudonym David Grayson and wrote or edited several books on Woodrow Wilson, including the comprehensive *Woodrow Wilson; Life and Letters*, a multivolume work published between 1927 and 1939. His spouse, Jessie Beal, was the daughter of Professor William J. Beal, who founded the W. J. Beal Botanical Garden. Today, Baker Hall houses part of the Department of Psychology as well as the Department of Anthropology.

Alumni Memorial Chapel

Calder, 1952

The Alumni Memorial Chapel sits atop an incline overlooking the Red Cedar River. A steep roof gable, square tower, and pervasive limestone door and window surrounds identify it as Collegiate Gothic. The front entrance features a segmental arch, a three-paneled stained glass window of "Faith, Hope and Love," and a decorative frieze that says "Alumni Memorial Chapel" in Gothic letters. The frieze also reads, "In honor of those who served their country" and "In memory of those who made the supreme sacrifice." In relief, in the frieze's center is an angel by Leonard Jungwirth who buoyantly proclaims "Pax" and "Amitas," or peace and amity. Jungwirth also produced several other campus sculptures including *The Spartan*, known today as "Sparty."

Vestibule walls contain the names of Michigan State alumni "who died in the armed forces" since 1861. From this cozy space, with its low ceiling, the view of the center aisle of the large assembly room is impressive. Tan Pewabic floor tiles link one space with another. The assembly room has an exposed rafter trussing system. Pendant lamps hang from these wooden beams to provide interior light that, on sunny days, is complemented by light shining through the stained glass windows. Along the east wall, glass panels depict aspects of civilization: work, abundance, community, freedom of the mind, diffusion of knowledge, leadership, truth, wisdom, beauty, and aspiration. West-wall panels depict moments in the history of Michigan State University: the legislative act of 12 February 1855 to establish an agricultural college, the College Hall dedication of 1857, the Morrill Act of 1862, the admission of women in 1870, the Farmer's Institutes of 1876, the founding of the School of Engineering in 1885, the Agricultural Experiment Station of 1887, applied science and liberal arts, student activities, and international peace. Odell Prather, Marguerite Gaudin, and Anthony Mako of the Willet Stained Glass Studios of Philadelphia designed the windows. They are registered in the Michigan Stained Glass Census.

Throughout the chapel, more than two dozen fragments of stone from damaged or ruined European cathedrals are embedded in the walls as if to link with the past and suggest hope for the future of the human spirit. There is even a brick from the White House. Other American architecture includes similar fragments. A notable Midwestern example is the Gothic-inspired Chicago Tribune Building of 1922, on Michigan Avenue in Chicago, by Howells and Hood.

Alumni and friends provided the funds for the Alumni Memorial Chapel and its pipe organ, furniture, and windows. Different graduating classes offered memorials such as the Class of 1954 gift of the window depicting the admission of women to State Agricultural College. The chapel serves as a place for personal and communal reflection, for weddings and other ceremonies for people of all beliefs, and as a reminder of the relationship between education and international peace and understanding.

GARY BOYNTON

Kresge Art Center

Calder, 1958 *Calder, 1973*
Calder, 1966

Unornamented brick surfaces and glass curtain walls with green spandrels and aluminum trim are prominent International Style characteristics. These are seen clearly on the north (front) facade. Northern light, which creates favorable conditions for painting and drawing, enters the north classrooms abundantly. The stairwells at the east and west ends, when illuminated at night, appear as "glass boxes" common to this style. The south facade, facing the Red Cedar River, is especially notable for its three cantilevered balconies. On its top balcony, multicolored sunshades separate one art studio from another and enliven spatial rhythms. From the Farm Lane Bridge, looking east, the successful siting of the Kresge Art Center to provide occupants with beautiful river views is most apparent.

The Kresge Art Center name derives from the Stanley S. Kresge Foundation, which funded this consolidation of art classrooms, studios, and gallery space in one building. During previous decades, the MSU Union and temporary classrooms south of the Red Cedar River housed depart-

mental activities. Howard Church, who was department chair from 1945 until 1961, traveled with Ralph Calder, the architect, to several colleges and universities to garner ideas suitable for adaptation here. Church wanted a building that was slightly more "modern" than the Collegiate-Gothic Music Building. As the International Style vocabulary reveals, his wish came true.

Calder also designed the 1966 and 1973 additions to provide the one-story east wing, separate Sculpture Annex, and what is now the North Gallery of the Kresge Art Museum. The Department of Art and Art History continues to occupy most of this building. The Kresge Art Museum, originally a part of the department, occupies the former Kresge Art Gallery space. Outdoor exhibition spaces include changing student and professional-artist exhibitions and permanent works such as *Untitled*, a Minimalist sculpture by Melvin Leiserowitz, emeritus professor, Department of Art and Art History.

Area Three: The Brody Complex, University Village, Spartan Stadium, and Other Athletic Facilities

The natural beauty of the Red Cedar River and surrounding trees and shrubs, interwoven with winding paths, provide the context for viewing and experiencing several multi-use athletic facilities, a continuing education center, and a large residential complex in this area.

From Spartan Stadium, walking west along the Red Cedar River leads to the intersection of Kalamazoo Street, Red Cedar Road, and Chestnut Road and the pedestal on which the well-known sculpture *The Spartan* ("Sparty") stands. Following the path between Jenison Field House and Old College Field offers another picturesque view of the Red Cedar River area and, beyond it, the Kellogg Center and the Brody Complex. Standing between Demonstration Hall and Munn Ice Arena, amidst the pines of the Sand Hill Plantation, provides a moment to contemplate the beauty of these tall trees and to hear the wind whistle through them. Glancing west from several places along Harrison Road always reveals the interplay of buildings and trees. Trees and shrubs accent the large abstract forms of the large athletic facilities—Jack Breslin Student Events Center, Munn Ice Arena, and Spartan Stadium.

Driving east along West Kalamazoo Street, the Red Cedar Natural Area visually welcomes visitors to campus.

These fifty acres of floodplain forest exhibit heavy regeneration stimulated by the loss of mature elms to Dutch Elm disease. Before reaching Harrison Road, University Village, a part of University Housing, appears on the south side of West Kalamazoo Street.

Easiest access: From Michigan Avenue, head south along Harrison Road; from Harrison Road, head west at Kalamazoo Street; from Harrison Road, head east at Kalamazoo Street or east at West Shaw Lane.

Boundaries: Michigan Avenue, the Red Cedar River, Red Cedar Road, West Shaw Lane, Marigold Avenue, Red Cedar Natural Area.

Predominant historical style, name or theme: Revivalist, Art Deco, International Style, and post-modern. Living-learning and athletic facilities amidst the trees and the Red Cedar River.

Date of oldest extant building in this area: 1923, Spartan Stadium. Original portion, 24,750 seats, then known as M.A.C. (Michigan Agricultural College) Field.

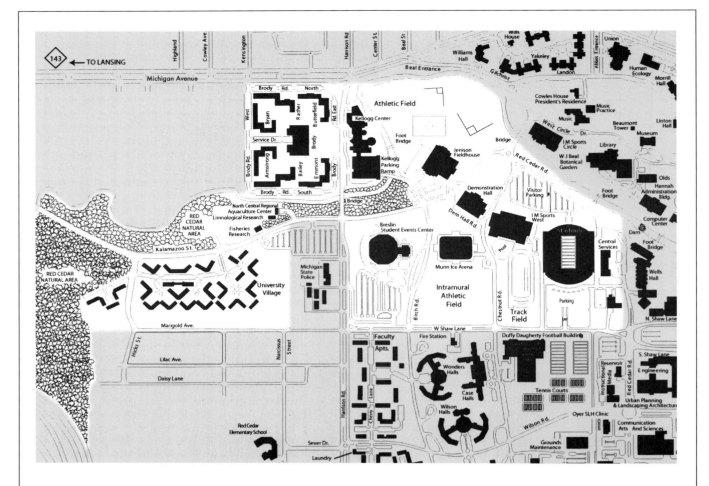

Selected Historical Sites or Markers, Public Art, and Natural Areas

Aquarius, Aries, Pisces, Zodiac reliefs, enamel, Brody Complex, Doris Hall and Kalman M. B. Kubinyi

> These three reliefs adorn the exterior facades of Butterfield Hall and Emmons Hall. The original commission called for the twelve signs of the zodiac to adorn the seven buildings that comprise this residential complex. Only *Aquarius* (Water Bearer) and *Pisces* (Fishes) on Butterfield Hall and *Aries* (Ram) on Emmons Hall reached completion. Their vibrant colors and fluid, energetic forms contrast vividly with the brick facades. Perhaps it was this contrast that led to their demise. Controversy surrounded the imagery and led the university to terminate the commission held by the artistic team of Doris Hall (1907–) and Kalman M. B. Kubinyi (1906–73).

John Kobs, relief, exterior of the Kobs Field announcer's stand

> This relief honors John Kobs, who was Michigan State's baseball coach (576-377-16) for thirty-nine seasons from 1925 until 1963. During those years, the Michigan State baseball teams had winning records for thirty-five seasons, including the 1945 Big Ten championship and, in 1954, a third-place finish in the College World Series. In 1966 Kobs was inducted into the American Association of College Baseball Coaches Hall of Fame. In 1969 the baseball diamond received the name Kobs Field.

Old College Field, between Jenison Field House and the Red Cedar River

> This is the location of the baseball field (Kobs Field), in its original location, as well as softball and soccer fields. On campus maps this entire area is sometimes known as "Athletic Field" or as "Old College Field." In other accounts a field to the west of Kobs Field is labeled Old

College Field. The college acquired this area in the late nineteenth century for a baseball diamond, cinder track, football field, grandstand, and bleachers.

Ralph H. Young, stone marker, just west of Spartan Stadium, north of Ralph Young Field

This stone marker reads:

> Dedicated to Ralph H. Young
> Coach and Director of Athletics
> Michigan State
> 1923–1954
> Devoted Friend of Track and Field.

Young lived from 1889 until 1962.

Red Cedar Natural Area, Kalamazoo Street

This is a fifty-acre floodplain forest.

Sand Hill Plantation, between Munn Ice Arena and Demonstration Hall

This outdoor laboratory for silviculture research and instruction is remarkable for its beauty and for the sense of calm it offers to those who stand amidst these pine, fir, and spruce trees. This plantation was originally part of the Woodbury Farm, which Michigan State acquired in 1913. The outdoor plaque states: "In order to curtail the wind erosion problem, this seemingly worthless ridge was converted into a research area demonstrating that sand-blows could be permanently controlled." In 1914, Frank Hobart Sanford, professor of forestry, planted the trees that now stand on this 3.76 acre site.

***The Spartan*, "Sparty,"** terra cotta sculpture, intersection of Kalamazoo Street, Red Cedar Road, and Chestnut Road, Leonard D. Jungwirth

"Sparty" is the symbol of the Michigan State University Spartans and one of the most prominent symbols of the entire university. He stands near several athletic facilities, highly visible, on a brick pedestal in a traffic island at the juncture of Kalamazoo Street, Red Cedar Road, and Chestnut Road.

While Sparty is often believed to be solid bronze, he is terra cotta. The clay figure was cast in three sections and fired in industrial kilns at the Grand Ledge Clay Products Company in Grand Ledge, Michigan. The

The Spartan, "Sparty," by Leonard D. Jungwirth, 1945.

hollow cast sections were fused on site, and then concrete cement was poured into the ceramic sections. Sparty is approximately ten feet tall, and he weighs several thousand pounds.

Sparty was dedicated 9 June 1945 and is the work of Leonard D. Jungwirth, a professor in the Department of Art and Art History. At the time the sculpture was erected, the popular media claimed it was the largest freestanding outdoor ceramic sculpture in the world. Stylistically, Sparty recalls ancient Greek sculpture with his formal posture and position atop a pedestal. Actually, he is truly a twentieth-century figure whose stylized contours also recall Cubism, Futurism, and other European modernist art, Russian academic sculpture, and American civic art of the 1930s and 1940s. The incised figures on the pedestal are engaged in football, basketball, and baseball while Sparty stands above them as an athletic prototype.

Sparty is well known on campus. He has become the subject of campus legends and the focus or backdrop for many events in campus life. Myriad stories circulate about what will happen when Sparty drops his helmet; he is the focus of pre-football Michigan State University Band drum rituals; and aside from Beaumont Tower he is the most photographed object of the campus built environment.

In 1926 George S. Alderton, sports editor for the *Lansing State Journal*, and Dale Stafford, sportswriter for the *Lansing Capitol News*, disavowed the new team name, "The Michigan Staters," and decided to find a new one. The Michigan Staters label had derived from a contest held on campus to update the college's team name, the "Aggies," because in 1925 the school name had changed from Michigan Agricultural College to Michigan State College of Agriculture and Applied Science. The sportswriters selected the "Spartans," which was a name submitted by Perry J. Fremont, a former Michigan State athlete who used it to write a newspaper account of a spring baseball game. It stuck. The Spartans of ancient Greece were courageous and self-disciplined and represent important aspirations for today's athletes.

In 1989 extensive restoration of Sparty included resealing the ceramic exterior, repointing the brick pedestal, and improving the traffic island and its lighting.

Varsity Club, stone marker, south of Spartan Stadium, on the north side of Red Cedar Road

Its bronze plaque commemorates students who died in World War I:

> *In memory of the members of the M.S.C. Varsity Club who gave their lives in the Great War.*
> E. E.Peterson '15
> I. F. Lankey '16
> F. M. Stewart '17
> O. N. Hinkle '19

M.S.C. refers to Michigan State College of Agriculture and Applied Science.

THOMAS KACHADURIAN

Jenison Field House

Munson, 1940

Large, brick, and Art Deco, this field house and main building block prominently display their importance. Formal symmetry and vigorous articulation of geometrical volumes complement flat and gabled roof lines. Prominent limestone courses accentuate horizontality while the projecting entrance pavilion stands proudly vertical. Atop the main building block, the 2001 renovation, with horizontal ribbing, accentuates the building's overall stolid character.

Four unadorned entryway piers rise uninterruptedly. Their smoothness contrasts with patterning found in the glass-brick limestone reliefs and metal-framed windows. The reliefs, with their stylized rhythms, depict respectively, from left to right, the skilled movement of a well-trained basketball, football, and baseball athlete. The entryway's subtle Art Deco detailing is evidenced in the interior overhead lighting and streamlined staircase railings. On the walls flanking the staircase are photographs of male and female Michigan State University Olympians and Pan-American athletes as well as coaches, press liaisons, and officers.

The Jenison Field House is named for Frederick Cowles Jenison (1884–1939), who was an engineering student at Michigan State, a successful businessperson, and an active alumnus. He bequeathed his entire estate to the university. A portion of his estate, along with Public Works

Administration support, was used to erect this building. A portrait of Mr. Jenison by an artist named Ferguson, which hangs in the field house, bears the inscription, "an ardent sportsman." Its inscription further reads, "Through almost daily visits to the campus he loved, he maintained throughout his life a keen interest in student affairs and in all athletic activities." Other hallway memorabilia include a plaque from the 1952 National Collegiate Football Championship, a painting of the 1954 Michigan State College Rose Bowl Team and Big Ten Co-champions, and other sports ephemera.

Jenison was built to serve male students at a time when women's athletic activities were housed solely in what is now Intramural Recreative Sports–Circle (IM Circle). Given its size, Jenison was also the site of many commencements, year-end comprehensive examinations in the former Basic College and, for a brief time after World War II, housing for veterans who arrived at Michigan State with G.I. Bill of Rights support. Until the completion of the Jack Breslin Student Events Center, Jenison was where the Michigan State basketball team played its home games. Jenison's facilities include an Olympic-sized swimming pool, over half an acre of gymnasium floor, handball courts, ticket and administrative offices, and an indoor track.

Kellogg Center

Sarvis, 1951, 1955, 1959
Calder, 1988

The original International Style building featured a seven-story rectangular block and various single-story extensions. Subsequent additions and a major 1988 renovation integrate the original hotel and office block, expanded conference and kitchen facilities, and a parking structure to form a sleek hotel and conference center. Tinted ribbon windows and smooth brick and limestone trim unify the overall design. The porte cochere, cantilevered and unadorned, stands in front of the glass-enclosed main entry and complements the original International Style concept.

This hotel and conference center supporting continuing education opened on 17 September 1951 as the first of approximately a dozen Kellogg Centers for continuing education on university campuses in the United States. With major support from the W. K. Kellogg Foundation, the center was conceived to accommodate thousands of Michigan residents who visit campus annually for special courses, seminars, and conferences, and to serve as a working laboratory for what is known today as the School of Hospitality Business. The Michigan Hotel Association provided funds for the center's furnishings. In 1948 MSU's Continuing Education program began. Soon after, the Kellogg Center became a focal point for Michigan State's commitment to public service as part of its land-grant mission.

The W. K. Kellogg Foundation provided a second major grant for the 1988 renovation. Today, the center has 165 guest rooms and suites, a 300-seat auditorium, more than thirty flexible meeting spaces, dining facilities, a parking ramp, and offices for units such as University Outreach and Evening College.

In the entrance lobby, a facsimile of an original portrait of W. K. Kellogg greets visitors. On a nearby wall is an original painting, *Cedar Creek Alluvial Fan*, 1997, by Irving Z. Taran, a professor in the Department of Art and Art History. The painting is on loan from the Kresge Art Museum. The Kellogg Center's main corridor includes many other original works of art.

From the entrance lobby, a staircase passes a fountain whose cascade leads to a ground-floor pool and an intimate seating area. On the surrounding walls are copies of 1924 and 1925 drawings by Ralph R. Calder, architect. Calder was a consulting architect for many aspects of campus development, and he created these drawings on a trip to Europe. His firm designed numerous campus buildings. The certificate he received as an Honorary Alumnus hangs here along with a photograph of him with former president John Hannah.

Brody Complex

The Brody Residence Hall Complex, with its central service (classroom-dining-office) building and six surrounding residence halls, occupies the southwest corner of Harrison Road and Michigan Avenue on the western edge of campus. The entire complex emphatically conveys the prominent characteristics of the International Style: brick curtain walls, smooth exterior surfaces, and geometrical simplicity. Brody Hall stands in the center, with each of its six, four-storied, residence halls positioned to define the perimeter of the complex. Ample lawns and landscaping between each hall and in front of the central Brody Hall create a park environment. Cantilevered staircases in all buildings are especially dramatic in the evening when the "glass-box" stairwells are illuminated. The view of the entire complex looking west from Harrison Road and the Kellogg Center reveals the masterful layout of this living-learning residence hall complex that serves 3,000 students.

Originally known as the Harrison Road Halls, each building now bears the name of a person important to Michigan State's history. Armstrong Hall is named for W. G. Armstrong, a student and farmer, master of the State Grange, treasurer of the National Grange, and long-time member of the State Board of Agriculture. Bailey Hall bears the name of Liberty Hyde Bailey, Class of 1882, who joined the faculty in 1885. He developed the idea for the first distinct horticultural laboratory in the United States; in 1888 this idea became the Horticultural Laboratory that today is known as Eustace-Cole Hall. Bailey was the author of more than sixty books and became a national leader in scientific agriculture. Brody Hall is named for Clark L. Brody, Class of 1904, county agricultural agent, executive secretary of the Michigan Farm Bureau, and member, 1921–59, and chair, 1932–38 and 1948–57, of the State Board of Agriculture (later Board of Trustees).

Claude S. Bryan is the person whose name adorns Bryan Hall. He held both D.V.M. and Ph.D. degrees and was a distinguished researcher of dairy hygiene. In 1946 he became dean of the College of Veterinary Medicine. Butterfield Hall recalls Kenyon L. Butterfield, Class of 1891, who served as president of land-grant colleges in Rhode Island and Massachusetts and from 1924 until 1928 at Michigan State. The college was known during his tenure as Michigan Agricultural College and then, beginning in 1925, as Michigan State College of Agriculture and Applied Science. In the 1890s Butterfield served as the first superintendent of the Farmers' Institutes, the predecessor of Farmers' Week, or the more recent ANR (Agriculture and Natural Resources) Week. Emmons Hall honors Lloyd C. Emmons, a professor of mathematics and statistics who also served as dean of Liberal Arts and director of the Michigan State University Museum. Howard C. Rather is the person for whom Rather Hall is named. He was an extension specialist, professor, and department head, although he is best remembered for his role as dean of Basic College.

Armstrong Hall
Calder, 1955

Armstrong Hall stands west of Brody Hall. Its irregular plan is the reverse of the Bryan Hall plan.

Bailey Hall
Calder, 1955

Bailey Hall stands southwest of Brody Hall, along the Red Cedar River. Its irregular plan is the reverse of the Rather Hall plan.

Brody Hall
Calder, 1954, 1955
Holmes and Black, 1979

Brody Hall has a colorful student history. It is the site for special events, informal meetings, classes, and daily meals. Often described as having the largest nonmilitary kitchen in the world, the facility is equipped to serve 3,000 students three meals a day. According to legend, students persist in referring to the mythical "Ma Brody" as the person who is responsible for the kitchen's success. At special meals throughout the year, they salute her.

Bryan Hall
Calder, 1954

Bryan Hall stands west of Brody Hall. Its irregular plan is the reverse of the Armstrong Hall plan.

Aries, "The Ram," from the Zodiac series by Doris Hall and Kalman M. B. Kubinyi, enamel relief, east facade of Emmons Hall, 1956.

Emmons Hall
Calder, 1955

Emmons Hall stands at the intersection of Harrison Road and the Red Cedar River. Its L-shaped plan is the reverse of the Butterfield Hall plan. On its east exterior is a polychromed enamel relief of *Aries* depicted as a white ram who is surrounded by red and turquoise abstract forms. Doris Hall and Kalman M.B. Kubinyi are the artists.

Butterfield Hall
Calder, 1954, 1962

Butterfield Hall stands at the corner of Michigan Avenue and Harrison Road. Its L-shaped plan is the reverse of the Emmons Hall plan. On its exterior are two polychromed enamel reliefs by Doris Hall and Kalman M. B. Kubinyi. On the north facade is a figure of *Aquarius* draped and immersed in blue and gray abstract shapes. On the east facade is *Pisces* depicted as red fish with turquoise eyes swimming amidst turquoise waves.

Rather Hall
Calder, 1954, 1962

Rather Hall stands northwest of Brody Hall, along Michigan Avenue. Its irregular plan is the reverse of the Bailey Hall plan.

University Village

Manson and Carver, 1953–55

Natural contours of the surrounding trees and park environment complement the spare, geometric International Style vocabulary of this apartment complex. Individual two-story apartment blocks stand in clusters surrounding cul-de-sac parking areas and greenspaces. This planning recalls the influence of the Garden City movement of the 1920s and its influence on the new American automobile suburb.

Metal casement windows, balconies, and flat roofs are other stylistic traits. Recessed panels of glass brick serve as decorative motifs while they function to protect exterior stairwells from the weather. Inside, compact configurations

of kitchen, bathroom, closets, and built-in bookshelves allow for maximal open floor space.

As these units and others in Spartan Village and Cherry Lane became available, the post–World War II trailers and other temporary housing disappeared. In 1955, the Western Michigan Chapter of the American Institute of Architects (AIA) presented an award to University Village in recognition of excellence in architectural design. Adjacent to the Red Cedar Natural Area, this residential complex continues to provide a convenient yet tranquil setting, a restful reprieve for faculty, staff, and student apartment dwellers.

Jack Breslin Student Events Center

Giffels/Hoyem Basso, 1989
IDS, Inc., 2001

With modernist formal purity and post-modernist colorful surfaces, the Jack Breslin Student Events Center stands affirmatively at the intersection of Harrison Road and Kalamazoo Street to welcome campus visitors. In brick, limestone, and glass, squares and rectangles rhythmically accentuate its extended-oval exterior. These brown, green, and off-white forms enliven the surface while affirming the green and white of MSU. Swaths of glazed green brick at the north and south sides are especially notable.

Four-color brick patterns soften the scale of the building's girth and offer visual surprises to delight the eye. Forming upright and inverted T shapes, they allude to internal steel and external skeletal framing. Inside, in daylight, glass brick panels provide natural lighting for the concourse and transform the overwhelming exterior scale into a fluid airy interior concourse.

The 254,000-square-foot building serves as an all-events center to accommodate men's and women's basketball, commencements, other university functions, concerts, trade shows, and conventions. Conceived in consultation with student groups and university administrators, the center provides space for activities formerly held at Jenison Field House. The center has full accessibility for disabled persons. For all entrants, sloping concrete walks replace steps and enhance the flow of up to 16,000 people to their seats. Remarkably, the arena offers unobstructed viewing with the farthest upper deck seats only 127 feet from the basketball court.

On the east side, a projecting wing houses a practice gymnasium and support services. Its south facade includes a head silhouette of a Spartan in full regalia incised in brick. "Paula '88" is the artist's signature.

Dedicated on 7 November 1989, the center honors an alumnus, Jack Breslin, known as "Mr. M.S.U." Breslin played football, basketball, and baseball, rendering him an appropriate namesake choice. Teacher, adviser, administrator, and institutional advocate, Breslin was vice president for state relations and a university liaison to the state legislature. He was from Battle Creek. A bronze plaque praising Breslin hangs in the center, a gift from his friends at the Kellogg Company in Battle Creek and the Calhoun County Alumni Club.

In 2001 the Board of Trustees approved the 37,747-square-foot Breslin Center east addition known as the Alfred Berkowitz Basketball Complex, planned to integrate with the original structure. Its cantilevered entrance canopy, with its green surface and arched shape, links visually with the main building. Variety in brick colors and a refined use of glass walls, glass brick, and aluminum trim also echo the original design. Green spandrels and green tinted glass recall other campus buildings.

The complex provides an auxiliary gymnasium, training and exercise faculties, offices, conference and video review rooms, and dining spaces for men's and women's basketball. The Berkowitz Foundation, founded by southeast Michigan businessperson and pharmacist Alfred Berkowitz, donated funds for the project. In honor of Berkowitz the complex bears his name.

GARY BOYNTON

Clarence L. Munn Ice Arena

Daverman Associates, 1974
Rossetti Associates, 1999

The architects designed Munn Ice Arena with a surrounding berm so it would blend harmoniously with the landscape and stand of pines known as the Sand Hill Plantation. This architectural and environmental feature is integral to the building's success. Modernist in its geometric simplicity and unadorned surfaces, this arena reflects a recurring contemporary interest in conceiving a building for use *and* site. Plants around the arena serve as teaching and demonstration gardens for botany, horticulture, and landscape architecture students and provide year-round visual appeal.

From a distance, the low-slung profile of the reflective metallic roof is prominent. At close range, belying its large scale, this huge horizontal sheath appears to float above its cast concrete and steel base. Entrance approaches are surprisingly intimate and lead the spectator into an unob-

structed, large, extended-oval interior. During the day, at the concourse level, a view directly across the recessed rink reveals sunlight filtering in through the entry doors. This light opens the interior and makes the roof appear to float from the inside. Daverman Associates created this bermed design to gain maximal ground insulation for the efficient temperature control essential for ice hockey. They also succeeded in producing a spacious interior.

The arena was designed to seat 6,355 fans for varsity hockey, student ice skating, and special campus events. Its lower level contains offices, locker rooms for varsity and intramural players, a physical therapy area, and a varsity club room. In 1999, V.I.P. seating was added. The building's name honors a former athletic director, Clarence "Biggie" Munn, who served as head football coach from 1947 until 1954 and as athletic director from 1954 until 1971.

THOMAS KACHADURIAN

Demonstration Hall

Bowd-Munson, 1928

Set amid deciduous trees and evergreens, this utilitarian gable-roofed Romanesque Revival building faces Demonstration Field, an expansive lawn. Demonstration Hall features a memorable tri-arched north entry whose prominent limestone voussoirs frame and accentuate each arch. Limestone-trimmed roundels also punctuate this north facade.

Like icing on a cake, brick and limestone arched corbeling trims the roof line. Large, metal-framed windows accentuate thin walls made possible by the building's skeletal construction. Although dressed in a historical style, "Dem Hall" is modern in its skeletal framing and characteristic of many gymnasia, halls, and field houses built on American college campuses in the early twentieth century.

The Morrill Act, establishing land-grant institutions such as Michigan State, called for military instruction. Demonstration Hall became the place for students to receive training in infantry, cavalry, artillery, equitation, and band. Prior to the erection of Demonstration Hall, on-campus military-training activities were usually based at the armory (1885) that once stood near the present site of the Music Building and Walter Adams Field.

From its opening day, with a seating capacity of nearly 5,000, an ice rink, and a riding arena, Demonstration Hall was used heavily. It became the home for military departments, athletic events, exhibitions of agricultural stock and equipment, and large meetings. Until nearby Munn Ice Arena opened in 1974, it was the "home ice" for the men's varsity hockey team. Today, Demonstration Hall is the home of the Department of Military Science. Demonstration Field continues to be a practice field for military training and the MSU Marching Band and a place for a variety of campus athletic and performance events.

GARY BOYNTON

Intramural Recreative Sports–West (IM West)
Sarvis, 1958

Brick, limestone, and glass, "IM West" is characteristically International Style. Its identical east and west entrances are particularly notable for their open framework, recessed glass curtain walls, and exposed stairwells.

IM West houses Michigan State classes and varied intramural sports and recreation programs. It has four gymnasia and more than two dozen courts for badminton, basketball, racquetball, squash, tennis, and volleyball. Steam and fitness rooms; archery, martial arts, table tennis, weightlifting, and wrestling facilities; and indoor and outdoor swimming pools complete the building's resources.

According to an undated publicity release, "From [former athletic director] Biggie Munn's original conception of a building that was light, airy and open, with centrally located showers and lockers leading through many different activity areas . . . to the location of storage rooms, . . . in line with adjacent gymnasiums for easy movement of equipment . . . every effort was made to create a facility that would efficiently serve intramurals, physical education, and limited varsity programs."

Originally known as the Intramural Sports Arena, IM West was designed so that its 2,000 bleacher seats, for fans of fencing, wrestling, and gymnastic varsity events, could be folded and stored after an event to accommodate the next floor activity. International Style advocates promoted the creation of universal spaces, adaptable to different needs. The IM West design reflects this architectural aspiration.

THOMAS KACHADURIAN

Spartan Stadium
Bowd, 1923
Munson, 1948, 1956, 1957

Monumental scale and bold, unadorned reinforced concrete enhances the visual strength of Spartan Stadium as the home of the MSU football team, the Spartans. Modernist in its simplicity, its sheer size has long made this stadium a prominent visual landmark for campus visitors. With a capacity of 76,000, the stadium ranks among the largest university-owned structures of its kind in the nation designed solely for football. Nevertheless, given its location in the heart of campus, it is often used for other university events. The view from the north tunnel entrance offers a memorable and comprehensive view of the field.

The original stadium, named M.A.C. (Michigan Agricultural College) Field, consisted of east and west stands with a capacity of 24,750. Bleachers filled the north and south ends. In 1935 the stadium became Macklin Field to honor John Farrell Macklin who was the first full-time athletic director from 1911 until 1916. At the dedication ceremony, President Shaw informed the crowd that the State Board of Agriculture (now Board of Trustees) recognized Macklin's "achievements as a distinguished athlete, coach, and exponent of the worth of athletic training as preparation for after-college activities."

The addition of 27,250 seats occurred in 1948, with 9,000 more added in 1956 to bring the total to 61,000 seats. The following year, with the completion of the upper deck and 15,000 more seats, Macklin Field became Spartan Stadium.

Director Stanley Kubrick used 76,000 screaming fans in Spartan Stadium attending the October 17, 1959, MSU–Notre Dame game in the gladiator scenes soundtrack of the Oscar-winning movie *Spartacus*. According to the summer 1991 *MSU Alumni Magazine*, Kirk Douglas, who starred as the Thracian slave-turned-gladiator, explained in his biography why MSU was picked: "'It's only natural for Spartacus to go to the Spartans for help.'"

Renovations during the 1990s included the addition of aluminum seating, waterproofing, expanded press box areas, computerized scoreboards, and new flagpoles. In 1998 a five-year program was undertaken to renovate the entire stadium structure. The west concourse restoration reached completion first, to be followed by the east con-

course restoration, including replacement of its 1923 seating and Column Repair 2000, a program to reinforce all columns that support the upper decks. In fall 2002, for the first time in thirty-two years, the playing field became natural grass. Grown at MSU's Hancock Turfgrass Center, south of Mount Hope Road, this experimental turfgrass reflects the research excellence of a land-grant institution.

On the south facade, facing Shaw Lane, three large green-and-white murals depict the Spartan home schedule flanked by players in action. On the west facade, three large bronze wall plaques document, respectively, the 1953 Big Ten and 1954 Rose Bowl Championships, the 1965 Big Ten and National Championships and 1966 Rose Bowl Championship, and the 1987 Big Ten and 1988 Rose Bowl Championships.

GARY BOYNTON

Central Services
Munson, 1948, 1952, 1956

Designed to house refrigeration rooms, kitchen preparation facilities, and a variety of university services, Central Services is visually plain. Its utilitarian, flat-roofed form includes metal-framed industrial windows and spare touches of contrasting trim. The original, main building offers a touch of aesthetic detail in the understated patterning of brick headers and stretchers that form alternating horizontal bands on the building's exterior.

Equipped with both enclosed and open loading dock bays, the building has met the changing demands of different university departments. In recent years the building has housed Automotive Services, Concessions, and Michigan State University Museum programs.

Power Plant – Shaw Lane

Erickson, 1948
Commonwealth, 1958

The gabled brick power station with its limestone trim is reminiscent of the Collegiate Gothic, an architectural style that was still in use for a few new campus buildings in the late 1940s. When this power plant was built at Red Cedar Road and South Shaw Lanes it was one of a few structures south of the Red Cedar River. For example, nearby at the corner of Farm Lane and South Shaw Lane, another Collegiate Gothic building, A.W. Farrall Agricultural Engineering Hall, was nearing completion. Clearly, maintaining visual consistency between academic and utilitarian structures was important.

The site was selected for proximity to then-existent railroad tracks and to make it feasible to raze the power plant and smokestack that stood north of the river near the present-day John A. Hannah Administration Building. That smokestack had structurally integral tan brick letters, "M" "A" "C," near its top, serving as a symbol of Michigan Agricultural College. Here, at the Shaw Lane Plant, the embedded letters are "M" "S" "C." Visible from the north and the south, they symbolize Michigan State College of Agriculture and Applied Science. The tower stands along a north-south axis. Beaumont Tower is to its north and the T. B. Simon Power Plant is to its south. As three sentinels, these towers watch over the campus and remind us of the past, present, and future.

From 1948 until 1975, when the Simon Power Plant opened, the Shaw Power Plant was the university's main power source. Today part of it serves as an electrical substation. The Erickson firm built the power plant, and the Commonwealth firm built the smokestack and the addition.

The Power Plant–Shaw Lane is named for its location on Shaw Lane. In turn, Shaw Lane was named to honor the eleventh president of Michigan State, Robert S. Shaw, who served in that capacity from 1928 until 1941.

Area Four: West Shaw Lane and Harrison Road

The explosion of post–World War II student enrollment led to the development of new residence halls, faculty housing, and service buildings in this area. From the 1950s to the late 1980s ambitious building projects reached completion south of West Shaw Lane, along Harrison Road to Service and Crescent Roads, and east to Chestnut Road.

Designed as living-learning centers, these new residence halls, when viewed as a group, form a veritable city. They are sets of complex services contained within sheaths of glass, steel, brick, and concrete. The South Complex, consisting of Case, Wilson, Wonders, and Holden Halls, has classrooms, student services, and residential rooms that became models for other campus buildings such as East Complex, along East Shaw Lane. Informed by the International Style, Wonders Hall (1963), Wilson Hall (1962), Holden Hall (1967) and, more subtly, Case Hall (1961) all have central large communal living spaces and wings for smaller residential, instructional, and meeting rooms.

In contrast to the gargantuan scale of Wonders, Wilson, and Holden Halls, both the Faculty Apartments and Cherry Lane Apartments seem human-scaled and intimate. Stylistically, they reflect the move from historically inspired style to the modern International Style, a transition that was in its final stages in American architecture during the 1940s and 1950s. The Faculty Apartments (1948) are Georgian Revival. They bear the names of Michigan State alumni who died in World War II. Cherry Lane Apartments (1956, 1961) are almost identical to those in Spartan Village (1957, 1958, 1966). With their International Style vocabulary, Cherry Lane Apartments relate directly to the area's other residential, office, and service buildings such as the Manly Miles Building (1959).

Easiest access: From Harrison Road, head east on West Shaw Lane; from West Shaw Lane, head south on Birch Road or Chestnut Road; from Harrison Road continue south and then east on Wilson Road, east on Service Road or east/west on Crescent Road; from Mount Hope Road, head north on Harrison Road and then east/west on Crescent Road, east on Service Road, Trowbridge Road, Wilson Road or West Shaw Lane.

Boundaries: Harrison Road, West Shaw Lane, Chestnut Road, Trowbridge Road, Farm Lane, and Mt. Hope Road.

Predominant historical style, name or theme: Georgian Revival and International Style. High-density living and services in a suburban park environment.

Date of oldest extant building in this area: 1948, Ungren Apartment Building (part of the Faculty Apartments).

These apartments are part of more than 2,500 campus units; Michigan State has the second highest number of on-campus apartments in the nation.

Today, this area contains a variety of support-services buildings including the Stephen S. Nisbet Building, University Housing, Physical Plant, Food Stores, and the T. B. Simon Power Plant. It also features several athletic facilities including the postmodernist Clara Bell Smith Student Athlete Academic Center and Hugh "Duffy" Daugherty Football Building and, along Mount Hope Road, the Forest Akers Golf Course and the Indoor Tennis Facility.

On 23 June 2000 the Board of Trustees approved a plan to create a new campus entrance. It agreed to extend Trowbridge Road from Harrison Road, past Cherry Lane Apartments, Holden Hall, Physical Plant, and Parking Ramp No. 5 to Farm Lane. An information center stands along this extension of Trowbridge Road. This new Trowbridge entrance allows easy campus access from

Trowbridge Road along a landscaped drive, improves traffic circulation when special campus events occur, and provides a place to welcome visitors.

Selected Historical Sites or Markers, Public Art, and Natural Areas

Trees in Cherry Lane and Spartan Village

As Cherry Lane Apartments neared completion, tenants and students planted some of the trees, whose descendants still stand between Harrison and Birch Roads. The sycamores along Crescent Road in Spartan Village originally grew in the area where the World War II barracks, used as student housing, once stood in and near the intramural field south of Munn Ice Arena.

Hugh "Duffy" Daugherty Football Building

Wakely-Kushner Associates, 1980
Sims-Varner and Associates, 1985
Gharfari Associates, 1997

The Hugh "Duffy" Daugherty Football Building bears the name of the legendary Michigan State football coach from 1954 until 1972, Hugh "Duffy" Daugherty. The predominantly one-story Brutalist brick building, with its emphatic horizontality, stands firmly on its flat ground. Its sloped walls and recessed ribbon windows enhance this sense of stability. Varietal trees and shrubs complement the irregular building plan. Its south entrance exterior displays a metal silhouette of the Spartan head insignia. Inside, a permanent wall exhibit of program covers from previous football games includes the 8 October 1956 *Time* magazine cover that features "Michigan State's Coach Daugherty." The hall between the south and west (main) entrances displays rows of photographs of Spartan All-Americans and members of the College Football Hall of Fame from Michigan State. The west entrance lobby proudly presents cases filled with football trophies, uniforms, and memorabilia. The original building design included classrooms, equipment storage, hydrotherapy rehabilitation, and training rooms still used today. Today the football building is part of

the postmodernist form, glass volumes, brick masses, and metal sheathing that boldly interrelate to form a multipurpose center for campus athletes. Built in four stages, this 179,743 square-foot complex is a visually compelling compilation of different architectural vocabularies.

When first conceived, the 1985 indoor practice field was supposed to be an expansive white pole barn. Subsequently, the Board of Trustees approved the wrapping of a portion of this building with brick to match the original football building, which serves to minimize its sheer size and relate it comfortably to other nearby south campus buildings. On its east facade, a row of large evergreens is particularly impressive.

The indoor practice field was funded as part of a major sports package for the Jack Breslin Student Events Center, indoor tennis facilities, and Jenison Field House renovations. The 1997 addition expanded services in anticipation of the need to complement the Clara Bell Smith Student Athlete Academic Center, then in the planning stages.

Clara Bell Smith
Student Athlete Academic Center
Gharfari Associates, 1998

The Clara Bell Smith Student Athlete Academic Center is 36,372 square feet and links with the Hugh "Duffy" Daugherty Football Building and the indoor practice field. It serves more than 800 students in all Division I sports and houses computer labs, study and tutorial rooms, student athlete support services, and the John H. McConnell Auditorium. Its two-story glass entry offers a light-filled space with the Spartan S embedded in its travertine floor. On the first wall visitors encounter, the large wall text reads:

> *I have had great coaches, but none greater than my mother. I have had great role models, but none greater than my mom. I have had great teammates and fans, but none greater than Clara Bell Smith. —Steve Smith.*

Surrounding the text is the Secchia Academic All-American Gallery consisting of portrait paintings of

Michigan State's Academic All-Americans. To the right is the Michigan State University Athletics Hall of Fame in a memorably designed, curved hallway. A historical diorama depicts significant moments and individual accomplishments in all sports, by male and female athletes, at Michigan State. Overhead banners and window wall plaques complete this visually compelling presentation.

Steve Smith, who was an All-American Michigan State basketball player in the late 1980s and early 1990s, donated this building in memory of his mother, Clara Bell Smith. After his Michigan State years, Smith entered the National Basketball Association (NBA) and played for the Atlanta Hawks and then for the Portland Trailblazers. When he made this donation to Michigan State it was one of the largest gifts any athletic alumnus had given to any American college or university.

THOMAS KACHADURIAN

Fire Station

Munson, 1955
Physical Plant, 1981

The simplicity of the International Style vocabulary is appropriate for this utilitarian building. Its L-shaped plan has a two-story section, and a one-story section that faces West Shaw Lane near the South Complex. Limestone trim neatly accentuates its rectilinear doors, windows, piered entrance, and overall form. When the engine-house doors are open, the lightness of the curtain walls is especially apparent.

South Complex

South Complex, built in the International Style, is characteristic of 1960s architecture. The educational philosophy underpinning its development was very innovative in its day. These halls are living-learning residences designed to foster a vital student life environment integrating housing, classrooms, faculty offices, and social facilities. Holden, Wilson, and Wonders Halls have kivas, a common meeting space in the round for instruction, performances, and hall meetings. This new approach to student life emerged in response to a recommendation from the 1959 Committee on the Future of the University. It recommended that "the education programs of the residence halls should be implemented to maintain a climate which primarily promotes academic, intellectual and cultural pursuits." This innovative approach attracted state funding.

The South Complex halls departed from past practice in other ways. The Board of Trustees named each hall for *two* people. Case Hall is named for Albert H. and Sarah A. Case. Albert was the 1901 State Agricultural College football captain, earning a bachelor of arts degree in 1902, and Sarah Avery Case was an instructor at State Agricultural College. They married in 1906. Albert Case became a mining executive and made his fortune in investments.

Both Albert and Sarah made significant gifts to Michigan State. Albert died in 1962, the year Case Hall opened. Case Hall is the home of James Madison College.

Holden Hall honors James and Lynelle Holden. James entered State Agricultural College in 1889. For thirty-eight years James played a key role in developing the Detroit Zoological Park. James and Lynelle also made significant gifts to Michigan State.

Wilson Hall bears the names of Alfred G. and Mathilda R. Wilson. Mathilda Wilson served as a member of the State Board of Agriculture (now Board of Trustees) from 1931 until 1937. The Wilsons, for whom Wilson Road is named, donated their 1,400-acre Meadow Brook Farms estate and $2 million to Michigan State in 1957 to create a branch campus in Oakland County near Rochester, Michigan. This later became a separate institution known as Oakland University.

Wonders Hall recalls Wallace K. and Grace Wonders. Wallace Wonders received his bachelor of science degree from State Agricultural College in 1902. He was a real estate claims adjuster and a price and rent investigator. He and Grace became Michigan State benefactors.

Case Hall

Sarvis, 1961
FTCH, 1987

Case Hall is the earliest living-learning center erected in this campus area. Lewis J. Sarvis created this International Style design with a multileveled, straight-line plan. He paid attention to fine detail as exemplified by the limestone coursing at the roof lines and a touch of expressivity in the central projecting gables. Case Hall features a lift-slab construction. In the 1960s this process was new to campus. Builders poured concrete slabs singly, stacked them like pancakes, and used hydraulic jacks to lift each slab. Then they anchored each slab to the steel infrastructure. The Case Hall design, with its access to the dining hall and offices without climbing stairs, is an early example of accessible design. Like those in other South Complex halls, residence hall rooms are arranged in suites of two adjoined by a bathroom.

Holden Hall

Calder, 1967

Holden Hall is the last of the three residence complexes Ralph Calder designed for South Complex. Holden Hall's plan, like that of Wilson and Wonders Halls, has central commons facilities and two prominent wings. Holden, however, is a more formal International Style building, with projecting piers that enframe the vertical bands of windows and taupe spandrels.

GARY BOYNTON

THOMAS KACHADURIAN

Wilson Hall
Calder, 1962

Wonders Hall
Calder, 1963

Wilson Hall and Wonders Hall share many similar characteristics although they are not identical. Each displays a
circular central classroom and student life area flanked by
two arced wings. The main entrance for each wing is located at the vertex of two angled facades. Thin limestone
planes flank each entrance. An angled six-story glass curtain wall reveals the internal post and beam construction.
Gray Mankato stone spandrels accent each floor level.
Characteristic of the International Style, other glass curtain walls link one facade with the next. They offer visual

relief from the stark brick facades patterned only with neat
rows of metal-framed windows. At the center of both
Wilson Hall and Wonders Hall, dining rooms, raised on
pilotis, offer airy views of the surrounding wings and continue the use of limestone and gray Mankato stone effec-
tively. In 1963, as Wonders Hall rose in the South
Complex, its twin, McDonel Hall, appeared as part of the
East Complex. The Ralph Calder firm designed both
buildings.

Faculty Apartments

Munson, 1948

Designed by different architectural firms, Faculty Apartments and Cherry Lane Apartments feature two distinct architectural styles, the Georgian Revival and the International Style. Yet despite their distinctly different outward appearance, both building groups are brick, two-storied, and similar in scale. They form semi-enclosed spaces for playground and other recreational activities in a park-like environment, close to central campus, between Harrison Road and Birch Road. Given the post–World War II scarcity of certain raw materials, the choice of brick was practical and cost-effective. In the 1950s and 1960s many faculty members who lived in Faculty Apartments referred to them as the "bricks."

Faculty Apartments: Bale III, Bauman, Crowe, Drake, Frang, French, Howland, Parker, Pelton, Rafferty, Ungren

In 1948 Munson designed the first phase as two-story apartment buildings in the Georgian Revival style, loosely reminiscent of one of the most long-lived styles in American architecture. Side-gabled entrances, doorways with segmental pediments and pilasters, quoins, cupolas, and brick contrasted with white trim are stylistic reminders. Doors and windows are not original; they were replaced in the 1980s for energy efficiency. Selecting a historical style seemed appropriate for this building complex whose entrances commemorate a male alumnus who died in World War II. The alumni are as follows:

Joseph L. Bale III, Class of 1946
H. Thane Bauman, Class of 1943
Edwin B. Crowe, Class of 1940
Royce A. (Allison) Drake, Class of 1927
Carol N. (Nelson) Frang, Class of 1943
Robert L. French, Class of 1944
Arthur John Howland, Class of 1941
Robert Parker, Class of 1943
Joseph A. (Allshouse) Pelton, Class of 1936
William T. Rafferty, Class of 1940 or 1941
Arthur K. Ungren, Class of 1932.

Cherry Lane Apartments

Manson and Carver, 1956
Manson, Wilson, and Jackson, 1961

Manson and Carver and the successor firm Manson, Wilson and Jackson used the International Style for these twenty-eight detached or adjoined, balconied units. These architects also designed University Village apartments (1953–55) and Spartan Village Apartments (1957, 1958, 1966), which explains why the Cherry Lane units are essentially identical to those found in the two other apartment complexes. All three complexes include one- and two-bedroom apartments. To create a sense of community and a safe recreational environment, the architects arranged the apartments to form contiguous greenspaces and cul-de-sac driveways.

THOMAS KACHADURIAN

Physical Plant
Physical Plant, 1963, 1969

Designed to blend with its architectural neighbors, the Physical Plant shops and office building display the flat roof, curtain walls, boxed eaves, and plain, exterior surfaces of the International Style. Gray and green Mankato stone panels and aluminum trim enliven the "front" or south facade and its overall pleasing proportions. This front entrance leads to offices and beyond to the two large wings, running north-south and east-west, that contain various technical shops. These are also accessible from the large nearby parking lot.

Physical Plant houses many critical campus services, such as Custodial Services, Engineering and Architectural Services, Maintenance Services, and the Power and Water Department. In 1965 former president John A. Hannah wrote in *Note a Thing Apart* that "Many factors and developments could be singled out as substantial contributors to the high regard in which this university is now held by universities everywhere. . . . The improving quality and magnitude of our physical plant is undoubtedly a factor."

THOMAS KACHADURIAN

Spartan Village

Manson and Carver, 1957, 1958, 1966

With its simple, geometric vocabulary, Spartan Village was one of three apartment complexes built to accommodate the burgeoning post–World War II university enrollment. Along with its predecessor, University Village (1953–55), and its approximate contemporary, Cherry Lane Apartments (1956, 1961), its overall plan and individual buildings embrace the International Style. Flat roofs, smooth exterior curtain walls, and metal casement windows are universal traits. Some units have brick exteriors while others feature enameled steel panels in bands of light green and buff trimmed with aluminum. Practical, maintenance-free, and seemingly "modern," these colored panels recall the nationwide use of similar materials in the 1950s, particularly for motels, gas stations, and restaurants. In 2001, several units near the CSX Railroad tracks were

demolished because renovation costs exceeded new construction costs. The area will become greenspace.

The overall plan is nonhierarchical and modular. Groups of buildings stand around cruciform or straight-line parking areas accessible from the curves of Crescent and Middlevale Roads. The Spartan Village School is part of the East Lansing Public Schools. Spartan Village also includes laundries (1957, 1958). The Spartan Village Child Development Center (1971), designed by the Hartwick firm, was superseded by a new gabled building bearing the same name in 2002. Tower, Pinkster, and Titus are the architects. Today, plenty of mature trees and shrubs help to create a park environment in this complex for students, staff, visiting scholars, and faculty. The sycamores along Crescent Road are especially beautiful.

GARY BOYNTON

Manly Miles Building

Sarvis, 1959

The Manly Miles Building has a symmetrical facade and a T-shaped plan with a four-storied central block and two lower projecting wings. Limestone coursing and blue-enameled spandrels accentuate refined exterior proportions. The main entrance facade features a cantilevered entrance canopy and recessed curtain walls, both exemplary characteristics of the International Style.

Manly Miles was the first professor of zoology at the Agricultural College of the State of Michigan from 1860 until 1875. He is referred to as the first professor of scientific agriculture in the United States. In 1865, he was appointed superintendent of the farm in addition to being professor of animal physiology and practical agriculture. As a born collector, he curated the collections in what was then the college museum. Known internationally as an investigator, he worked on the forefront of advanced agriculture. A consummate teacher and scientist, he published books titled *Stock-Breeding, Experiments with Indian Corn, Silos and Ensilage,* and *Land Drainage.* He wrote papers for *Popular Science Monthly, American Naturalist,* and the American Association for the Advancement of Science. Today, the Manly Miles Building serves as the home of several administrative and academic units, including the Michigan State University Press.

Stephen S. Nisbet Building

Warren-Holmes, 1973

Projecting bays with recessed copper-tinted windows give this Brutalist building its distinctive undulating exterior. Textured concrete, used as coping and for the ground level, controls the vertical rhythms of the facades. Windows read as voids instead of as the glass sheaths seen in the Manly Miles Building across the street. In the Nisbet lobby and on its exterior, the overt display of textural variety in concrete and brick is characteristic of Brutalism. This stylistic characteristic reveals the influence in American architecture of the internationally known Swiss-French architect,

Le Corbusier. Extensive tinted glass recalls the prevalent use of this material in 1970s corporate buildings.

This building bears the name of Stephen S. Nisbet from Fremont, Michigan. In 1961 Nisbet was the elected chairperson of the Michigan Constitutional Convention. From 1963 until 1970 he served as a member of the Board of Trustees. His other professional experiences included positions as president of the Michigan Education Association, member of the State Board of Education, and vice president for public relations, Gerber Products.

University Housing
Manson, Jackson, Kane, 1962

This one-story, brick International Style office building, with its curtain walls and simple post-and-beam construction, blends with many other campus designs of the 1950s and 1960s. It is the first of several university services buildings found along the aptly named Service Road.

University apartment and residence hall assignments are determined here. At one time this building was named Married Housing. Initially, campus housing that was not residence hall housing was for faculty and married students, including many World War II veterans. In April 1945, President John Hannah addressed a letter, "To

Whom It May Concern," in which he noted that the number of veterans on campus was 303 and that the number would increase to 5,000 or more following the end of the war. At that time, there were few rental properties in East Lansing and certainly not enough to serve large numbers. In anticipation of housing demand, within a year or two of Hannah's letter, construction began for Faculty Apartments, Phillips and Snyder Halls, and Gilchrist, Landon, and Yakeley Halls. With the completion of other apartments and residence halls during the 1950s, the need for a separate housing office became urgent.

Robert D. Angell University Services

Margerum, 1988
Physical Plant, 1998

Purchasing

Mayotte-Webb, 1969

Stores

Frantz and Spence, 1950
Physical Plant, 1963, 1964, 1969, 1987

This utilitarian International Style structure is actually a complex of one-story buildings linked to fulfill university services: Stores, Purchasing, Mail Processing, and University Services Administration. Unadorned surfaces and flat roofs are dominant. The center section has six cargo loading and unloading bays. In the west portion, exposed post-beam construction and ribbon windows set flush with the brick sheathing below are characteristic stylistic traits.

The building name honors Robert D. Angell, who began working in Purchasing in 1935 and retired in 1981.

GARY BOYNTON

Food Stores

Manson, Kane, Jackson, 1964

This one-story, flat-roofed, unadorned brick structure complements other nearby service buildings and pays homage to the International Style. A cantilevered entrance canopy, green enameled spandrels, and windows set flush with exterior walls are typical stylistic traits.

In 80,331 square feet, Food Stores holds extensive food supplies for residence halls and other university needs. This building contains one of the largest freezers in the United States.

T. B. Simon Power Plant

1965, Benjamin, Woodhouse, Guenther   *1993, Black and Veatch*
1974, 1976, Commonwealth   *1998, FTC&H*
1981, Commonwealth Associates

This massive complex consisting of main building, gallery and transfer tower, cooling towers, and two 275-foot smokestacks is the source of steam for heat and electricity for all campus buildings. The importance and scale of this operation is enhanced by the bold, plain, brick curtain walls trimmed with Indiana limestone and the slightly recessed windows and green-gray spandrels.

The north tower displays white letters spelling "MSU." These letters appear on both the north and south sides of the tower; they are visible from many campus and off-campus vantage points, making this structure a prominent Lansing area landmark.

The complex bears the name of Theodore "Ted" B. Simon, who was assistant construction engineer 1946–51, construction engineer 1951–56, superintendent of buildings and utilities 1956–64, director of physical plant 1964–73, and assistant vice president for physical plant 1973–84. He oversaw the planning and growth of much of the post–World War II campus development, including the residence halls.

Area Five: Farm Lane, North and South Shaw Lanes, Wilson and Trowbridge Roads

This area, south of the Red Cedar River between Spartan Stadium and Farm Lane, reflects the growth pattern of Michigan State University in the second half of the twentieth century. The last vestiges of the Collegiate Gothic and touches of High Tech styling and postmodern design complement the predominant influence of the International Style. This stylistic range reflects developments in American architecture as a whole. Consistency of scale and purposeful siting of these buildings foster a sense of spaciousness while the frequent use of brick as exterior sheathing increases a sense of visual unity.

Particularly notable is the way the buildings near the Red Cedar River foster a park environment. From Erickson Hall, the International Center, and Wells Hall, ample views of the Red Cedar River environment and its scenic rapids and duck-feeding area abound. The tree-covered space between Erickson and Wells Halls south of the International Center is also part of the

new Campus Center. This center is actually a student-inspired set of events that occur in buildings in a campus area that today serves as a main hub or "center" of campus activity.

The area south of the International Center and north of Anthony Hall–Engineering Building is in transition. Some will recall that before 1997 the Livestock Judging Pavilion stood in this space bordered by North and South Shaw Lanes. This pavilion was a 1938 Public Works Administration project. In the late 1930s new barns emerged on south campus to replace those originally found north of the Red Cedar River. This created the need for a new judging pavilion and site for livestock association meetings close to the barns. Decades later, due to the existence of the barns and the Pavilion for Agriculture and Livestock Education, south of Mount Hope Road, the need for the 1938 pavilion passed. Today, a row of brick and limestone pylons mark the former pavilion's site and form a visual link

> **Easiest access**: From Farm Lane, south of the Red Cedar River, head west on North Shaw Lane, Wilson Road, or Trowbridge Road; from West Shaw Lane, head north/ south on Red Cedar Road or east on South Shaw Lane.
>
> **Boundaries**: Red Cedar River, Farm Lane, Canadian National Railway, Trowbridge Road, Red Cedar Road.
>
> **Predominant historical style, name or theme**: Collegiate Gothic, International Style, High Tech, and postmodern. Classrooms, laboratories, special meeting places, and services west of Farm Lane.
>
> **Date of oldest extant building in this area**: Anthony Hall, 1955 (original portion).

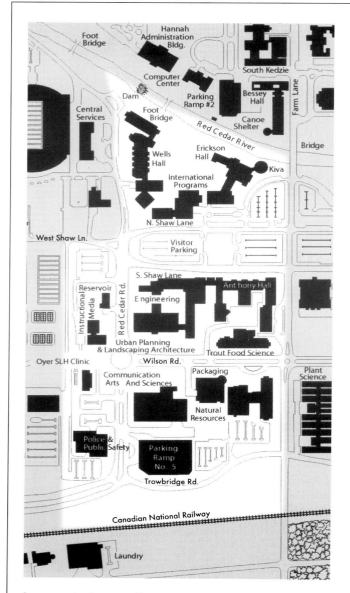

improves traffic circulation while it more precisely defines the perimeter of this thickly vegetated demonstration area.

Selected Historical Sites or Markers, Public Art, and Natural Areas

Campus Center, uses the facilities of Wells Hall, the International Center, Erickson Kiva, and the Engineering Building

During the academic year, the Campus Center offers programming inspired by student interest on Friday, Saturday, and Sunday evenings. Entertainer and band performances and movies are among the most popular events.

Fish and Wildlife Demonstration Area, south of the Natural Resources Building, north of the railroad tracks

The Fish and Wildlife Demonstration Area was developed with the cooperation of the Daughters of the American Revolution, Michigan State University Division of Campus Park and Planning, Department of Fisheries and Wildlife, United States Soil Conservation Service, Michigan Department of Natural Resources, Michigan Commercial Nurseries, and the Associated Students of Michigan State University (ASMSU) Funding Board.

Frederic Reeve Memorial Garden, northwest of the International Center

These beddings include rhododendrons, azaleas, and other acid-soil plants. On 16 January 1970 the Board of Trustees approved this garden's name to honor Professor Frederic Reeve who loved flower gardens. He referred to them often in his teaching about beauty in courses such as the University College Great Issues course. In 1959 he became a full professor in the Department of American Thought and Language and in Justin Morrill College.

Livestock Judging Pavilion Site, between North Shaw Lane and South Shaw Lane, north of the Engineering Building and south of the International Center

Twelve pylons with pyramidal crowns define a walkway

between Anthony Hall–Engineering and the International Center. To the east, young crabapples line Farm Lane recalling the beauty of the mature predecessors they replaced.

The northernmost boundary of this area is the Red Cedar River. From the Farm Lane Bridge, which spans the Red Cedar, spectators can see Erickson Hall just beyond the river's south shore. A glance toward the river's north shore reveals the Canoe Livery Service, fondly known to some as the Red Cedar Yacht Club.

The southernmost boundary is the Canadian National Railway and the Fisheries and Wildlife Demonstration Area. The decision to extend Trowbridge Road south of Parking Ramp No. 5 and Communication Arts and Sciences to Farm Lane changed this area. The road between North Shaw Lane and South Shaw Lane at the site of the former Livestock Judging Pavilion. Alternating bands of limestone, concrete, and brick make up each pylon. These bricks, from the razed Livestock Judging Pavilion, symbolically link campus life, past and present.

Just west of the twelve pylons, benches, plantings, and a curved brick parapet join together to form a pleasant area to sit and reflect. The creation of this area is integral to the Campus Beautification Project. The parapet plaque reads:

The Campus Beautification Project is an effort to plant hundreds of trees south of the Red Cedar River. This endeavor honors the legacy left by Profs. William J. Beal and Ernest E. Bogue in the late 1800s, when they made the same effort on the north campus, creating the environment that all who know MSU cherish.

These trees will add to the richness and beauty of this campus for future generations of Spartans.

Actually, the plaque should read late 1800s to early 1900s, because Bogue was at Michigan State from 1902 until 1907.

The southernmost pylon bears a plaque that reads:

Judging Pavilion Site
This plaque marks the former site of the MSU Judging Pavilion, built in 1938 and replaced by the Pavilion for Agriculture and Livestock Education in 1997. For nearly 60 years, the Judging Pavilion was dedicated to the advancement of Michigan's livestock industry through education, exhibition and livestock distribution. On April 14, 1993, Governor John Engler signed into Law Act 19 of the Public Acts of 1993, which provided funding for the Agriculture Initiative, enabling the university to undertake a campus-wide modernization of research, teaching and demonstration facilities to better serve Michigan's livestock industry. The Animal Agriculture Initiative was the result of the foresight, drive and leadership of the governor, the bipartisan efforts of the Michigan Senate and House of Representatives, Michigan agriculture and Michigan State University.

From the north, the fifth pylon reads:

On this site stood The Livestock Judging Pavilion. For six decades, 1938–97, the Livestock Judging Pavilion served as a focal point for many activities within the College of Agriculture and Natural Resources. At this site, thousands of students learned how to evaluate and judge farm animals. Serving as a laboratory for courses offered by the Department of Animal Science and a forum for student events, the pavilion provided young people the opportunity to develop their skills. Some of them eventually became state and national agricultural leaders. Animal events included the Block and Bridle Club Horse Show, Little International Livestock show, MSU Rodeo, and visits by collegiate judging teams from other universities. The Judging Pavilion offered many college, high school and elementary students their first exposure to the MSU campus. It also provided opportunities to bring Michigan's finest industry leaders and livestock managers together with faculty and students. At these summits, important agricultural issues were discussed and future trends developed. Initially, draft horse competitions were the most popular activity. By the 1950's, beef, dairy, poultry, sheep and swine events had gained in popularity. In later years, youth activities, centered around 4-H and the Future Farmers of America program, were predominant. The bricks highlighting these columns were preserved when the pavilion was razed in May of 1997, as a reminder of its legacy. The spirit and mission of the pavilion lives on with the new pavilion for agriculture and livestock education which was constructed on Farm Lane in 1996.

Red Cedar River, rapids and duck-feeding area, Red Cedar Road, north of Wells Hall along the banks of the Red Cedar River

Although the Red Cedar River has always been integral to campus life, the creation of a current park and seating area for access to the rapids and the local resident duck population dates from the late 1960s, the time when the John A. Hannah Administration Building was nearing completion. Looking north across the river provides a comprehensive view of this building.

GARY BOYNTON

Wells Hall

Harley-Ellington, 1967
Harley-Ellington, 1970

Simple, unadorned, geometrical form characterizes this sprawling International Style brick complex of more than 250,000 square feet. Wells Hall has four functionally discrete, yet linked, sections that form a long south-north nexus.

The southernmost three-story wing has deeply recessed windows that enhance the drama of its positioning at a forty-five degree angle from its neighbor, the A wing. Inside, the Vernon G. Grove Research and Mathematics Library features unusual skylight illumination that pervades a large, open, three-story-high reading room. The A wing is a seven-story classroom and office block and is home to

the Department of Mathematics, the Department of Linguistics and German, Slavic, Asian and African Languages, and the English Language Center. The one-story B section has three large lecture halls and computer labs. The northernmost section, the C wing, offers three stories of classrooms and offices along the Red Cedar River. When weather is severe, students and faculty often walk from one end of Wells to another to enjoy its controlled climate.

Vernon Grove (1890–1967), for whom the Research and Mathematics Library is named, was a professor of mathematics in 1920–58. He was an ardent supporter of

Above: **First Wells Hall, 1877, burned 1905.** *Right:* **Second Wells Hall, built 1907, razed 1966. Stood on the site of the present-day Library.**

and participant in "mathematics research and scholarship."

The present Wells Hall is actually the third building on campus to bear this name. The first Wells Hall stood from 1877 until it burned in 1905, and the second stood from 1907 until 1966, when it was razed to make room for the 1967 addition to the library. Each prior Wells Hall was a student residence. Like its predecessors, the present Wells Hall is named for Hezekiah G. Wells who served as a member, and often as president, of the State Board of Agriculture (now Board of Trustees) in 1861–83. Wells, a lawyer and a judge from Kalamazoo, Michigan, was instrumental in founding the Agricultural College of the State of Michigan and, in subsequent years, in convincing the Michigan legislature that the Agricultural College of the State of Michigan should remain on its present site and not move to Ann Arbor to become part of the University of Michigan.

DERRICK TURNER

International Center

Calder, 1964   *Ralph Calder and Associates, Inc., 2003*
Calder, 1980

Unadorned, brick, and multileveled, the International Center is characteristically International Style. Its L-shaped plan has a classroom-office block and a large, sprawling two-story wing that includes the main entrances. From either the south entrance (North Shaw Lane) or the north entrance, visitors pass through glass doors and ascend stairs to an expansive lobby whose glass walls keep the space visually open. Although some internal spaces have been reconfigured, in the dining area, the view of the wooded park north of the building remains superb. In the 1990s, the south entrance was expanded but the International Style vocabulary still predominates throughout the building.

Michigan State University developed its commitment to international study, research, and outreach in the 1950s. The decision to erect this building still serves as a symbol of this commitment. International Studies and Programs is housed in the classroom-office block. Its international

branch library and meeting room, the Crossroads Food Court, and the Michigan State University Bookstore occupy the two-story wing. The meeting room is the site of faculty and student governance group meetings. It was formerly known as the Con-Con Room because it commemorated the Michigan Constitutional Convention of 1961 and 1962 held at the Lansing Civic Center.

Located where temporary retrofitted World War II army buildings once stood, the International Center continues to be a lively nexus of campus academic, cultural, and social life. Its most recent addition is a 10,000-square-foot expansion of the classroom-office block named for Delia Koo, an alumnus who created the Volunteer English Tutoring Program in 1983 and worked to promote educational opportunities for international students. The Delia Koo International Academic Center includes the classroom-office block and the library.

THOMAS KACHADURIAN

Erickson Hall

Calder, 1957, 1964, 1974

With its rambling plan, Erickson Hall is perfectly situated for its site. Its windows face the Red Cedar River, Farm Lane, and the wooded park area to the west. This fine example of the International Style features wide expanses of glass complemented by green spandrels and brick. From Farm Lane, the glass-enclosed stairwell near the main entrance is an impressive sight. Its transparent glass walls reveal the cantilevered staircase and affirm a favorite International Style characteristic—the demonstration that this is an architecture of volumes not masses, as the lightness of curtain walls hung from a skeletal frame reveal. Another notable feature is the circular kiva, with its simply patterned copper roof, which has been the site of many lectures, concerts, and rallies. Not surprisingly, a glance east across Farm Lane to the Kresge Art Center reveals many stylistic similarities. Calder designed both.

The building is named for Clifford E. Erickson (1907–63) who was dean of the College of Education when the first portion of this building was erected. He served as dean in 1953–61 when he was appointed provost. Prior to that appointment, in 1951–53, Erickson was the second faculty member to serve as dean of the Basic College which, at one time, provided the general education program required of all Michigan State students. Erickson was the author or co-author of numerous books and papers on guidance, school counseling, and instructional television.

Anthony Hall

Munson, 1955   *Bei Associates, 1997*
Physical Plant, 1964

This Collegiate Gothic design displays characteristic gabled pavilions, hipped dormers, and prominent limestone trim. Interesting stylistic details include end gables with parapets. The Munson architectural firm designed both Anthony Hall and A. W. Farrall Agricultural Engineering Hall (1948) to face north and to occupy, respectively, the east and the west corners of South Shaw Lane and Farm Lane. Until the completion of the 1997 Anthony Hall addition these two Collegiate Gothic buildings were comparable in scale and size.

The 1997 addition is revivalist, as its South Shaw Lane facade, with its gables, reveals. Its overall massing reaffirms the scale of the original Anthony Hall and maintains a similarity in height to the Engineering Building. It is the new link between the original Anthony Hall and the Engineering Building. Visual continuity among these buildings is conveyed by the horizontal bands of limestone (Anthony) or aluminum (Engineering) trim and windows that, although stylistically different, run at the same height from one section to another. Another section of the 1997 addition links Anthony Hall with the Dairy Store.

Ernest L. Anthony (1888–1966), for whom the building is named, was a professor of dairy science who served as dean of agriculture 1933–53. He taught dairy farm management, published several editions of Clarence Eckles's *Dairy Cattle and Milk Production*, and was a strong proponent of continuing education.

GARY BOYNTON

Engineering Building

Giffels-Rossetti, 1962   *Albert Kahn Associates, 1996*
Albert Kahn Associates, 1989

The original building on this site faces South Shaw Lane and displays the spare, refined International Style vocabulary of its era. Especially notable are the aluminum-trimmed ribbon windows, which emphasize the thinness of the exterior walls, and the glass stairwell near Red Cedar Road. With a sense of nuance characteristic of the International Style, the viewer is reminded that the inner skeleton, not the outer wall, supports the building. Prominent green and teal spandrels complement the red brick and recall the same use of materials as nearby Erickson Hall.

The 1989 addition enlarged this facility by 200 percent, formed a squarish plan with a central courtyard, and created the first postmodernist building on campus. The introduction of historicist detailing as a gabled entrance pavilion with a roundel window suggests postmodernist appropriation. A rich interplay of textures, colors, voids, and solids enlivens these Wilson Road exteriors. Expanses of glass-brick walkways, replete with bright blue trim, are notable. An architectonic sculpture stands in the courtyard. It is dedicated to Tau Beta Pi, the engineering honor society, and has brick and limestone piers that support its aluminum-trussed top.

With the completion of the 1996 historicist addition, the Engineering Building and Anthony Hall were linked. At that time, other interior renovations to accommodate

innovative directions in manufacturing and materials research and applications were also completed. Inside the new South Shaw Lane entrance, in the addition, is a plaque to inform all who enter that this is the "Site of The Herbert H. and Grace A. Dow Institute for Materials Research in the College of Engineering." A variety of metal paneling and beveled glass in the vestibule visually affirm this scholarly commitment to materials research. On 5 April 2001 the Masonry Institute of Michigan and the Michigan Chapter of the American Institute of Architects presented the 2000 M Award for Excellence in Masonry Design to the architects, Albert Kahn Associates, and the Dow Institute for Materials Research, Michigan State University.

In 1885 the first building for the newly established mechanical and engineering department was built. In 1907 a new engineering building was completed and the 1885 building continued to be used for engineering shops. When a fire destroyed this building, R. E. Olds paid for the erection of an identical building in 1916, known as Olds Hall. The Electrical Engineering Building, now known as the Computer Center, was built in 1948. With the completion of the new Engineering Building in 1962, it became possible, gradually, to move all engineering facilities south of the Red Cedar River to the present location.

G. Malcolm Trout Food Science and Human Nutrition Building
Kahn, 1966

Simple, unadorned, and geometric form, hallmark of the International Style, is emphatically evident in this building. Slightly recessed paired windows and their off-white stone spandrels alternate with tan-gray mullions to form a pervasive dark-light pattern across the facades. The cantilevered rectangular canopy over the front entrance reads "Food Science" and is otherwise unadorned. The modest entrance vestibule leads directly to offices and laboratories and thereby signals that this is a building whose three levels are devoted to serious teaching and research. Located just south of Anthony Hall, this building houses the Department of Food Science and Human Nutrition.

Originally named Food Science, on 26 October 1992 the Board of Trustees dedicated this building as the G. Malcolm Trout Food Science and Human Nutrition Building to honor an accomplished Michigan State

University professor of food science. From 1928 until 1966 G. Malcolm Trout (1896–1990) contributed significantly to the diary science industry and particularly the development of new processes for the manufacture of yogurt and cheese. Most important, in the early 1930s he contributed to the research needed to make homogenized milk a reality by linking the processes of pasteurization and homogenization. In 1950 Michigan State University Press published his book, *Homogenized Milk: A Review and Guide*. Internationally known, Trout served as the official United States delegate to the XII, XIII, and XIV World's Dairy Congresses held, respectively, in Stockholm, the Hague, and Rome. He received the Michigan State Distinguished Faculty Award in 1961 and the American Dairy Science Association Award of Honor in 1964.

GARY BOYNTON

Urban Planning and Landscape Architecture–Instructional Media Center

Calder, 1966

Curtain walls, unadorned brick surfaces, and lime-stone coping all contribute to the simple, geometric vocabulary of this International Style complex. These two building blocks link via an enclosed passageway. Each building has paired windows with aluminum frames separated by gray, metal spandrels.

The three-story block houses the programs in Urban and Regional Planning and Landscape Architecture, and the two-story block houses the Instructional Media Center.

GARY BOYNTON

Herbert J. Oyer Speech and Hearing Clinic

Harley-Ellington, 1968

A deeply recessed main entrance, pronounced coping at the roof line, and vertical brick patterning all contribute lively surface rhythms. These attributes and the emphatic display of materials are characteristic of late 1960s Brutalist architecture. Notable are the tall, narrow windows that enliven this symmetrical design. They read as voids and enhance the dark-light contrast of window to facade.

Originally called the Audiology and Speech Sciences Building, the building was renamed the Herbert J. Oyer Speech and Hearing Clinic in honor of a professor and

chair of audiology and speech sciences. As a scholar and leader, Herbert J. Oyer (1921–2000) published *Visual Communication* in 1961 and directed the creation of clinical speech and hearing programs at four hospitals and health care facilities in Michigan. He also helped plan research programs in speech and hearing in Nigeria and India. In 1969 Oyer won the Distinguished Faculty Award. In 1971 he became dean of the College of Communication Arts, and five years later he became dean of the Graduate School.

Public Safety

Manson, Jackson, Kane, 1975   *Physical Plant, 1992*
Physical Plant, 1981

The International Style flavor of the original design is evident in the smooth, brick curtain walls of the front entrance facade and the cantilevered entrance canopy. Two additions have heightened the geometrical boldness of the exterior and expanded the floor plan from 27,000 to more than 37,000 square feet.

In 1928 Michigan State had one police officer who worked from 8 A.M. to 5 P.M. From 1950 until 1975 the Department of Public Safety was housed in post–World War II Quonset huts. When this building opened, there were forty-two sworn personnel, four service officers, and six civilians in the Records Division. The loan used to pay for construction costs was repaid using revenue derived from campus parking fees. Today this building houses the Department of Police and Public Safety, including its Police Bureau and Parking and Safety Bureau. Its exterior signage now reads "MSU Police and Public Safety."

THOMAS KACHADURIAN

Communication Arts and Sciences

Harley Ellington Pierce Yee Associates, 1981

Bold expanses of brick surfacing and recessed ribbon windows form the only exterior ornament of this large High Tech building. The architects noted the need to protect the radio and television studios from noise and placed them in the center of the two-story building block. Then, they positioned the five-story office and classroom portion to wrap around the west, south, and east side of this block to act as a buffer against airborne noises from the railroad and power plant.

Several building entrances provide access for pedestrians and those who arrive by car. The northwest entrance, with its angled facade, seems visually to acknowledge its location on the traffic circle. The south entrance originally faced a large parking lot, which was replaced by the 2001 opening of Parking Ramp No. 5. Inside, a thermal storage

system for recovering and storing heat allows for energy recycling and efficiency. Among the building's facilities are Studio A (5,400 square feet); Studio B (2,410 square feet); offices; lecture halls; and laboratories for design, listening and viewing, editing, reporting, and screening.

The College of Communication Arts, now known as the College of Communication Arts and Sciences, existed for a quarter century, at various sites, before this building became the home for its departments in 1981. On a first-floor wall are the names of those in the Michigan Journalism Hall of Fame. Another occupant is Broadcasting Services (Instructional Television, Radio Talking Book, WKAR-TV, and WKAR-AM/FM). WKAR-TV had previously been in a Quonset hut on the site of the Jack Breslin Student Events Center.

Packaging Laboratory
Calder, 1964
Calder, 1987

Visible framing, a flat roof, and the cantilevered canopy of a north entrance mark this one-story building as International Style. The 1987 addition complements the original one-story design sensitively. It features subtly patterned brick and simple forms, most notably the slope roof of the new north entrance and the circular auditorium.

Inside the original portion of the building a rectangular courtyard, open to the fresh air, contains trees and shrubs and offers a place to view a sculpture entitled *Wind Song* by Francesco Acitelli, a Detroit artist. Its nonobjective, geometric, limestone form rises from a granite base. The new north entrance leads to a lobby and seating area outside the auditorium. Light enters softly through the glass below the slope roof to create a dramatic effect. On display are examples of celebrated packaging designs by School of Packaging graduates. A wall plaque acknowledges the support of the Shenkai Corporation for the 1987 addition.

Known today as Packaging, MSU commissioned this building solely to house the School of Packaging. In June 1964 the journal *Modern Packaging* called the structure the world's first building dedicated to educating students of packaging.

Natural Resources

Kahn, 1966

Unadorned forms, flat roofs, and the cantilevered east entrance canopy are International Style characteristics. The overall plan approximates an H shape that becomes comprehensible when walking around or through the building. Brick, limestone, and concrete define exterior contours subtly. The Farm Lane facade of the large four-story classroom, office, and laboratory block offers a prominent grid pattern. Paired windows and spandrels create a formal overall rhythm.

Wooden entrance doors hint at what the visitor will find inside. In the Department of Forestry area the walls display wood paneling selected to represent a range of genus and species. The one-story north entrance lobby area includes a large stuffed polar bear, *Thalarctos maritimus*, which observes all who enter. According to a descriptive label, Mr. Koepplinger, from Oak Park, Michigan, shot the bear at Point Barrow, Alaska, in 1957.

Originally conceived as the Forestry-Conservation Building when built, this building became Natural Resources. It houses the Departments of Fisheries and Wildlife, Forestry, Park Recreation and Tourism Resources, and Resource Development.

Area Six: Farm Lane, North and South Shaw Lanes, Wilson Road, and Bogue Street

Visitors who stand at the southeast corner of Farm Lane and South Shaw Lane find themselves in front of the A. W. Farrall Agricultural Engineering Hall (1948). It is Collegiate Gothic in inspiration and recalls many pre–World War II buildings on campus. Looking east toward Bogue Street, north to the Red Cedar River, and south to the Baker Woodlot, visitors will see the predominance of the International Style that reflects the enormous growth of Michigan State in the 1950s and 1960s. These visitors will notice significant changes, too. Newer additions to the landscape of this campus area include several 1980s and 1990s High Tech and postmodernist designs. In scale, the most outstanding is Biomedical-Physical Sciences, a huge academic building transforming the campus skyline. It affirms that this area is a major center for basic and applied scientific research.

Shaw Hall (1950) was a stylistic precursor for many International

Style buildings soon to arise along the South Shaw Lane and Wilson Road corridors in this campus area. It is the only residential complex in this area where academic and research facilities and public gardens intermingle.

Stylistically, Shaw Hall's low-slung design contrasts with several exemplary high-rise academic buildings nearby, such as Eppley Center (1961) in the Business College Complex, Chemistry (1963), and Biomedical-Physical Sciences (2001), the tallest academic building on campus.

In this area, some architectural and natural or landscaped sites provide visual contrasts to the large-scale International Style buildings with their cool, clean lines and the newer High Tech and postmodernist buildings. Abrams Planetarium (1963) and the original Cyclotron (1963) are small in scale. The Horticulture Demonstration Gardens and the 4-H Children's Garden (1993), C. E. Lewis Landscape Arboretum, and seventy-eight-acre

---

Easiest access: From Farm Lane, head south from the Red Cedar River, then head east on South Shaw Lane or east on Wilson Road; from Bogue Street, head west on North Shaw Lane or Wilson Road

Boundaries: Red Cedar River, Farm Lane, Mount Hope Road, and Bogue Street

Predominant historical style, name or theme: International Style, High Tech, and postmodern. Residence halls, classrooms, laboratories, gardens, an arboretum, and a woodlot.

Date of oldest extant building in this area: 1948, A. W. Farrall Agricultural Engineering Hall.

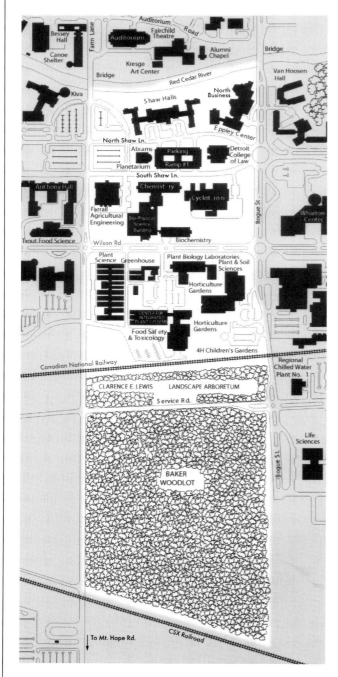

age interdisciplinary scientific collaboration. The Waterfowl Breeding Marsh, just east of Farm Lane, complements the Fisheries and Wildlife Demonstration Area across the street. This marsh, Food Safety and Toxicology, and the Horticulture Demonstration Gardens occupy the remaining land north of the Canadian National Railway tracks between Farm Lane and Bogue Street.

Selected Historical Sites or Markers, Public Art, and Natural Areas

Baker Woodlot, south of Service Road between Farm Lane and Bogue Street

In its seventy-eight acres, this forest woodlot has mixed upland hardwood trees including beech and maple, vernal ponds, and rich herbaceous flora. In 1941 this forest became Baker Woodlot to honor two early foresters at Michigan State—James Fred Baker and Harry Lee Baker. James was a professor of chemistry, and on 1 October 1907, he accepted the position of chair of the Department of Forestry. Harry became the first State Forester in Florida. On 5 June 1999 Baker Woodlot received the designation of Rachana Rajendra Neo-Tropical Migrant Bird Sanctuary to honor Rachana Rajendra. A resident of Okemos, Michigan, Rachana was a lover of birds and nature who died in an automobile accident. As a Category One natural area, Michigan State manages this site with the highest level of protection and the lowest level of use.

Clarence E. Lewis Landscape Arboretum, north of Service Road between Farm Lane and Bogue Street

This six-acre instructional arboretum serves students in landscape horticulture and visitors interested in ornamental trees, shrubs, ground covers, and perennials. The site began as the campus nursery, which explains why specimen trees lend a mature appearance. It contains several unique gardens and collections. The Mawby Fruit Collection features trees and small fruits grown in Michigan and a demonstration of training systems for dwarf fruit trees and grapes. On 12 May 2000 Michigan State dedicated the Kathleen D. and Milton E. Muelder Japanese Garden, which displays plants of Asian origin. Ceramic Shisa lion-dogs flank the garden's

Baker Woodlot offer verdant areas with significant and diverse selections of plants for public study and enjoyment.

Plant Science Greenhouses (1949 to 1998), Plant Biology Laboratories (1966, 1968, 1985), and the large High Tech Plant and Soil Sciences building (1986) testify to the ongoing commitment of Michigan State to theoretical and applied plant research. Food Safety and Toxicology (1997) links with the Center for Integrative Plant Systems, formerly the Pesticide Research Center (1969), to encour-

entrance; they are gifts from the University of Ryukyus in Okinawa, Japan. Other unique gardens include the Martha and Harold Davidson Bees, Butterflies, and Hummingbirds Garden; the Sensory Garden; the Yvonne Wilson Native Plant Garden; the Jane L. Smith Conifer Garden; and the Central Court in memory of Judith A. Schubert.

Clarence "Clancy" E. Lewis attended the 10 July 1984 dedication ceremony at which the arboretum received his name. Lewis, who died the following year, was an internationally known landscape horticulturalist who joined Michigan State in 1957, after teaching at the State University of New York at Farmingdale. He retired from the Department of Horticulture in 1972. Among his many awards was the Arthur Hoyt Scott Garden and Horticulture Award in recognition of his thirty-five years of teaching. He also received the Award of Merit from the International Society of Arboriculture. He wrote more than 500 articles, contributed photographs to national publications such as *American Forests* and the *New York Times*, served as a contributing author for the *New York Times Garden Book*, and advised the *Encyclopedia Britannica*.

Foyer Garden, on Wilson Road, outside Plant and Soil Sciences

Amien A. Carter, Class of 1949, donated this intimate garden with seating to honor his siblings, Samuel Synge Carter and Dorothy Carter Mayhew.

Horticulture Demonstration Gardens, west of Bogue Street, south of Plant and Soil Sciences, and north of the Canadian National Railway

In size and complexity, these demonstration gardens surpass the Old Horticulture Gardens and the former greenhouses that once stood between Old Horticulture and Student Services. Here, in seven and a half acres, amid Roman-inspired arches or pergolas and winding or straight pathways are brilliant annuals, herbaceous perennials, and occasional sculptures. Gardens fill the grounds surrounding Plant and Soil Sciences, Food Safety and Toxicology, Plant Biology Laboratories, the Center for Integrative Plant Systems, and the Plant

Science Greenhouses in order to integrate the study of plants with public enjoyment.

In the Amien A. and Florence M. Carter Annual Garden, west of Plant and Soil Sciences, sculptures, a fountain, and a pool form a straight line. At the west end stands *Windows*, a cast concrete sculpture by Professor Melvin Leiserowitz. When illuminated, the low-relief images become more pronounced. To the east is the circular Post Gardens Fountain with its low and continuous cascade of water. Farther east is *Sunseed* by O. V. Shaffer. Its burnished form gently reflects light and suggests flight. Farther east is the Reflecting Pool, which reminds us that horticulture is "a science and an art." Finally, the bronze figure of *Liberty Hyde Bailey* stands within a tan cast concrete "Roman Arch" portico dedicated to Jacob Van Namen. Linda Ackley, a Department of Art and Art History graduate, produced this representational sculpture in 1993. It honors Liberty Hyde Bailey (1858–1954), a leader in American horticulture. He was chair of the Department of Horticulture in 1885–88.

The Michigan 4-H Children's Garden is scaled for the height of children and planned thematically to inspire the imagination. A spherical sculpture, *Small World Globe*, is one of several focal points. It was created by Richard W. Storey, a 1945 graduate in veterinary medicine.

Metamorphosis II, 1965–66, by Subrata Lahiri, on South Shaw Lane in front of the Cyclotron

When Subrata Lahiri was a student in the Department of Art and Art History and a cyclotron employee, he produced this bronze sculpture to convey the activity of the cyclotron in which atoms are changed into electrified particles and then accelerated in a magnetic field. The top signifies the past, the center the present, and the bottom the future. *Metamorphosis I* is at the University of Tokyo and *Metamorphosis III* is at the University of Arkansas.

Waterfowl Breeding Marsh, east of Farm Lane, just north of the Canadian National Railway

Cattails surround this marsh frequented by waterfowl and other birds.

Abrams Planetarium

Calder, 1963

In its International Style, Abrams Planetarium complements nearby Shaw Hall and Erickson Hall and reflects the skill of the Calder firm that designed these three buildings. Particularly notable is the stylistic similarity of the planetarium's copper dome to the Erickson Hall dome.

The planetarium's International Style traits include its unadorned entrance canopy, coping set flush with the roof line, and vertical glass window panels. Its curtain wall features Flemish bond brickwork whose headers extend beyond the wall surfaces to form a decorative pattern.

Abrams Planetarium is found in the center of campus just east of Farm Lane and south of Shaw Hall and the Red Cedar River. Original plans linked the planetarium to the south side of the Michigan State University Museum. In 1962, however, plans changed and the following year the building arose on its present site with a new design. Visitors who attended the 1964 dedication ceremony entered the planetarium chamber through the permanent exhibition hall and a black-light art gallery. Their eyes would adjust gradually to the darkness as they approached the domed sky theater. Its 252 seats face a stage at the front of the theater. This arrangement allows for versatility in scheduling lectures and other activities. Although a more up-to-date star projection system operates today, at the time of its dedication, the theater housed the first Spitz Space Transit Planetarium star projection instrument.

The planetarium was the Michigan State University Development Fund's initial Capital Fund project. Talbert and Leota Abrams, who were already friends of the Michigan State University Museum, funded the building. Talbert Abrams was a pioneer aviator and businessperson and, in 1961, recipient of an honorary degree from Michigan State.

Abrams Planetarium offers special exhibits and a variety of educational programs. It has a reputation as a pioneer in astronomical and space education and as a training site for planetarium educators. It received a renovation in 2000 to assure its continued educational success.

Shaw Hall

Calder, 1950

Flanking the Red Cedar River, Shaw Hall marks a radical shift in the architectural design of residence halls at Michigan State from the historically inspired mode of the East Circle and West Circle Complexes to the International Style. It was also a significant shift for the architectural firm of Ralph R. Calder, which had been partially or fully responsible for the West Circle Drive Tudor designs of Williams (1937), Campbell (1939), Landon (1947), Gilchrist (1948), and Yakeley (1948) Halls.

Shaw Hall is a large (258,943 square feet) building with a markedly horizontal design. Its East Hall and West Hall entrances face curved North Shaw Lane driveways. Here, the familiar International Style vocabulary is evident in the curtain walls, ribbon windows, and cantilevered staircases.

Shaw Hall blends, by design, into the slope of land along the Red Cedar River. Today, prolific large trees and shrubs affirm this blending. To adapt to this sloped terrain, the interior plan has two "main" floors—one on the north

side and one on the south. The north side, with its extensive fenestration and patios, offers magnificent views of the Red Cedar River from indoors or outdoors. In honor of its fiftieth birthday, Michigan State announced plans in 2000 for extensive interior renovations.

Shaw Hall derives its name from Robert Sidey Shaw, who served as the eleventh president of Michigan State, 1928–41. In 1908 he became the first dean of the Division of Agriculture. From 1921 until 1928 he served as acting president of Michigan State three times. In 1928 the State Board of Agriculture appointed Shaw as president. He acted to manage resources astutely during the Depression, encourage the development of liberal arts programs to complement applied sciences and technical areas, and establish the position of dean to strengthen graduate studies. East, West, North, and South Shaw Lanes also bear his name.

Business College Complex

Eppley Center
Calder, 1961

In the International Style, the Eppley Center delights the eye with the refined proportions of its symmetry, glass and stone curtain wall, and pilotis (supporting piers). The slight bulges of the buff-colored stone wall panels align directly with each piloti to add a subtle rhythm to the facade. A discrete cornice caps the facades in the same shade of aquamarine used for the entryway lettering, "Eugene C. Eppley."

Eppley (1884–1958) was a self-proclaimed "hotel man," philanthropist, and patron of education. The Eugene C. Eppley Foundation, Inc., provided buildings funds to honor Eppley and support graduate training in the fields of hotel, restaurant, and institutional management.

The Eppley Center also has a small office and classroom building linked to its west facade. This small building has a notable International Style glass entry on its Red Cedar River side. The Eppley Center also links to the large North Business Building to form the Business College Complex. The Eli Broad College of Business and its Eli Broad Graduate School of Management call the entire Business College Complex home.

THOMAS KACHADURIAN

North Business Building

Harley Ellington Pierce Yee Associates, Inc., 1993

The North Business Building, also known as North Complex, houses the Eli Broad College of Business; it offers 135,400 square feet of space dedicated to teaching, administration, and research with state-of-the art acoustics and other technological advancements. The design, sophisticated with its interplay of brick, concrete, and glass, renders the High Tech stylistic label appropriate. The glass-enclosed cantilevered stairwell at the north end is one of several notable architectural features. In the center stairwell, a bronze bust of Richard J. Lewis stands. He was dean of the college in 1974–93. Nancy Leiserowitz of Mason, Michigan, produced this bronze in 1993.

Eli Broad, a Michigan State alumnus and highly successful businessperson, provided the funding for the entire North Business Building. He graduated with a bachelor's degree in accounting in 1950. The name of the College of Business became The Eli Broad College of Business and The Eli Broad Graduate School of Management in recognition of Broad's generous gift to the university.

Michigan State University–Detroit College of Law

SSOE, Inc., 1997

With 191,388 square feet, the Michigan State University–Detroit College of Law prominently faces east toward the intersection of North Shaw Lane, South Shaw Lane, and Bogue Street. Its east pavilion, capped with a barrel vault, offers a distinctive High Tech exterior. Bold brick and limestone piers surround an inner glass sheath. Retaining walls, along the east facade, feature reliefs. The south relief depicts Education as a man, in profile, who faces the building and holds a book and the lamp of knowledge. The north relief depicts the same subject as a woman. Viewers can also see these reliefs from inside the Gast Business Library.

Gerald R. Ford, former president of the United States, gave the keynote address at the 21 April 1998 dedication of the Law and Business Library Building. Renamed in 1999, it is the home of the Michigan State University–Detroit College of Law. The law school is affiliated with Michigan State University in what President Peter McPherson has called a "unique partnership." As noted, it is also the home of the Gast Business Library. Marcella Gast Schalon, a Michigan State graduate (B.A. 1946; M.A. 1947), and Warren E. Gast provided library funds. The library honors William C. Gast, who attended Michigan State in 1923 and 1924. He became a businessperson and is known for saying "real business success can be found only through the sharing of goals and information."

The Gast Business Library occupies the first floor, the law library the next two floors, and the Michigan State University–Detroit College of Law classrooms the top two floors. With extensive hookups for laptop computers, the Clif and Carolyn Haley Moot Courtroom, a computer lab-oratory, and four 100-seat tiered classrooms, this is a technologically advanced learning center. Aesthetically, the moot courtroom's barrel vault serves as an external crown while hallway windows offer panoramic campus views. In recognition of its accomplished design, Michigan State University and its Physical Plant received the Engineering Society Outstanding Achievement Award for Building Design and Construction in 1999.

The main or South Shaw Lane entrance faces the Business College Complex. In its vestibule an Art Deco light fixture hangs overhead. It recalls the original Detroit College of Law Building at 130 East Elizabeth Street in Detroit. Other artwork merits attention. On the fourth floor are reliefs of King John (1167–1216) and Justinian (483–565). An atrium provides sunlight to a ramped hallway that leads to a reception area containing concrete columns and a prominent Art Deco relief figure of Justice. Holding a sword, at rest, in her right hand and a balanced scale in her left hand, she originally stood over the entrance of the Detroit College of Law Building. On her garment are historical scenes pertaining to the foundations of law. They depict King Hammurabi (1792–50 B.C.E.), the she-wolf and the founding of ancient Rome, and probably the presentation of the Magna Carta (1215). On the third floor are reliefs of Moses and Hammurabi and figures of Education identical to the ones that grace the exterior retaining walls. In their simplicity and stylized curves, all of the new reliefs complement the figure of Justice and serve as visual reminders of the law school's institutional history.

Cyclotron

Black, 1963, 1968

Holmes and Black, 1978

Physical Plant, 1979

Commonwealth Associates, 1982

N.S.C.L., 1985

HEPY, 1988, 1996

Harley Ellington, 1999

The original Cyclotron (1963) is still discernible at its courtyard entrance. Here, at close view, are the International Style characteristics of ribbon windows, cantilevered entrance canopy, and roofs ending flush with wall planes. A notable addition to the building's courtyard is the 1965–66 abstract bronze sculpture, *Metamorphosis II*, by the artist Subrata Lahiri. The sculpture's form and title suggest change in both scientific research and the facility's continual upgrades.

The Cyclotron's additions adapt to the needs of a major nuclear science research facility known as the National Superconducting Cyclotron Facility. The laboratory houses two Michigan State–built superconducting cyclotrons: the K500 (the world's first) and the K1200 (the world's most powerful). It is the premier, university-based nuclear science research facility in North America. Scientists from the United States and abroad visit to conduct research. Doctoral students train here and undergraduates gain exposure to developments in advanced physics research and technologies. Superconductivity and applications in cancer treatment are among the topics visitors will learn about during scheduled facility tours.

GARY BOYNTON

Chemistry

Ralph R. Calder, 1963

Precise proportions characterize this large, rectangular International Style building. From a passing car or a pedestrian's path, viewers can discern how the projecting piers neatly divide the glass curtain walls into controlled rhythms. Gray slate spandrels and fieldstone accents provide visual variety. An unadorned, cantilevered north entrance canopy includes letters that spell "CHEMISTRY." End facades display pilotis and unadorned brick "skins" that encase stairwells. On the south side, a one-story fieldstone wing with narrow windows sits atop a cantilevered base. Inside, the Renaud Lecture Hall honors Harold E. and H. James Renaud of Lansing, Michigan, who began sponsoring the American Chemical Society (ACS)—Renaud Lectures in 1958.

The Chemistry Building is one of several classroom and research facilities built in this area during the 1960s to support the creation of a campus science center and Michigan State's growing research reputation in the biological, chemical, and physical sciences. Since its opening, this building has housed the Department of Chemistry. Its proximity to the Cyclotron, Biochemistry, and the razed Biological Research Center fostered interdisciplinary research initiatives among faculty from different disciplines. From this research tradition, plans emerged to link Chemistry to the Biomedical-Physical Sciences building to enhance research exchange and teaching opportunities. By 2001 this linkage was complete.

GARY BOYNTON

A. W. Farrall Agricultural Engineering Hall

Munson, 1948
Progressive Arch, 1999

Twin gabled pavilions, hipped dormers, a slate roof, and prominent limestone coursing highlight this simplified Collegiate Gothic design. The unadorned, limestone entrance pavilion has subtle setbacks reminiscent of Art Deco. A plain segmental arch and tripartite window crown the recessed entry door. Other windows have industrial-grade metal frames. Glazing a large percentage of the wall elevations hints at future stylistic change as non-load-bearing walls became more prevalent in the soon-to-be prolific International Style. Like its neighbor, Anthony Hall (1955), this is one of the last buildings on south campus to maintain the red brick and stone vernacular so prominent on north campus and on campuses nationwide in the first half of the twentieth century.

Originally known as Agricultural Engineering, the building was rededicated and named A. W. Farrall Agricultural Engineering Hall on 23 June 1985, to honor Arthur W. Farrall (1899–1986), who was department chairperson in 1945–64. An internationally known inventor and researcher, Farrall contributed significantly to the development of Michigan State's reputation as a world leader in agricultural engineering.

In 1999 the Agricultural Engineering Shop, formerly located south of the A. W. Farrall Agricultural Engineering Hall, was demolished to clear space needed for the Biomedical-Physical Sciences Building. That same year, the hall received a 4,000-square-foot addition to provide updated facilities.

Biomedical-Physical Sciences

SHG of Detroit, 2001

With six stories and an observation deck, "The Science Building" or "Bio-Physical Sciences" is a bold, complex structure sheathed in glass, aluminum, and brick. Visible framework, exposed mechanical and cooling towers, and interior details such as stainless-steel railings affirm the High Tech style. Most notable is the building's atrium, capped in glass, forming a prominent north-south, light-filtered, internal axis and meeting place. Conference rooms and walkways provide expansive internal views. On sunny days the building's external aluminum surfaces offer crisp reflections of nearby windows. At other times these same aluminum surfaces, which are subtly textured, convey a luminescent sheen.

Biomedical-Physical Sciences is visually compatible with the International Style vocabulary of the nearby Chemistry and Biochemistry Buildings and is linked with them via underground tunnels and elevated walkways to create the largest research complex on campus. With 368,000 square feet, it is the largest academic building on campus. It was designed to house the Department of Physics and Astronomy, Department of Physiology, Department of Microbiology and Molecular Genetics, several research centers, and a branch library. Technologically advanced, the building design includes classrooms, research laboratories with independent ventilation systems, office and conference rooms, and an astronomy observation deck including telescope hookups on the rooftop level. On its west facade, a two-story physics wing includes a large machine shop. The Southern Astrophysical Research (SOAR) telescope viewing room provides live images of stars transmitted from the SOAR telescope in the Andes Mountains in Chile. Department of Art and Art History faculty artworks enhance the interior space.

As the Biomedical-Physical Sciences Building arose it dramatically changed the silhouette of campus buildings against the day and evening skies. It dominates the south campus skyline and is visible from north campus, Hagadorn Road, and Harrison Road. From its observation deck, there are spectacular views of the entire campus and, in the distance, the skyline of the city of Lansing. In 1999, before construction began on this site, the Biology Research Center (1962) and an agricultural barn (1929) stood here. With the completion of Biomedical-Physical Sciences, there is a hub of advanced research activity on the "science campus." In addition to Chemistry and Biochemistry, nearby buildings include Abrams Planetarium, the Cyclotron with its National Superconducting Cyclotron Laboratory, Food Safety and Toxicology and the National Center for Food Safety and Toxicology, Center for Integrative Plant Systems, Plant Biology Laboratories, Plant Science Greenhouses, and Plant and Soil Sciences.

DERRICK TURNER

Biochemistry

Harley-Ellington, 1964

This International Style building, like others dating from the 1960s, is a self-contained grouping of rectangular volumes clearly defined as user spaces, technical support, or entrances and passageways. It is so strictly symmetrical that the huge, limestone sheaths that enclose the stairwells look as though they are bookends defining the building's length. Honeycombed facades distinguish the exterior. They achieve their three-dimensionality with three layers: recessed rows of windows and spandrels, brick sheathing, and outer spandrels that project beyond the brick sheathing.

Biochemistry continues to function as a research and teaching facility. In addition to classrooms, laboratories, and offices, it houses the Mass Spectrometry Laboratory and the Macromolecular Structure Facility. On the entry level, travertine floors enhance design quality. A variety of deciduous trees and conifers dot the grounds surrounding the building and contrast pleasingly with its essentialist geometric vocabulary. Underground and elevated walkways link this building with Biomedical-Physical Sciences.

THOMAS KACHADURIAN

Plant Biology Laboratories

Black, 1966, 1968
Hoyem-Basso, 1985

Large, volumetric forms intersect to shape the plan of this International Style building complex known today as Plant Biology. Along its Wilson Road facade, tall windows with green, reflective spandrels form precise limestone-trimmed verticals; these projecting verticals serve as surface texture on this unadorned brick building. Flat roofs and a cantilevered entrance canopy are other recognizable stylistic traits. On the first floor, green travertine flooring subtly suggests plant life.

Plant Biology Laboratories has office, research, and teaching facilities. It has been home to the Department of Botany and Plant Pathology (now the Departments of Plant Biology and Plant Pathology). The building houses some of Michigan State's internationally known plant research programs including the Michigan State University Department of Energy (DOE) Plant Research Laboratory.

Its ground floor is the site for the Michigan State University Herbarium that attracts scholars and visitors from around the globe. With more than 530,000 specimens, this collection features a worldwide collection of all plant groups, as well as lichenized and non-lichenized fungi. In the mid-1990s the Beal-Darlington Herbarium and the Cryptogamic Herbarium combined to form the Michigan State University Herbarium. The original herbarium dates from 1863, when Dr. Dennis Cooley, a physician, donated his private collection. Then Dr. William J. Beal added his own collection and new specimens until he retired in 1910. From 1914 until 1945 Dr. H. T. Darlington served as curator. The Cryptogamic Herbarium dates from 1958, with Dr. Henry Imshaug as its first curator.

Plant Science Greenhouses

West Range

Headhouse
Munson, 1949
Physical Plant, 1956

Greenhouses
Physical Plant, 1949, 1956, 1958, 1963
Kilgore, 1981

East Range

Headhouse
Black, 1966

Greenhouses
Opdyck, 1966
Black, 1966
Mayotte, Crouse, Dhaen, 1980
Physical Plant, 1998

The West Range greenhouses and its headhouse stand along Farm Lane, and the East Range greenhouses and its headhouse stand just behind them to the east. A row of crabapple trees lines their Wilson Road facades. Both greenhouse ranges are dedicated to plant research. Primary users have been the Department of Botany and Plant Pathology (now the Department of Plant Biology and the Department of Plant Pathology), the Departments of Crop and Soil Sciences, Entomology, Forestry, and Horticulture and the United States Department of Agriculture (USDA).

The West Range headhouse is an asymmetrical, one-story Colonial Revival design that faces Farm Lane. Prominent stylistic traits include its pedimented portico, sets of twin columns, eight-over-eight double-hung sash windows, and shutters. The headhouse's design seems more residential than academic, but it continues to serve administrative, plant potting, and other workspace needs in support of greenhouse research. Its scale and style are reminiscent of Michigan State's scientific agricultural past. Greenhouses flank the headhouse and form a row along Farm Lane. Once the industry standard and the style for all campus greenhouses, this utilitarian design still serves contemporary botanical research. New greenhouses, including those linked to nearby Plant and Soil Sciences, include advanced technological features.

DERRICK TURNER

Center for Integrative Plant Systems
Kingscott, 1969

Headhouse
Kingscott, 1967

Greenhouses
Kingscott, 1967

The architects designed the main building in the International Style. Its projecting piers and paired vertical windows with brown spandrels create the basic facade ornamentation. Located amidst the Horticulture Demonstration Gardens, the building's direct links to greenhouses and to Food Safety and Toxicology foster interdisciplinary research.

Although the building's official name is the Center for Integrative Plant Systems, it is known today as the Center for Integrated Plant Systems. Its former name was the Pesticide Research Center. Administered by the College of Agriculture and Natural Resources with support from Michigan State Extension and the Michigan Agricultural Experiment Station, the center is an interdisciplinary research and extension unit. Faculty from the Colleges of Agriculture and Natural Resources, Natural Science, and Social Science conduct research on ecologically based integrated crop management, pest management, and the use of biotechnology. Anthropod, Nematode and Plant Disease Diagnostics and the Center for Electron Optics are among the center's service facilities.

Food Safety and Toxicology

Harley Ellington, 1997

Prominent limestone courses and patterned brickwork create bold horizontal rhythms across the facades of this High Tech building. Gabled east and west entrances display even livelier limestone and brick detailing. Each gable has a segmental arch for its entry with another segmental crowning arch above it. On the second story, metallic glass brick covers the north side of the west entrance and south side of the east entrance. From outside, these bricks offer silver reflections. Surprisingly, from inside, these bricks are translucent. They allow users of the second-floor lounge areas to experience a soft interior light. Ironically, this design reminds the viewer that the visually stolid limestone and brick exterior merely envelops the inner framework rather than supports it. On the second floor a long hallway, with a window at each end, leads from the west to the east lounge area. East and west lounge windows provide spectacular views of the Horticulture Demonstration

Gardens to the east and south campus to the west.

Food Safety and Toxicology was dedicated on 24 October 1997. It houses the National Food Safety and Toxicology Center at Michigan State. The United States Department of Agriculture furnished more than half the building funds for this three-story, 124,318-square-foot structure. According to the 1996 President's Report, it is "one of the world's foremost research centers, focusing on new ways to identify and eliminate or reduce chemical and microbial hazards in food." The center also strives to improve knowledge and understanding of food safety through public education.

Food Safety and Toxicology links to the Center for Integrative Plant Systems via an accessible hallway. Set back from Farm Lane, a curved driveway leads past the Waterfowl Breeding Marsh to its west entrance.

GARY BOYNTON

Plant and Soil Sciences
Giffels/Hoyem-Basso, 1986

Of gargantuan scale, Plant and Soil Sciences stands emphatically at the corner of Bogue Street and Wilson Road. Passersby, especially when they are close, may feel overwhelmed by its sheer size. Sleek brick sheathing encases this High Tech form to create abstract shapes and wall openings. A cantilever on the Wilson Road facade dramatically punctures surrounding space. Ribbon windows acknowledge floor levels and recall the earlier International Style. Internally, fifty-nine environmentally controlled research spaces serve plant and soil sciences basic and applied research.

With a roughly L-shaped plan, Plant and Soil Sciences is well suited to its site. Its scale, design, and color complement the Clifton and Dolores Wharton Center for Performing Arts (1982) that stands northeast across the traffic circle. At different times in the day the sun's rays cause strong dramatic shadows that heighten the stark geometry of both buildings.

In the entrance atrium, plaques dating from 1987 describe the Consulting Engineers Council of Michigan Award of Merit, the Engineering Society of Detroit Outstanding Achievement Award, and the Professional Engineers in Education Outstanding Engineering Achievement Award. In the entrance hall, an anonymous painting of Liberty Hyde Bailey (1858–1954), the well-known horticulturalist, greets visitors.

Included in the teaching greenhouse portion of Plant and Soil Sciences is the popular Butterfly House, formerly housed in greenhouses that once stood north of Old Horticulture. It has twenty species of butterflies, all native to Michigan. Today, the Plant and Soil Sciences greenhouses, used for teaching, extend into the Horticulture Demonstration Gardens. Until 1987 these gardens existed between Student Services and Old Horticulture. With approval of the Plant and Soil Sciences design, it became possible to expand special demonstration garden areas and add the 4-H Children's Garden. As a landscape design, the Horticulture Demonstration Gardens recall classically inspired architectural elements of which the entrance pergola is a prime example. On the north (Wilson Road) side of Plant and Soil Sciences is the Foyer Garden.

Before Plant and Soil Sciences opened, the site for many of the academic and research activities in this area was the Soil Science Building (1913), which once stood at the north end of Farm Lane. Before it was Soil Science, the building was the campus dairy. Milk trucks used to ride from the campus farms along the aptly named Farm Lane to deliver milk to this dairy.

Area Seven: Bogue Street, East Shaw Lane, and Wilson, Service, and Hagadorn Roads

High-rise East Complex residence halls, a performing arts center, recreational facilities, medical and life sciences buildings, and several natural areas are prominent in this area whose extant buildings date from 1957 to the present.

Undergraduate and graduate International Style residence halls (Owen Graduate Hall, McDonel Hall, and Holmes Hall) stand along the picturesque Red Cedar River west of the Beal Pinetum and south of the Sanford Natural Area. They face East Shaw Lane and the elegantly landscaped High Tech Wharton Center for Performing Arts, the compact Intramural Recreative Sports–East, and the north side of the monumental Akers Hall, one of four buildings positioned to form the circular cluster at the easternmost campus edge: Akers Hall (1964), Hubbard Hall (1966), Fee Hall (1964), and Conrad Hall (1964).

Even from a half mile away, at the intersection of Wilson Road and Farm Lane, looking east, these huge residence hall blocks are prominently vis-

ible. In their immensity, style, and position on a wide expanse of flat land, they are reminiscent of the modernist dreams for ideal high-rise communities such as those presented in the influential Plan Voisin for the 1920s renewal of Paris by the Swiss-French architect, Le Corbusier. Here, however, the setting is suburban, not urban.

With the completion of the sleekly curved design for the Clifton and Dolores Wharton Center for Performing Arts (1982), a High Tech stylistic phase emerged in this campus area. Later, the Veterinary Medical Center, with its 1991 addition, would present a postmodernist view complete with a fresh interpretation of a historical element, the gabled roof. Perhaps the most stark indication of a break from a strict adherence to an International Style was first seen in the Brutalist vocabulary of the modular Clinical Center (1976), with its precast concrete sections and overall utilitarian, no-frills appearance.

Given the large scale of the build-

> **Easiest access:** From Bogue Street, head east on East Shaw Lane, Wilson Road, or Service Road; from Hagadorn Road, head west on East Shaw Lane, Wilson Road, or Service Road.
>
> **Boundaries:** Red Cedar River, Hagadorn Road, Mount Hope Road, and Bogue Street.
>
> **Predominant historical style, name or theme:** International Style, Brutalist, High Tech, and postmodern. Residence halls, performing arts, and three medical schools.
>
> **Date of oldest extant building in this area:** 1957, Van Hoosen Hall.

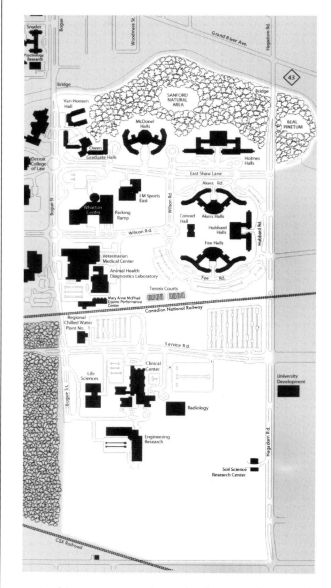

Selected Historical Sites or Markers, Public Art, and Natural Areas

Beal Pinetum, 1896, east side of Hagadorn Road, across from the Sanford Natural Area and south of the Red Cedar River

Often overlooked by passersby, three acres of Michigan white pine border the Red Cedar River and the east side of Hagadorn Road across from the Sanford Natural Area. Today, this stand of trees is recognized as one of the earliest forest test plantings in Michigan. William J. Beal, professor of botany, planted the trees in 1896. In 1996, one hundred years after they were planted, 370 of them were still standing, an average of 101 feet high. Hardwoods also grow in their midst below the pine canopy. Professor Beal, for whom the pinetum is named, taught at Michigan State from 1870 until his retirement in 1910. In 1873 he established what is now known as the W. J. Beal Botanical Garden, just west of the present library.

Orpheus, 1979, by Melvin Leiserowitz, plaza in front of the main (north) entrance of the Clifton and Dolores Wharton Center for Performing Arts

Dedicated on 25 May 1979, this Cor-ten and stainless steel sculpture received its name from Orpheus, a mythological Greek musician and poet whose music was so overwhelming that it purportedly could move inanimate objects. The sculptor, Melvin Leiserowitz, was a faculty member in the Department of Art and Art History. Leiserowitz manipulated simple geometric shapes so they would invite passersby to walk through and around the sculpture. Thirty-five-feet high, its circles, curves, and angles are pleasurable to view as pure form and as a means through which to explore the stark geometry of the Wharton Center itself. Former president Clifton R. Wharton Jr. funded the sculpture from fees earned as a member of the board of directors of the Ford Motor Company and the Burroughs Company.

Sanford Natural Area, west side of Hagadorn Road, across from the Beal Pinetum and south of the Red Cedar River from Bogue Street to Hagadorn Road

This forty-two-acre floodplain and upland forest is part

ings in this campus area, the randomly arranged trees and shrubs often appear small whereas in older parts of campus, such as the Circle Drive Area, trees are often as tall as the surrounding buildings. This distinction is in part related to the older age of some trees in campus areas that developed earlier, but it is also reflective of the ongoing commitment to maintaining a diverse campus-park environment. Here, in addition to occasional trees and shrubs there are two large natural areas to the north—the Beal Pinetum, bordering the east side of Hagadorn Road and the Red Cedar River, and the forty-two-acre Sanford Natural Area along the Red Cedar River, between Hagadorn Road and Bogue Street.

of the original 677 acres of forested land purchased in 1855 from A. R. Burr of Lansing to establish the Agricultural College of the State of Michigan. Originally called North Woodlot, then Woodlot No. 1, and later River Woodlot, it became the Sanford Woodlot in 1941. Professor Paul A. Herbert, then head of the Forestry Department, renamed this land to honor Frank Hobart Sanford (1880–1938), the second full-time forester the college appointed. He earned a bachelor of science degree in 1904 and a master of science degree in 1913 and served on the forestry faculty in 1906–20. The Sanford Natural Area is an outdoor laboratory for biological study, a lovely place to walk and reflect, and a stunning backdrop for the residence halls that line the south bank of the Red Cedar River. In this natural area, from 1915 until 1960, a simple structure known as the Sugar House served as the site where sap was boiled to make maple syrup.

Veterinarians, 1999, by James Cunningham, in front of the Veterinary Medical Center

"Veterinarians. Caring for Animals and the Public Health" is the inscription below this sculpture. The text includes the 1969 Veterinarian's Oath of the American Veterinary Medical Association (AVMA), and it is signed, "Jim Cunningham 99." Professor James Cunningham is from the Departments of Physiology and Small Animal Clinical Sciences. Standing five feet high, the sculpture's burnished stainless steel surfaces reflect brightly on sunny days. A bronze eagle, a dog, and a Zebu cow intertwine with one another to form a bold and lively image. A bronze circle symbolizes the cycle of life. It conveys the intense commitment of veterinarians to improve the lives of all animals.

THOMAS KACHADURIAN

Van Hoosen Hall

Manson and Carver, 1957

This low-slung, International Style residence hall complex has an irregular U-shaped plan and delineates the west end of the Sanford Natural Area. Enveloped by trees, the hall gives the impression of being a cozy environment in which to study and live. Originally, Van Hoosen Hall was a women's cooperative residence with thirty-six apartments. Today, it is a graduate student residence hall serving as an extension of Owen Graduate Hall next door. As Van Hoosen Hall neared completion, its architects, Manson and Carver, had already completed or designed other International Style campus residences such as University Village, part of Cherry Lane, and Spartan Village.

Van Hoosen Hall honors Sarah Van Hoosen Jones (1892–1972) who was a State Board of Agriculture member in 1943–55. Van Hoosen was the board's representative to the Association of Governing Boards of State Universities and Allied Institutions in 1944–55 and the association's president in 1955. She was the first woman in the United States to earn a doctorate in animal genetics (University of Wisconsin, 1921) and to receive the Michigan Master Farmer Award (1933). After completing her service as a board member, Van Hoosen Jones donated her 350-acre Centennial Farm to Michigan State in 1956.

GARY BOYNTON

Owen Graduate Hall

Calder, 1961, 1965

This International Style graduate residence offers sophisticated stylistic nuances. Cantilevered, polychromed balconies enliven unadorned brick facades and windows. The canopied main entrance stands at a forty-five-degree angle from the main building block and South Shaw Lane. It offers a humanly scaled one-story entrance to this 312,810 square-foot structure. From its airy interior, frequent appealing views include the spectacular scene of the Sanford Natural Area in the Woodland Room dining facility.

Floyd W. Owen Graduate Hall recognizes the institutional commitment to graduate study. It became the graduate residence center. Before its completion, graduate students lived in two ground-floor precincts in Mason Hall or Abbot Hall and in half of Armstrong Hall or Mayo Hall. The building honors Floyd W. Owen (1882–1956) of Maple Rapids, Michigan. A Class of 1902 graduate, Owen was a successful businessperson who returned to Michigan State to study sociology and psychology and earn a doctor of philosophy in 1930. In his will Owen bequeathed monies to Michigan State that were later used to help in the construction of this graduate center. As a dedicated alumnus, he was also a leader in coordinating donations for the Alumni Memorial Chapel (1952).

East Complex

The East Complex contains five large residence halls and a classroom building. The same architectural firm, Ralph Calder and Associates, designed these International Style buildings, built between 1963 and 1966. The firm had completed the Owen Graduate Hall immediately west of McDonel Hall in 1961. The university sorely needed these buildings. By the early 1960s the student population of Michigan State University was 20,000, an increase of 5,000 over the preceding five years. By decade's end, the number would be approximately 30,000. McDonel Hall (1963), Akers Hall and Fee Hall (1964), Holmes Hall (1965), and Hubbard Hall (1966) offered cost-effective and practical solutions for student housing. Their central dining facilities, large and small classrooms, offices, and counseling and conference rooms promoted the "living-learning" environments for which Michigan State became well known.

East Complex halls honor people notable in the life of Michigan State University and the state of Michigan.

Akers Hall honors Forest H. Akers and his spouse, Alice Akers. Akers was a vice president of the Chrysler Corporation and the sales manager of its Dodge Division. From 1940 until 1958, during the years of extensive campus development, he served as a member of the State Board of Agriculture. The university golf courses, Forest Akers Golf Course West and East, also bear his name. Conrad Hall recalls the first dean of women and a professor of French, Elisabeth A. Conrad, who served in 1928–45. The naming of Fee Hall recognizes Harry A. Fee and Jessie T. Fee for their development of Hidden Lake Gardens in Tipton, Michigan. Their 1945 gift of this natural resource to Michigan State came with an endowment for its care and maintenance.

Holmes Hall pays tribute to John C. Holmes, a Detroit businessperson, horticulturalist, and secretary of the Michigan State Agricultural Society. In the 1850s, Holmes strongly encouraged the Michigan legislature to approve the creation of a separate college of agriculture in Michigan and to appropriate funds for land and buildings. On 12 February 1855 Governor Kingsley S. Bingham signed the law to establish the Agricultural College of the State of Michigan. One of the first two buildings funded was a dormitory, Saint's Rest, located, before it burned, near the present Michigan State University Museum. It is appropriate that one of today's residence halls bears Holmes's name. Hubbard Hall recognizes Bela Hubbard, a Detroit farmer and geologist. In 1849 Hubbard accepted the request of the Michigan State Agricultural Society to develop a proposal for an agricultural college. He recommended a scientific agricultural college to provide a broad liberal education in the natural and social sciences, literature, and the fine arts to "add greater lustre and dignity to life." His vision became Michigan State University. McDonel Hall honors Karl H. McDonel and his spouse, Irma N. McDonel. Karl McDonel was secretary to the State Board of Agriculture (later Board of Trustees) 1941–60. He played a key role in the planning and financing of buildings, from Berkey Hall to the Brody Complex.

GARY BOYNTON

Akers Hall
Calder, 1964

Akers Hall stands south of East Shaw Lane on Akers Road. Its architectural twin, Fee Hall, stands farther south along Fee Lane. Each complex has a V-shaped plan with a large central section and wings. At the end of each wing is a curved wing. The result is two large International Style complexes whose lengthy interior corridors and bold exterior coursing create a sense of continuous movement. Taupe spandrels add rhythmic variety. Akers Hall and Fee Hall serve as student residences and as classroom buildings.

THOMAS KACHADURIAN

Conrad Hall
Calder, 1964

Conrad Hall, a simple, one-story International Style building, faces Wilson Road. It completes the circular cluster that Akers Hall, Fee Hall, and Hubbard Hall form. In its horizontality, Conrad reaffirms the flatness of the ground on which it rests. Inside, a 439-seat auditorium is on the south and the Michigan State University Archives and Historical Collections is on the north. Straight ahead, through the floor-to-ceiling windows, is a view of a grassy area and Hubbard Hall, the tallest residence hall on campus.

GARY BOYNTON

Fee Hall
Calder, 1964
Physical Plant, 1972

Fee Hall, the architectural twin of Akers Hall, stands along Fee Lane near Hagadorn Road. The Colleges of Human Medicine, Osteopathic Medicine, and Veterinary Medicine have offices here.

Holmes Hall

Calder, 1965

Holmes Hall prominently faces East Shaw Lane while its north facade takes full advantage of the Sanford Natural Area as its backdrop. Its east hall and west hall entrances are notable for their glass curtain walls and rows of taupe spandrels. This International Style residence and classroom building is the home of Lyman Briggs School, founded in 1967. Since that year this residential program, administered by the College of Natural Science, has focused on mathematics and basic sciences education. Holmes Hall is also the central office for the Michigan State University Housing and Food Services, one of the largest on-campus university residence systems in the United States.

Hubbard Hall

Calder, 1966

Hubbard Hall, with twelve stories and a penthouse level, is the tallest residence hall. Its north hall and south hall facades parallel Hagadorn Road, the easternmost edge of campus. Characteristic of the International Style, alternating glass and brick panels create a steady pattern of voids and planes. Taupe and white spandrels enhance facade and stairwell rhythms as they define floor levels. Projecting piers and hoodmolds above the topmost windows create a pleasing three-dimensional effect. Fieldstone parapets offer textural contrast and define the space at the buildings' ground level.

McDonel Hall

Calder, 1963

McDonel Hall is similar in its plan, brick and limestone exterior, and International Style to Wilson Hall (1962), and it is identical to Wonders Hall (1963). These likenesses provide a visual link to South Complex and another campus area. McDonel Hall stands just west of Holmes Hall facing East Shaw Lane. Like Holmes Hall, its northern living and classroom areas benefit from beautiful views of the Sanford Natural Area.

THOMAS KACHADURIAN

Intramural Recreative Sports–East (IM East)
Calder, 1988

Smooth, brick surfaces and no applied ornamentation recall the International Style. An assured, asymmetrical horizontality lends an air of visual fluidity. This pronounced horizontality or "rootedness to the ground" is reminiscent of the work of Frank Lloyd Wright, a major American twentieth-century architect.

From the East Shaw Lane sidewalk or the window of a passing car, the north entrance facade appears solid and modestly scaled. Prominent limestone coursing overpowers the deep window and entry apertures. From Wilson Road, looking west, the complexity of this building's form

emerges. Again, limestone coursing enlivens the varying heights of the building's volumes.

"IM East" was designed to house sports and leisure activities for the nearby 8,000 graduate and East Complex residence-hall students. It is at most a ten-minute walk to any of these residences. The complex is barrier-free and includes four basketball courts, a four-lane running track, eight paddleball-racquetball courts, two squash courts, a large weight training and fitness facility, and a multipurpose room.

GARY BOYNTON

Clifton and Dolores Wharton Center for Performing Arts

Candill, Rowlett, Scott, original concept
Harley, Ellington, Pierce, Yee Associates, 1982

Huge scale and monumental impact characterize this High Tech brick-and-glass performing arts center. It includes a 2,500-seat proscenium-stage Catherine Herrick Cobb Great Hall and a 600-seat theatre-in-the round Pasant Theatre. Precise, unadorned exterior outlines, planes, and rounded corners are stylistically High Tech. An irregular plan and discontinuous exterior surfaces captivate and reveal a postmodernist sensibility. The Houston, Texas, architectural firm Candill, Rowlett, Scott developed the original design and the Southfield, Michigan, firm Harley, Ellington, Pierce, Yee Associates provided the construction supervision.

On the interior, the emphatically curved stairwell leading to the Grand Tier offers a memorable spatial experience to visitors. From the Grand Tier itself, spectacular campus views appear through the expansive windows.

Among the notable works of art seen inside is the *Four Muses* with its four large multicolored banners. George Ortman, a Cranbrook Academy of Art faculty member, produced them for a commission from Catherine Herrick Cobb. Paintings by Department of Art and Art History faculty James Adley, Clifton McChesney, and Irving Taran also grace interior walls.

In 1986 Thomas Kehler, then the director of Campus Park and Planning, designed the surrounding landscape. For this design, Michigan State received a National Landscape Award from the American Association of Nurserymen. Integral to this landscape design is *Orpheus*. Melvin Leiserowitz of the Department of Art and Art History produced this large, nonobjective, sculpture in stainless steel for the entry plaza. Its bold geometric shapes reflect the surroundings and enhance how the sculpture

Orpheus, by Melvin Leiserowitz, Cor-ten and stainless steel, 1979.

GARY BOYNTON

complements both landscape and building. *Three Graces,* a large ceramic sculpture near the center's entrance, is the work of Mark Chatterley, a graduate of the Department of Art and Art History.

The center bears the names of Clifton Wharton and his spouse, Dolores Wharton. He served as Michigan State's fourteenth president in 1970–78. She was an active member of many arts and business boards of directors. The Whartons were vital supporters of campus cultural programming and well aware of the need to raise funds and build an on-campus performing arts center.

The Great Hall was the site for the final presidential debate of the 1992 presidential campaign. Today, local, national, and international groups and individuals and Michigan State University students and faculty perform on Wharton's stages to serve the mid-Michigan area.

THOMAS KACHADURIAN

Veterinary Medical Center

Harley-Ellington, 1965
GBKB, 1989, 1991

Now known as the Veterinary Medical Center, the university built this sprawling complex in stages. The initial brick International Style building, whose exterior sign says "Veterinary Clinic," stands at the corner of Wilson Road and Bogue Street. Along its north facade is the Small Animal Clinic entrance and prominent limestone courses that separate identical rows of windows. These narrow windows or "lights" have black spandrels and projecting limestone surrounds. The 1991 addition features a post-modernist entry, with concrete columns and a gabled metal roof, ironic as a historical referent and contemporary in its boldness. Brick facades and prominent limestone coursing optically integrate this addition with the original 1965 building. *Veterinarians*, a 1999 bronze and stainless steel sculpture by Professor James Cunningham, greets visitors.

Inside, a dramatic wood, glass, and travertine stairway leads to the second-floor seating and exhibition area. From here, visitors can see the entry roof's apex and trees in the distance. Among the displayed items is a bronze sculpture, *Birth of a Purebred*, by Steve Streadbeck. It depicts three figures and a calf and was a gift from the Bad Axe Medical Center, Bad Axe, Michigan. The entire complex is home to the College of Veterinary Medicine. It is the only college of its kind in Michigan and one of twenty-seven nationally. Among the complex's facilities are the Office of the Dean, Animal Health Diagnostic Laboratory, Large Animal Clinic, Small Animal Clinic, Veterinary Teaching Hospital, Mary Anne McPhail Equine Performance Center, and various laboratories and classrooms.

Mary Anne McPhail Equine Performance Center

Avance Construction, 2000

The most recent facility in the Veterinary Medical Center is the Mary Anne McPhail Equine Performance Center. Dedicated on 7 June 2000, this low-slung brick structure with gabled roofs and a porte-cochere complements the center's other buildings. Its green metal roof and white trim enhance the attractive "clubhouse" appearance. The center adds 18,000 square feet and increased capacity for clinical evaluation, research, and teaching on equine performance. Diagnosis of problems and the performance of sports horses are specialties. As an expert horsewoman and dressage judge, Mary McPhail, Class of 1955, is the equine center's namesake. She and her spouse, Walter McPhail, are longtime supporters of the college. With the completion of the Mary Anne McPhail Equine Performance Center the technologically advanced Veterinary Medical Center is an outstanding choice in the United States for undergraduate, graduate, intern, and residency programs in veterinary medicine.

Regional Chilled Water Plant No. 1

Calder, 1971, 1976   *HEPY, 1991*

Hoyem-Basso, 1985   *Scales and Associates, 1993*

Starkly geometrical, this rectangular block has a limestone and concrete exterior. Its simple functional appearance suits its role as a campus utility. Nearby trees and shrubs provide contrasts of color and form.

Life Sciences

Calder, 1971

Life Sciences is two large, rectangular blocks linked by a large, two-story, glass entryway. It stands confidently on Bogue Street, east of the Baker Woodlot near trees and shrubs that accent its pristine geometric vocabulary. Boldly scaled limestone piers and recessed ribbon windows and entryways form pronounced light-and-dark patterns to reveal a Brutalist influence. Refinements include subtle value changes in the concrete panels that sheath the exteriors. More than 200,000 square feet enable Life Sciences to serve as the home of the College of Nursing and as a site for life sciences teaching.

GARY BOYNTON

Clinical Center

Calder, 1976   *Threshold/GE, 1988*
Torke/Maslowski, 1985

The Clinical Center complex contains many of the Michigan State University Health Team campus clinical practice sites. Its buildings stand along Service Road, east of Life Sciences. Architects planned the original main office block as a set of modules that could adapt to expansion and reallocation of internal space. Inside, different medical specialties still use color coding to distinguish one module or building area from another.

Modular planning also appears externally in the use of vertical metal facade panels and precast concrete towers. This stark presentation of structural members and materials is Brutalist in style and industrial in feeling. The Clinical Center was supposed to have limestone facing, but for economical reasons, concrete became the final choice. Interestingly, the pale gray metal and concrete modules accentuate the distinction between support spaces (staircases, smokestack, etc.) and useable spaces (offices, clinics, etc.). In this regard, the architects may have been familiar with Louis Kahn's well-known modular and extremely rational design for the Richards Medical Research Building (1965) at the University of Pennsylvania. Occasional nearby conifers and shrubs offer welcome relief from the unadorned exterior surfaces.

THOMAS KACHADURIAN

Radiology

Redstone-Tisco Architects, 1998

Tuscan-inspired columns frame each entrance and provide postmodern flavor. These sturdy columns support bold canopies and accent the symmetrical plan. Above the flat roof line, the apex of the central skylight appears. Inside, twelve columns continue the historical reference as they surround the skylight. Gently filtered light enters and dramatically calls attention to the green, gray, and white terrazzo flooring.

The 16 October 1998 dedication of the Radiology Building positioned Michigan State to become one of five General Electric research centers recognized nationally for radiological research and advances in imaging technology.

THOMAS KACHADURIAN

Research Complex–Engineering
Physical Plant, 1986

Physical Plant designed Research Complex–Engineering to blend unobtrusively with its surroundings. A subtle berm ensconces this predominantly single-story structure. Two wings meet to form an L-shaped plan. At this juncture are a second story and a pitched roof entrance. Taupe metal paneling hangs above eight-by-eight-inch bricks to produce a tidy, utilitarian exterior. The Division of Engineering Research and the Office of Radiation, Chemical and Biological Safety are among the building's occupants.

Area Eight: South of Mount Hope Road

This area, with 3,139 acres, includes the James B. Henry Center for Executive Development, Forest H. Akers Golf Course, and experimental farms, research facilities, and natural areas essential for a major land-grant research university. Among the areas preserved primarily for observation are Bear Lake Natural Area, Biebesheimer Woodland, Minnis Woodland, and Toumey Woodlot. The latter is a virgin beech-maple forest. It holds the United States Department of the Interior designation of National Landmark.

In 1997 the Pavilion for Agriculture and Livestock Education opened at the southwest corner of Farm Lane and Mount Hope Road just west of the Hancock Turfgrass Research Center. The pavilion replaced the razed Livestock Judging Pavilion that once stood between North and South Shaw Lanes south of the International Center. Beyond the Pavilion, farther south, are research and teaching centers for dairy cattle, beef cattle, poultry, swine, purebred beef, horses, and sheep.

Easiest access: From Harrison Road, Farm Lane, or Hagadorn Road, head south; from Harrison Road, Farm Lane, or Hagadorn Road, head north.

Boundaries: Approximate area is east of Interstate 496 (U.S. 127), north of Interstate 96, south of Mt. Hope Road, and west of Hagadorn Road.

On 12 September 2001 leaders from Michigan State University, the State of Michigan, and the agriculture industry met for a groundbreaking to initiate construction of the new Animal Health Diagnostic Laboratory (AHDL) at the corner of Forest and Beaumont Roads. As MSU President McPherson spoke, attendees learned that "the new AHDL will play a critical role in meeting current and future challenges facing public and animal health." When complete, this 150,000- square-foot laboratory will be the largest and most comprehensive veterinary diagnostic facility in the United States.

In October 2001, just east of Interstate 496, the James B. Henry Center for Executive Development opened to support certain master's and continuing education programs of the Eli Broad College of Business. This technologically advanced facility was planned to create the kind of professional learning environment James B. Henry, former dean of the college, encouraged.

Planning for these facilities signals the

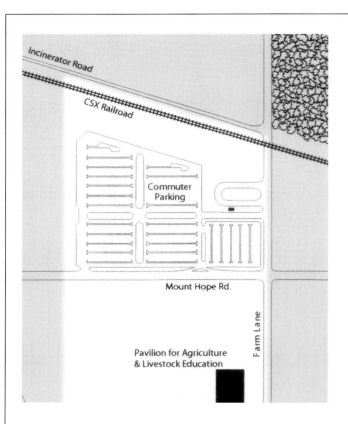

continuing institutional commitment to the use of carefully selected campus space south of Mount Hope Road to support research and training while preserving natural areas for education about and stewardship of the earth.

Pavilion for Agriculture and Livestock Education

Hobbs and Black, 1996

From a distance, across open fields, the white pavilion appears large and utilitarian. Nevertheless, with direct access from the parking lot, the modestly scaled, curved glass entryway welcomes visitors as they pass through a row of stone-faced piers. Once inside, wide ramped passageways lead easily to the auditorium, exhibit area, classrooms, and the show arena.

To help revitalize animal agriculture in Michigan, architects designed the pavilion to include 66,240 square feet of exhibition space within its overall 187,000 square feet. With unobstructed viewing, its show arena seats 2,000 people. The exhibit area fits 368 animal stalls easily removed to adapt to special activities such as trade shows. The auditorium seats 400 people and is popular for auctions and livestock industry events. This facility replaces the Livestock Judging Pavilion (1938) that once stood between North and South Shaw Lanes, north of the Engineering Building and south of the International Center.

Livestock Judging Pavilion, 1938, razed 1997. Designed by Bowd-Munson.

Epilogue

In these early days of the twenty-first century, as you experience the buildings of the Michigan State University campus park, remember that the campus was quite different a hundred years ago and that it will be quite different in a hundred years from now.

Then, think of the year 3000. "When we try to tally the architecture that will be around in the year 3000, it is of places, rather than buildings, that we are likely to think. . . ." For while we may be able to preserve some buildings, what "counts" is the "plan at human scale."[1] The plan here is the campus. It is our living place. Use it, change it for the better, and cherish it always.

Students walking in campus center area, with Wells Hall in the background, 2002.

Notes

Preface

1. Arnold Hauser, *The Philosophy of Art History* (New York: Alfred A. Knopf, 1959), 3.

2. Ibid.

3. John Seaman, *Only Connect . . . Art and the Spectator in the Italian Renaissance*, Bollingen Series 35, no. 37 (Princeton: Princeton University Press for The National Gallery of Art, 1992), 261.

The Campus Park of Michigan State University

1. Richard Dober, *Campus Architecture: Building in the Groves of Academe* (New York: McGraw-Hill, 1996), 174.

2. John Gallagher, "Best Campus Design May Be Spartan's," *Michigan Monthly* (October 1996): 15.

3. Dober, *Campus Architecture*, ix.

4. Anne Matthews, *Bright College Years: Inside the American Campus Today* (New York: Simon and Schuster, 1997), 128–29.

5. Dober, *Campus Architecture*, x.

6. Roger B. Finch, "Rensselaer Polytechnic Institute, 1971," in Dober, *Campus Architecture*, 47.

7. James Howard Kunstler, *Home from Nowhere* (New York: Simon and Schuster, 1996), 36.

8. Ibid., 37–38.

9. Ibid., 38–39.

10. Dober, *Campus Architecture*, 161.

11. Peter Drucker quoted in Robert Lenzner and Stephen S. Johnson, "Seeing Things as They Really Are," *Forbes* 159, no. 5 (10 March 1997): 127.

12. Theophilus Abbot, "The Orchards," Department Reports, *First Biennial Report of the Secretary of the State Board of Agriculture of the State of Michigan from September 1, 1880 to September 30, 1882*, 51, Michigan State University Archives and Historical Collections. President Abbot notes, "The greenhouse and borders near it are a great attraction to visitors."

13. Dober, *Campus Architecture*, 174. Dober speaks of "place making" and "place marking."

14. Minutes of the Board of Education, 21 January 1857, Michigan State University Archives and Historical Collections. The State Board of Education was the responsible governing body in 1857.

15. Herbert Andrew Berg, *The State of Michigan and the Morrill Land Grant College Act of 1862* (East Lansing: Michigan State University, 1965), 35. "Liberal and practical" is a phrase drawn directly from the Morrill Act.

16. W. J. Beal, *History of the Michigan Agricultural College* (East Lansing: Michigan Agricultural College, 1915), 267. The quotation is from Henry A. Haigh, Class of 1874.

17. Berg, *The State of Michigan*, 35.

18. Beal, *History of the Michigan Agricultural College*, Appendix C. This is the legislative text for State of Michigan, Act No. 140, Laws 1863, concerning the selection and care of lands for the endowment of colleges for the benefit of agriculture and the mechanic arts.

19. Ibid., 6.

20. Records of the State Board of Education Concerning the Agricultural College, 1855, Michigan State University Archives and Historical Collections; Harold W. Lautner, *From an Oak Opening: A Record of the Development of the Campus Park of Michigan State University, 1855–1969*, vol. 1 (East Lansing: Michigan State University, 1978), 1:12; Beal, *History of the Michigan Agricultural College*, Appendix A. These pages contain the legislative text to establish an agricultural college, State of Michigan, Sessions Laws of 1855, Act No. 130, approved 12 February 1855.

21. Board of Education Minutes, 3 January 1856, Michigan State University Archives and Historical Collections. The plans called for a central building with an east and a west wing. It became College Hall, and only its west wing was funded. It included the campus museum.

22. Richard Baxter, *The Saints' Everlasting Rest* (London: The Epworth Press, 1962), 29. This is an abridged version of the original 1650 publication. Richard Baxter (1615–91) was an English minister who said that "rest is the end and perfection of motion." Baxter's text was published in England, Scotland, and the United States and translated into Welsh, Gaelic, German, and French. The New York edition appeared in 1856, the same year the funding for Saint's Rest was approved, although copies were available in the United States since colonial times.

23. Berg, *The State of Michigan*, 4.

24. Beal, *History of the Michigan Agricultural College*, Appendix B. This is selected legislative text for State of Michigan, Act No. 188, Laws 1861 concerning the reorganization of the Michigan Agricultural College. The establishment of the State Board of Agriculture as the college's governing body is also included.

25. *Academic Programs 2000–2002*, Michigan State University, East Lansing, Michigan, 69.

26. Board of Education Minutes, 16 November 1855 and 3 January 1856, Michigan State University Archives and Historical Collections.

27. Letter, O. C. Simonds to the State Board of Agriculture, 1 May 1906, Michigan State University Archives and Historical Collections. Simonds was the principal of O. C. Simonds and Company, a landscape architecture firm in Chicago. He was hired as a campus consultant in 1905.

28. Beal, *History of the Michigan Agricultural College*, 261. Beal notes that "A good many native trees of the original 'oak opening' are still standing where they stood when the wild land was purchased for the use of the College."

29. J. Fenimore Cooper, *The Oak Openings* (1848; New York: Hurd and Houghton, 1866), 10. See also Lautner, *From an Oak Opening*, 1:ii.

30. Lautner, *From an Oak Opening*, 1:16.

31. Board of Education Minutes, 3 September 1856, Michigan State University Archives and Historical Collections.

32. Board of Education Minutes, 9 April 1861, Michigan State University Archives and Historical Collections.

33. *Eleventh Annual Report of the Secretary of the Board of Agriculture of the State of Michigan for the Year 1872* (Lansing, Mich.: W. S. George and Co., 1873), 16, Michigan State University Archives and Historical Collections; see also Beal, *History of the Michigan Agricultural College*, 260. A landscape gardener in the nineteenth century would be called a landscape architect today.

34. Lautner, *From an Oak Opening* 1:42.

35. *The Nineteenth Annual Catalogue of the Officers and Students of the State Agricultural College of Michigan* (Chicago: Baker Company, 1875), plan opposite page 42, Michigan State University Archives and Historical Collections.

36. Paul Venable Turner, *Campus: An American Planning Tradition* (New York: Architectural History Foundation; Cambridge, Mass.: MIT Press, 1987), 146.

37. Theophilus Abbot, "The Park," Department Reports, *Annual Report of the Secretary of the State Board of Agriculture of the State of Michigan from September 1, 1880 to September 30, 1882*, 50, Michigan State University Archives and Historical Collections.

38. Beal, *History of the Michigan Agricultural College*, 261–62.

39. Lautner, *From an Oak Opening* 1:56.

40. The State Register of Historic Sites (1979) lists "Laboratory Row" as Agriculture Hall, Chittenden Hall, Cook Hall, Linton Hall, Marshall Hall, and Old Botany. Eustace-Cole Hall, formerly known as Eustace Hall and, before that, the Horticultural Laboratory, is a separate State Register of Historic Sites listing (1971).

41. Madison Kuhn, *Michigan State: The First Hundred Years* (East Lansing: Michigan State University Press, 1955), 182.

42. Board of Agriculture Minutes, 27 May 1899 and 17 July 1900, Michigan State University Archives and Historical Collections. The quotation is from the 17 July 1900 minutes.

43. Board of Agriculture Minutes, 28 December 1905, Michigan State University Archives and Historical Collections.

44. O. C. Simonds, *Landscape-Gardening* (New York: Macmillan Company, 1920), 277.

45. Board of Agriculture Minutes, 20 June 1906, Michigan State University Archives and Historical Collections. The board approved Simonds's recommendations at this meeting.

46. Letter, O. C. Simonds to the members of the State Board of Agriculture, 1 May 1906, Michigan State University Archives and Historical Collections.

47. "The Campus," Department Reports, *Forty-fifth Annual Report of the Secretary of the State Board of Agriculture of the State of Michigan and Nineteenth Annual Report of the Experiment Station from July 1, 1905 to June 30, 1906* (Lansing, Mich.: Wynkoop Hallenbeck Crawford Company, 1906), 34, Michigan State University Archives and Historical Collections.

48. Board of Agriculture Minutes, 22 June 1908, Michigan State University Archives and Historical Collections.

49. Board of Agriculture Minutes, 7 May 1913, Michigan State University Archives and Historical Collections.

50. Board of Agriculture Minutes, 24 June 1913, Michigan State University Archives and Historical Collections. The minutes mention "Mr. Olmstead of Boston," which refers to one of the firm's principals. Olmsted Brothers became the successor firm to the Frederick Law Olmsted Sr. firm in 1898. Its principals were Olmsted Sr.'s stepson and partner, John Charles Olmsted and his son, Frederick Law Olmsted Jr.

51. Actually, Frederick Law Olmsted Sr. and Calvert Vaux designed Central Park. John Olmsted became a full partner in 1884. Frederick Jr.'s apprenticeship began with the World's Columbian Exposition project.

52. Frederick Law Olmsted Sr., *A Few Things to be Thought of Before Proceeding to Plan Buildings for the National Agricultural Colleges* (New York: American News Company, 1866), 10. See also Laura Wood Roper, *FLO: A Biography of Frederick Law Olmsted* (Baltimore: Johns Hopkins University Press, 1973), 310. In his role as an advisor to *The Nation*, Olmsted was an advocate for separate agricultural schools. His firm developed designs for several other land-grant institutions including what are now Iowa State University and Ohio State University.

53. Olmsted, *A Few Things*, 11.

54. Ibid., 12, 14, 15, 19.

55. It is not always apparent whether the board is referring to John Charles Olmsted (1852–1920) or to Frederick Law Olmsted Jr. (1870–1957), although it was Olmsted Jr. who visited the Michigan State campus in 1922. By that time, however, John Olmsted was deceased.

56. Letter, Olmsted Brothers to the State Board of Agriculture, 10 May 1915, 2–4, Michigan State University Archives and Historical Collections. The long quotation is on page 4.

57. Letter, Olmsted Brothers, 5.

58. Letter, Olmsted Brothers, 9–10.

59. Lautner, *From an Oak Opening* 1:123. The actual letter is reproduced here.

60. Edwyn Bowd, the campus architect, and others also recommended on numerous occasions that College Hall be razed because it was structurally unsound. The symbolic importance of the building made it difficult for the board to recommend its demolition. It did approve the idea of renovating it, but it collapsed before the work could be done.

61. Letter, Olmsted Brothers, 13; Board of Agriculture Meeting Minutes, 18 June 1919, Michigan State University Archives and Historical Collections. In its 1915 report the firm made this recommendation. In June 1919, it specified that this building should be the library.

62. William H. Wilson, *The City Beautiful Movement* (Baltimore: Johns Hopkins University Press, 1989), 1.

63. Architectural contributors to the City Beautiful movement strove to elevate city life for the good of all. They favored elaborate civic plans to achieve this social goal.

64. Turner, *Campus*, 245.

65. Ibid., 245.

66. Board of Agriculture Meeting Minutes, 18 October 1916, Michigan State University Archives and Historical Collections.

67. Board of Agriculture Meeting Minutes, 6 February 1922, Michigan State University Archives and Historical Collections.

68. Board of Agriculture Meeting Minutes, 26 June 1923, Michigan State University Archives and Historical Collections.

69. Board of Agriculture Meeting Minutes, 21 November 1923, Michigan State University Archives and Historical Collections.

70. Charles Z. Klauder and Herbert C. Wise, *College Architecture in America and Its Part in the Development of the Campus* (New York: Charles Scribner's Sons, 1929), 44.

71. Lautner, *From an Oak Opening* 1:150.

72. Board of Agriculture Meeting Minutes, 6 February 1922, Michigan State University Archives and Historical Collections.

73. Leland M. Roth, *A Concise History of American Architecture* (New York: Harper and Row, 1979), 232.

74. Beaux-Arts planning favors broad vistas and spatial arrangements with prominent axes, symmetry, and a sense of hierarchy. Beaux-Arts design placed emphasis on the rational formal plan. The name derives from the Ecole des Beaux Arts in France, the school of art and architectural training.

75. Justin L. Kestenbaum, *Out of a Wilderness: An Illustrated History of Greater Lansing* (Woodland Hills, Calif.: Windsor Publications, 1981), 110.

76. The International Style developed originally in the 1920s. It favored simple geometric form, open rather than contained spaces, and no historical detailing.

77. A G.I., "government issue," is a person enlisted in or a veteran of any of the U.S. armed forces. The G.I. Bill of Rights provided educational assistance after World War II.

78. Lautner, *From an Oak Opening* 1:146.

79. For a listing of a range of planning and grounds responsibilities and the names of those who fulfilled these responsibilities since 1855, see Lautner, *From an Oak Opening* vol. 1, Appendix A.

80. Harold W. Lautner, *From an Oak Opening: A Record of the Development of the Campus Park of Michigan State University, 1855–1969*, vol. 2 (East Lansing: Michigan State University, 1978), 2:6; a cantonment is a temporary structure for housing troops.

81. Temporary buildings, using wartime materials, and gardens from the World War II era were called "victory" buildings or gardens.

82. Lautner, *From an Oak Opening* 2:9.

83. Richard Dober, *Campus Planning* (New York: Reinhold Publishing Corporation, 1963), 1–12. Dober speaks of the challenges of post-1945 campus planning.

84. Quonset hut is a trade name for a prefabricated, corrugated metal structure with a semi-circular roof. Quonset huts are portable.

85. See Harold W. Lautner, Map, "Campus of Michigan State College," 1947, Michigan State University Archives and Historical Collections.

86. Lautner, *From an Oak Opening* 2:30.

87. Ibid., 2:31.

88. Ibid., 2:22.

89. Ronald T. Flinn, assistant vice president for Physical Plant, e-mail to Linda O. Stanford, 14 June 2001.

90. Lautner, *From an Oak Opening* 2:33.

91. Ibid., 2:54.

92. Ibid., 2:42, 92 (campus plan), 93 (land use plan).

93. Ibid., 2:90.

94. Ibid., 2:70.

95. Ibid., 2:70.

96. Roth, *Concise History of American Architecture*, 265. The quotation is Roth's. See Ebenezer Howard, *Garden Cities of To-morrow* (London: Faber and Faber, 1946). It was originally published in 1898 as *Tomorrow, a Peaceful Path to Real Reform* and offered the essential ideas that underpinned the Garden City movement.

97. Kenneth Frampton, *Modern Architecture: A Critical History* (New York: Oxford University Press, 1980), 47; Roth, *Concise History of American Architecture*, 266. The quotation is from Roth. It is interesting to note that in the era of post–World War II planning, a population of 32,000 was within the range of the projected size of many public university campuses.

98. Roth, *Concise History of American Architecture*, 267.

99. Lautner, *From an Oak Opening* 2:70–71.

100. A baby boomer is a person born between 1946 and 1960.

101. Dober, *Campus Planning*, 3; Lautner, *From an Oak Opening* 2:224. The source is Fall Term Enrollment Reports, Office of the Registrar.

102. Kuhn, *Michigan State*, 466; Physical Plant Division, *Building Data Book*, Michigan State University, August 1998, 33.

103. Baron earned a master of landscape architecture at Harvard University in 1939. He worked as a landscape architect with several firms and the Tennessee Valley Authority, and as a utilities noncommissioned officer during World War II.

104. Lautner, *From an Oak Opening* 2:219.

105. Ibid., 2:143.

106. Ibid., 2:134.

107. Michigan State University Ordinances, 37.00 Wildlife, http://www.msu.edu/dig/DOCUMENTS/ordinances.html (last visited 25 March 2002).

108. "Michigan State University Natural Areas," Division of Campus Park and Planning, Michigan State University, http://www.cpp.msu.edu/nat_area/index.htm (last visited 25 March 2002).

109. Michigan State University, "Campus Development Plan," 1966.

110. "Campus Development Plan," 4–5.

111. "Campus Development Plan," 5.

112. "Campus Development Plan," map 5, 14.

113. "Campus Development Plan," 23.

114. "2020 Vision," Division of Campus Park and Planning, Michigan State University, http://www.2020vision.msu.edu/ (last visited 25 March 2002). This website shows possible projected changes to the campus plan and pros and cons of different possibilities.

115. "Campus Development Plan," 35–36.

116. "Campus Development Plan," 36–37.

117. Dober, *Campus Planning*, 9.

118. Lautner, *From an Oak Opening* 2:246–47.

119. Ibid., 2:198, 297.

120. Michigan State University, Zoning Ordinance, 1968, iv. Today, the director of the Division of Campus Park and Planning reports directly to the vice president for finance and operations and treasurer, who in turn, reports directly to the president.

121. Michigan State University, Zoning Ordinance, 1968, 1.

122. A teach-in is an extended lecture or discussion on an important and often controversial topic. A sit-in is a protest people organize by occupying a place (sitting) and refusing to move.

123. Dober, foreword, *Campus Planning*, n.p.

124. Dober, *Campus Planning*, 45.

125. Anne Matthews, "2050: A Place Odyssey," *Historic Preservation* 51, no. 5 (September/October 1999): 64.

126. Ibid., 65.

127. "2020 Vision."

128. John Berger, *Ways of Seeing* (New York: Penguin Books, 1977), passim. See also, 8. "The way we see things is affected by what we know or what we believe."

129. Meyer Schapiro, "Style," in *Anthropology Today*, ed. A. L. Kroeber (Chicago: University of Chicago Press, 1953), 287.

130. John Berger, *About Looking* (New York: Pantheon Books, 1980), 197. Both quotations are on this page.

131. Dell Upton, *Architecture in the United States* (New York: Oxford University Press, 1998), 12, 249.

132. Robert Mugerauer, "Derrida and Beyond," in *Theorizing a New Agenda for Architecture: An Anthology of Architectural Theory 1965–1995*, ed. Kate Nesbitt (New York: Princeton Architectural Press, 1996), 184–97; see especially p. 187.

133. Retirees Luncheon, College of Arts and Letters, Michigan State University, October 1991.

134. E-mail, Frederick L. Honhart, director, Michigan State University Archives and Historical Collections, to Linda O. Stanford, 8 November 1999. The first time green was used as a school color was at the 1887 football game with Olivet. Another account reveals that in 1903 green and white became the colors under Chester Brewer who was the first full-time athletic director. See also: *Wolverine*, Michigan Agricultural College, 1912, n.p. The 1911–12 football, baseball, and basketball teams are called The Green and

White; Board of Agriculture Minutes, 20 May 1925, 2. The report of the color committee was accepted. This committee purportedly recommended green and white as the college's colors; "A Matter of Tradition," *Spartan Stadium Sidelines*, 7 October 1978. This article cites the records of the campus Athletic Association and its approval of a green monogram to be worn by athletes who participate in intercollegiate sports. (All articles are courtesy of the Michigan State University Archives and Historical Collections.)

135. Kermit H. Smith to George Kooistra, memorandum, "Official University Colors," 28 March 1979 (courtesy of the Office of the Registrar). Smith writes, "The official colors and specifications for the green color [Hunter Green 5007] were adopted by the Faculty in June 1925 as part of the discussion and approval of the design of the hoods for advanced degree recipients." See also note 134.

136. Beal, *History of the Michigan Agricultural College*, 150.

137. Ibid., 152.

138. Ibid.

139. Helen Lefkowitz Horowitz, *Campus Life* (Chicago: University of Chicago Press, 1987), 201.

140. Beal, *History of the Michigan Agricultural College*, 152. The quotation is from James Y. Clark, Class of 1885, 1 October 1883.

141. "The Third Imperative," *Policy Perspectives* 9, no. 1 (November 1999): 1.

142. Lefkowitz Horowitz, *Campus Life*, 185.

143. "The Third Imperative," 8.

144. Ibid., 1.

145. Ibid.

146. Campbell Hall, Clara Smith Student-Athlete Academic Center, Conrad Hall, Cowles House, Gilchrist Hall, Landon Hall, Mary Ann McPhail Equine Performance Center, Mayo Hall, Paolucci Building, Van Hoosen Hall, Yakeley Hall, Williams Hall.

147. Bernard Michael Boyle, "Architectural Practice in America, 1865–1965—Ideal and Reality," in *The Architect, Chapters in the History of the Profession*, ed. Spiro Kostof (New York: Oxford University Press, 1977), 328, 330; see also 309–44.

148. Eric Fernie, *Art History and Its Methods: A Critical Anthology* (London: Phaidon Press, 1996), 331.

Epilogue

1. Vincent Scully, "Tomorrow's Ruins Today," *New York Times*, 5 December 1999, http://www.nytimes.com/library/magazine/millennium/m6/ruins-scully.html (last visited 25 March 2002), 5 of 6.

Historical Facts About Michigan State University

The Sower by Lee Lawrie, north facade, Beaumont
Tower, ca. 1928.

Architects of Extant Buildings

Listings of architects' names and architectural firms vary, and they might change as time passes. Architects may practice alone or, more often, as a member of an architectural firm. The name of an architectural firm may be one person's name, a number of names, or even an acronym. For architects who designed more than one campus building, there may be more than one name listed below. For example, Ralph Calder is listed as "Calder," "Ralph R. Calder," and "Ralph Calder Associates." Some architectural firms use punctuation, such as commas, hyphens, or slashes in their names, to help define the relationship of the firm's partners. In some instances an architect's first name or initials are listed in parenthesis to provide further information although this first name may not be part of the firm's name.

What follows is a list of the architects or architectural firms responsible for new construction or additions to the buildings listed in *MSU Campus—Buildings, Places, Spaces*. In a few instances, the Physical Plant Division at Michigan State is responsible for new construction or additions and is listed simply as Physical Plant.

Albert Kahn Associates
Appleyard (William D.)
Architects Four
Avance Construction
Bei Associates
Benjamin, Woodhouse, Guenther
Black
Black and Veatch
Bowd
Bowd-Munson
Calder
Candill, Rowlett, Scott
Commonwealth
Commonwealth Associates
Daverman Associates
Donaldson-Meier
Eberle Smith
Erickson
Frantz and Spence
Freeman/Smith
FTCH
FTC&H
GBKB
George Lohman
Gharfari Associates
Giffels/Hoyem Basso
Giffels/Hoyem-Basso
Giffels-Rosetti
Harley Ellington
Harley-Ellington
Harley Ellington Design

Harley Ellington Pierce Yee Associates
Harley, Ellington, Pierce, Yee Associates
Harley Ellington Pierce Yee Associates, Inc.
HEPY
Hobbs and Black
Holmes and Black
Hoyem-Basso
IDS, Inc.
Johnson, Samuel
Kahn (Albert)
Kilgore
Kingscott
Malcomson and Higgenbotham
Malcomson, Calder, Hammond
Malcomson, Trout, Higgenbotham
Manson and Carver
Manson, Jackson, Kane
Manson, Kane, Jackson
Manson, Wilson, and Jackson
Margerum
Marsh (Charles H.)—Arnold
Mayotte, Crouse, Dhaen
Mayotte-Webb
McNamee, Porter, Seely
Munson (O.T.)
N.S.C.L.
Opdyck
Physical Plant
Pond and Pond
Pratt-Koepka

Progressive Arch
Ralph Calder Associates
Ralph Calder and Associates, Inc.
Ralph R. Calder
Redstone-Tisco Architects
Sarvis
Scales and Associates
Scott (J.J.)
Sedgewick-Seller
SHG of Detroit
Sims-Varner and Associates
SSOE, Inc.
Threshold/GE
Torke/Maslowski
Tower, Pinkster, and Titus
Wakely-Kushner Associates
Warren-Holmes

Classes Began: May 14, 1857

Sixty-three students, five faculty, and three now nonexistent buildings (College Hall, 1856; Saint's Rest, 1856; and a brick horse barn)

Dedication Date: May 13, 1857

Founding Date: February 12, 1855

As the Agricultural College of the State of Michigan

Governing Body

1855   State Board of Education
1861   State Board of Agriculture
1959   Board of Trustees

Morrill Act: 1862

To grant lands to each loyal state to support a college "where the leading object shall be, with excluding other scientific and classical studies and including military tactics, to teach such branches of learning as are related to agriculture and the mechanic arts . . . in order to promote the liberal and practical education of the industrial classes in the several pursuits and professions of life."

Name Changes

1855   Agricultural College of the State of Michigan
1861   State Agricultural College
1909   Michigan Agricultural College
1925   Michigan State College of Agriculture and Applied Science
1955   Michigan State University of Agriculture and Applied Science
1964   Michigan State University

National Landmark, U.S. Department of the Interior

Toumey Woodlot, listed 1976

National Register of Historic Places

Central School, 325 West Grand River, East Lansing
    Now: Child Development Laboratories, listed 4/10/86
Horticultural Laboratory
    Now: Eustace-Cole Hall, listed 9/3/71

Presidents

1	Joseph R. Williams	1857–1859
2	Lewis R. Fisk	1859–1862
3	Theophilus C. Abbot	1862–1884
4	Edwin Willits	1885–1889
5	Oscar Clute	1889–1893
6	Lewis G. Gorton	1893–1895
7	Jonathan L. Snyder	1896–1915
8	Frank S. Kedzie	1915–1921
9	David Friday	1921–1923
10	Kenyon L. Butterfield	1924–1928
11	Robert S. Shaw	1928–1941
12	John A. Hannah	1941–1969
13	Walter Adams	1969–1970
14	Clifton R. Wharton Jr.	1970–1978
15	Edgar L. Harden	1978–1979
16	Cecil Mackey	1979–1985
17	John Di Biaggio	1985–1993
18	Gordon Guyer	1993–1994
19	M. Peter McPherson	1995–present

State Register of Historic Sites

W. J. Beal Botanical Garden, listed 4/28/87

Central School, 325 West Grand River, East Lansing, listed 12/19/84
    Now: Child Development Laboratories

College Hall (Marker), at Beaumont Tower, listed 3/25/55

Horticultural Laboratory, listed 3/3/71
    Now: Eustace-Cole Hall

Laboratory Row, East and West Circle Drives, listed 9/10/79
    Now: Agriculture Hall, Chittenden Hall, Cook Hall, Linton Hall, Marshall Hall, and Old Botany

President's Residence/No. 4 Faculty Row, listed 9/25/85
    Now: Cowles House

Student Population

1857	63	1957	20,730
1900	627	1967	42,053
1927	1,047	1977	47,383
1937	5,212	1987	42,096
1947	15,208	1997	42,603

Works Progress Administration Buildings

During the 1930s, when Franklin D. Roosevelt was president of the United States, his "New Deal" administration initiated several governmental programs to abate the severity of the Depression. Many people think of all government-sponsored art and architecture programs of this time period as Works Progress Administration (WPA) programs. Actually, the WPA funded utilitarian projects including sidewalks, roads, bridges, and parks. The Public Works Administration (PWA) undertook large construction projects and provided partial funds for public buildings. The Federal Art Project (FAP), a WPA subsidiary, functioned at the state level to support art education programs and artists who produced sculptures, easel paintings, and murals.

WPA, PWA, and FAP works exist on the Michigan State University campus. The WPA provided funds for workers to build campus roads, bridges, drainage and grading, and sidewalks. Some WPA workers completed interior projects such as painting and redecorating Agriculture Hall, Beaumont Tower, Computer Center (then known as Electrical Engineering), Human Ecology (then known as Home Economics), Marshall Hall (then known as Bacteriology), and North Kedzie (then known as Kedzie). Workers also reconditioned specimens and exhibits for what is now the Michigan State University Museum.

	ARCHITECT OR ARTIST	SPONSOR
Abbot Hall (East Circle Complex)	Bowd-Munson, 1938	PWA
Auditorium	Munson, 1940	PWA
Band Shell (razed)	See: *Three Musicians* (*below*)	WPA/FAP, Class of 1937
Campbell Hall (West Circle Complex)	Malcomson, Calder, Hammond, 1939	PWA
Children Reading, ca. 1938 north exterior stairs, Williams Hall (West Circle Complex)	Clivia Calder Morrison	WPA/FAP
Exterior reliefs, Music Building, 1940	Samuel Cashwan	WPA
Giltner Hall	Bowd-Munson, second addition, 1938	PWA
Jenison Field House	Munson, 1940	PWA
Livestock Judging Pavilion (razed)	Bowd-Munson, 1938	PWA
MSU Union, 1936	Bowd-Munson, completion of original building and east wing, 1936	WPA
Michigan State College, Abbot Entrance Marker	Samuel Cashwan	WPA/FAP, Class of 1938
Music	Calder, 1940, building only	PWA
Olin Memorial Health Center	Calder, 1939, building only	PWA
Soil Science Lab/Tool Shed	Agricultural Engineering	PWA
Three Musicians, Music courtyard. Relocated here, this sculpture and a similar (razed) sculpture once flanked the former Band Shell stage.	Samuel Cashwan	WPA/FAP, Class of 1937

Glossary

archivolt: ornamental trim or molding along the exterior curve of an arch.

Art Deco: a style, especially popular in the 1920s and 1930s, which featured setback facades, low reliefs, and stylized decoration. Conceived as "modern" interpretations of historical form, the style's inspirational sources included jazz, Futurism, and Egyptian and Mayan art.

Arts and Crafts: a style of the late nineteenth and early twentieth centuries that valued simplicity of construction, integrity in the use of materials, and fine handiwork.

atrium: an interior, skylighted space.

attic or **attic story**: a story above the cornice of a building.

balustrade: a railing system including individual columns between a top rail and a bottom rail, found, for example, on the edge of a balcony or a porch.

barrel vault: an arch extended to form a half cylinder.

bay window: a window that projects from an exterior wall.

Beaux-Arts Classical: a style of the late nineteenth and first quarter of the twentieth centuries known for its large, detailed exteriors. Projecting pavilions, large columns, and pronounced symmetry are prevalent.

belt course: a horizontal band that runs around a building's exterior or a room's interior.

blind arcading: a row of arches affixed to a building's facade as decoration with no openings in the arches.

block: a large building or a large rectangular section of a building.

boxed eave: a hollow, open extension of an eave.

bracket: an architectural member that projects from a wall or roof and supports weight from above.

brick header: a brick laid with its end, rather than its length, exposed.

brick stretcher: a brick laid with its length, rather than its end, exposed.

Brutalism: a style, most evident in the 1950s and 1960s, known for its direct expression of materials and textures such as unadorned concrete. Le Corbusier, the well-known Swiss-French architect, and Alison and Peter Smithson, English architects, were early advocates of this approach.

buttress: brick, stone, or other material shaped and adhered to a wall at an angle to support the wall.

cantilever: a projecting bracket, canopy, or other architectural member that is supported only at the point of attachment to a building.

cartouche: an oval or oblong shield or scroll.

casein: a strong adhesive made from milk curd, mixed with paint for use in creating murals, as well as other applications.

casement window: a window that opens outwardly.

castellation or **castellated**: having turrets (small towers) and battlements (a roof line wall with indentations) like a castle.

City Beautiful movement: a development in city planning of the late nineteenth and early twentieth centuries founded on the belief that well-designed cities and civic improvements are essential to improving the quality of life.

Classical or **Classicism**: an approach to architectural design and decoration inspired by ancient Greece and Rome.

Collegiate Gothic: a style featuring Gothic characteristics found at Oxford University and Cambridge University in England and used often for American college and university architecture during the late nineteenth century and the first half of the twentieth century. Gabled roofs, roof dormers, prominent window surrounds (trim), and stone courses are common.

Colonial Revival: a style that borrows from the colonial period in American culture. Gabled or hipped roofs, board siding or brick facades, louvered shutters, sidelights framing entry doors, balconied entry porches are characteristic.

conical: shaped like a cone.

coping: a cap or top layer of a wall.

corbel gable: a gable with a stepped or indented edge.

corbeling: projecting stones that extend progressively farther from the wall that supports them.

cornice: projecting trim above the topmost main story of a building.

course or **coursing**: a layer of stone, brick, or other material laid to form a horizontal row.

crenelation: a pattern of repeated indentations, for example, along the top of a wall.

cross gable: a gable whose face is set parallel to the ridge of a roof.

crown molding: trim that finishes the top of certain structural members. In an interior room, crown molding is trim that covers the juncture of the wall and the ceiling.

cul-de-sac: a dead-end street.

cupola: a small domed structure on a roof.

curtain wall: an exterior wall that is not load-bearing. It hangs from, rather than supports, the skeletal framework.

dentil: a small, tooth-like block that joins with others to form a band of molding.

Doric or **Doric Order**: refers to the design of a column, its base, shaft, and capital, and the horizontal member (entablature) it supports. Developed by the Dorian Greeks, the order features fluted columns. Column capitals have sloped sides topped by a square block.

dormer: a projection from a sloped roof that often contains a window.

double-hung sash: a window with two vertically sliding sections each covering a different portion of the window.

eave: horizontal edge of a roof that usually projects beyond the walls.

Ecole des Beaux Arts: the major school of art and architecture in France in the nineteenth century. The architectural program of study focused on the development of an ideal building plan using a classical vocabulary.

end gable: a gable. The term is sometimes used to place emphasis on the fact that the gable is at the terminus of a long double-sloping roof.

entablature: a horizontal beam or member supported by columns in Classical architecture.

FAP: *see* Federal Art Project.

Federal Art Project: Known as the FAP, this 1930s program was a subsidiary of the Works Progress Administration in the New Deal administration of Franklin D. Roosevelt. The FAP functioned at the state level to support art education programs and artists who produced sculptures, easel paintings, and murals.

finial: a decoration at the tip of a spire or post.

Flemish bond: a style of brickwork in which the headers (end) and stretchers (length) alternate.

floriated: decorated with flower (floral) patterns.

fluted: the grooves or furrows that run along the length of a column.

frieze: a horizontal decorative band.

gable: the triangular section at the end of a double-sloping roof.

gallery: a long, covered section of a building's exterior.

Georgian Revival: a style, used often for residences, that was inspired by direct borrowing from the Georgian Style of the eighteenth century. Symmetry, classical detailing, dormers, columns, and entrances with pediments are common.

Gothic: a style developed in Europe for cathedrals in the late Middle Ages, featuring ribbed vaults, pointed arches, and flying buttresses, which allow for a lightness of effect achieved with thin walls and expansive windows.

Gothic Revival: a style popular 1830–60, inspired by the Gothic. Features are elaborate pitched roofs, prominent dormers, and pointed arches.

High Tech: a style that emerged in the 1970s and 1980s to reaffirm the values of modernism and of a society focused on high technology. It is characteristic to display forthrightly the engineering, via exposed structure and prefabricated parts, that made a building possible. Delight in the exhibition of highly polished industrial-grade finishes and new materials is characteristic.

High Victorian Romanesque: *see* Romanesque Revival.

hipped dormer: a dormer whose roof slopes inward from four sides.

hipped roof: a roof that slopes inward from four sides of a building.

hoodmold: projected molding over a window.

International Style: a style that flourished from the 1920s to the 1970s worldwide as an architecture of volumes rather than masses. Flat roofs, windows set flush with the outer wall, smooth wall surfaces, ribbon windows, and no applied decoration or historical detailing are typical. Essential geometric form and steel skeletal framing are manipulated to present walls as nonsupporting screens within multifunctional spaces.

Italianate: a style from the 1840s to 1880s that drew its inspiration from Renaissance and Romanesque borrowings. Symmetry, wide eaves, large brackets, and cupolas are among the most prominent characteristics.

lancet: a very narrow window with a pointed arch.

lantern or **lantern tower**: the crown of a roof or a dome with windows or perforated walls.

light: a window, often a tall narrow one.

lintel: a horizontal member that can support the weight above it.

load-bearing: a wall or other vertical member that can support itself as well as an imposed load from the overall building structure.

modernist or **modernism**: an approach to architectural design that emerged in the early twentieth century and retained its vitality until the 1970s. It favored a universal vocabulary based on essential geometric form and the abandonment of ornamentation and historical styles.

mullion: a vertical member that separates one window in a series from another.

Neo-Classical or **Neo-Classicism**: a style prevalent 1900–20 that drew its inspiration from Roman and especially Greek architecture. Symmetry and monumental scale are the norm. Large porticos and columns and prominent attic stories are common.

oriel or **oriel window**: a projecting bay window.

Palladian window: a large window divided into three sections with the central section being the largest.

parapet: a low wall often at the edge of a roof, balcony, terrace, or grassy area.

parapeted gable: a gable that has a low wall projecting up from its edges.

pavilion: a detached section of a building complex, or a prominent section of a facade. Often, a pavilion is a central or terminal section and is defined by projection, height, or roof treatment.

pediment: a triangular or curved area over a doorway.

Pewabic: refers to Pewabic Pottery, founded in 1903 in Detroit by Mary Chase Perry (Stratton). The company developed a national reputation for its unique iridescent glazes used for vessels, tiles, and architectural detailing. In 1965 Michigan State University accepted Pewabic Pottery as a donation. The pottery was administered by the Continuing Education Program from 1968 until 1976 and by University Extension from 1976 until 1981, when ownership was transferred from Michigan State to the Pewabic Society.

pier: a vertical post or support; it is usually square whereas columns are round.

pier buttress: a vertical support that receives the thrust of a buttress.

pilaster: a pier that is attached or integral to a wall.

piloti (pl. pilotis): a supporting pier that gives the appearance of raising a building on stilts.

pinetum: a stand of pine trees planted, in part, for botanical study.

pinnacle: the top; a decorative top; a finial.

porte cochere: a cover over a driveway near or attached to the side of a building to provide protection from the weather.

portico: a porch or walkway whose roof is supported by columns.

post: a round or square vertical; a column.

post and beam: a skeletal framing method in which horizontal beams rest on vertical posts and, in turn, support the vertical posts above them.

Postmodern, postmodernist or **postmodernism:** a movement that began in the late 1960s as a reaction against modernism and particularly against the universality of the International Style. It favors complexity of form and historical borrowing often for whimsical or ironical reasons.

Public Works Administration: Known as the PWA, this 1930s program was formed in the New Deal administration of Franklin D. Roosevelt. The PWA undertook large construction projects and provided partial funds for public buildings.

PWA: *see* Public Works Administration.

pyramidal: having four sloping sides that meet at a single apex.

quatrefoil: a square, squarish, or circular pattern divided into four parts by arcs that intersect.

Queen Anne: a style prominent 1880–1910 that features steeply pitched roofs with irregular shapes, asymmetrical plans, and large front gables. Bay windows, patterned masonry and shingles, and prolific eclectic ornamentation are common.

quoin: a stone placed at the corner or edge of a wall to reinforce or to decorate.

relief: a carved or raised surface of a wall or plaque.

relieving arch: an arch above a window or door that helps to shift the weight of the wall to either side of the window or door.

reveal: space between a window or door and the outer wall, showing the wall's thickness.

revivalist: an adjective describing a building whose style is inspired by borrowing from past styles.

ribbon window: one of a row of windows that form a horizontal band across the facade of a building.

Richardsonian Romanesque: *see* Romanesque Revival.

Romanesque Revival: This style flourished between 1840 and 1900. It favors the heaviness and semicircular arches reminiscent of medieval Romanesque architecture. Monochromatic brick and stone exteriors, towers with pyramidal roofs, and stringcourses are prevalent. Two related styles are listed below:

  Richardsonian Romanesque was popular between 1870 and 1900 and features wide, round arches, rough-faced masonry, towers with conical roofs, and asymmetrical plans refined by and later named for Henry Hobson Richardson, a prominent American architect.

  High Victorian Romanesque was popular between 1870 and 1890. Differences include a preference for polychromatic exteriors made possible with a variety of textured stone, brick, and other materials.

roof dormer: *see* dormer.

roundel: a small round window.

rusticated: masonry or other materials finished with deep beveled edges to look like individual stones with smooth or rough surfaces.

sash or **sash window:** any window, but usually a double-hung window with vertical slides.

segmental arch: an arch in which its inner curve is less than a half-circle.

Shingle Style: an American style popular 1880–1900 using shingles to cover whole or partial exteriors. This creates a fluid exterior surface to complement gable roofs, projecting bays, groups of (window) lights, and eaves held close to the walls.

sidelight: an unmovable vertical glass panel on the side of a door.

spandrel: in recent architecture, the space between the top of a window and the sill of the window above it.

steel-cage construction: a steel skeleton or framework used for tall buildings consisting of columns and beams. This skeleton supports the walls and transmits the load and stresses to the foundation.

stepped cross gable: a cross gable with a stepped edge; *see* cross gable.

stop: the termination of a strip of molding; molding against which a door ceases to move.

stringcourse: a horizontal band of stone or brick set into the actual facade of a building.

style: a constant form; a set of identifiable traits that distinguish one building from another.

surround: a border, frame, or trim that encircles a window or door.

taupe: a brownish-gray color.

terrazzo: marble or stone chips set in mortar and highly polished; usually used for flooring.

tesserae: small squares of stone, glass, or enameled tile.

tracery: a curvilinear framework within a window made of wood, metal or other materials to form a pattern.

transom: a horizontal bar or frame that separates a door from a window above the door.

travertine: a kind of limestone used for flooring and wall facing.

trefoil arch: an arch whose inner curve has three lobes.

tripartite: having three parts.

triptych: a painting or a mural with three panels.

trussing system: a framework using triangles for stability.

tympanum: the triangular or segmental area above a doorway that is enclosed by an arch.

Tudor: steeply pitched roofs, side gables, cross gables, narrow windows, large chimneys, and Renaissance inspired detailing are characteristic. In public buildings, the similarity to the Collegiate Gothic may be evident, but the Renaissance rather than Gothic detailing is a distinguishing trait.

Tuscan or **Tuscan Order**: refers to the design of a column, its base, shaft and capital, and the horizontal member (entablature) it supports. The Tuscan order, developed by the Romans, is a simplified version of the Greek Doric Order. Tuscan columns are not fluted and they support a plain horizontal member (entablature).

voussoir: a wedge-shaped stone in an arch.

Works Progress Administration: Known as the WPA, this 1930s program was an agency in the New Deal administration of Franklin D. Roosevelt. The WPA funded utilitarian projects including sidewalks, roads, bridges, and parks. The Federal Art Project was a subsidiary.

WPA: *see* Works Progress Administration.

Further Reading

These books and articles are recommended because they are readily available and they provide useful information about and insights into the Michigan State University campus park.

Beal, William J. *History of the Michigan Agricultural College.* East Lansing: Michigan Agricultural College, 1915.

Berger, John. *Ways of Seeing.* New York: Penguin Books, 1977.

———. *About Looking.* New York: Pantheon Books, 1980.

Galik, Mark. "Alumni Memorial Chapel. MSU's Forgotten Soul, Part One." *The Graduate Post* 4, no. 1 (fall 1996): 14–18.

———. "Alumni Memorial Chapel. MSU's Forgotten Soul, Part Two." *The Graduate Post* 4, no. 2 (spring 1997): 12–18.

Hannah, John A. *A Memoir.* East Lansing: Michigan State University Press, 1980.

Kestenbaum, Justin, ed. *At the Campus Gate: A History of East Lansing.* East Lansing, Mich.: East Lansing Bicentennial Committee, 1976.

Kuhn, Madison. *Michigan State: The First Hundred Years.* East Lansing: Michigan State University Press, 1955.

Turner, Paul Venable. *Campus: An American Planning Tradition.* New York: The Architectural History Foundation; Cambridge, Mass.: MIT Press, 1987.

Upton, Dell. *Architecture in the United States.* New York: Oxford University Press, 1998.

Prometheus by Samuel Cashwan, south porch, MSU Union, 1949.

Index of Buildings, Places, Spaces

This index includes references to the sacred space and oak opening, the place where Michigan State University began as the Agricultural College of the State of Michigan, and to the buildings, selected historical sites or markers, public art, and natural areas that comprise Areas 1 to 8 of this book.